but unofficial

The Complete Guide to the Willem C. Vis International Commercial Arbitration Moot

Editor:
Jörg Risse

Authors:
Markus Altenkirch
Ragnar Harbst
Annette Keilmann
Lisa Reiser
Jörg Risse

4th edition

2017

C. H. BECK · HART · NOMOS

Published by
Verlag C. H. Beck oHG, Wilhelmstraße 9, 80801 München, Germany,
eMail: www.beck.de

Co-published by
Hart Publishing, Kemp House, Chawley Park, Cumnor Hill, Oxford, OX2 9PH,
United Kingdom,
online at: www.hartpub.co.uk

and

Nomos Verlagsgesellschaft mbH & Co. KG, Waldseestraße 3–5
76530 Baden-Baden, Germany,
eMail: www.nomos.de

Published in North America (US and Canada) by Hart Publishing,
c/o International Specialized Book Services, 930 NE 58th Avenue,
Suite 300, Portland, OR 97213-3786, USA, eMail: orders@isbs.com

www.beck.de

ISBN 978 3 406 71443 6 (C. H. BECK)
ISBN 978 1 50992 036 5 (HART)
ISBN 978 3 8487 4468 8 (NOMOS)

Printed in Germany by
Beltz Bad Langensalza GmbH
Am Fliegerhorst 8, 99947 Bad Langensalza
Typeset by
Reemers Publishing Services GmbH, Krefeld
Cover: Imogen Linnemann

Foreword

This book has been prepared for the use of student participants in the Willem C. Vis International Commercial Arbitration Moot. I will assume that the reader of this foreword is, therefore, one of those students or is an advisor to a team of students.

The book, sponsored by Baker & McKenzie, on preparing for participation in the Vis Moot, is a welcome addition to the literature on mooting. There are a number of books on the general subject, but only a handful that are particularly useful in regard to the Vis Moot. The Vis Moot is different from almost all other moots in a number of ways, which make the insights of former participants particularly useful.

A major reason why most of the existing literature on mooting is not very helpful in preparing for the Vis Moot is that the Vis Moot is international. To be sure, there are other international moots, the Jessup in public international law being the most prominent. The Vis Moot shares a number of characteristics with them, but there are a number of features that make it unique.

The Vis Moot attempts to replicate an international commercial arbitration. It was the first international moot on a private law subject. In the case of the Vis Moot, the underlying dispute is always in regard to an international sale of goods subject to the United Nations Convention on Contracts for the International Sale of Goods (CISG). Until about twenty years ago, an international sale of goods or other private law dispute (with the exception of maritime disputes) were almost automatically litigated in national courts. It would have been unthinkable to have an international moot in which the forum for settlement of the dispute was a national court. It required the development of international commercial arbitration as the preferred forum for settling commercial disputes before an international moot such as the Vis Moot was feasible, and that is a surprisingly recent development.

To be sure, it is not possible to replicate an arbitration completely. To start with, there is no client interview in which the lawyer first learns of the dispute when a client tells him its side of the story. That introduces us to one of the two fundamental differences between the study of law and the practice of law. The first is that the lawyer, and the students fulfilling the role of lawyers in the Moot, represents a client. It is the lawyer's task to present the client's side of the story before a court or an arbitral tribunal. The student in the Moot is not attempting to learn the law but to apply the law. Naturally, one must learn the law before attempting to apply it. In the Vis Moot, the students learn about the law of international arbitration as well as deepen their knowledge about the law of contracts as found in a contract for the sale of goods. Secondly, the facts are seldom neatly packaged presenting an illustration of an important point of law or an interesting question of interpretation, as they are in the classroom. It is imperative that the students and lawyers thoroughly understand the facts as they become evident. However, the facts in the Vis Moot, as in real disputes, are often convoluted and not particularly clear. The student/lawyer must make as rational a story in favor of the client as possible from the facts given. Furthermore, there will always be documents, presented as exhibits in the Moot, that are the location of the details that strengthen or weaken the client's case. It is tempting to overlook them, but one does so at one's peril. The use of one word rather than another in a letter may be the key to winning or losing the case.

Of course, the other party to the dispute also has a story to tell that will differ in important details from that of the first party. In order to fully understand what happened and the legal consequences that flow from there and to make the most effective argument possible for the client, it is necessary to understand both sides of the story. In the Vis Moot that is accomplished by having every team represent both the claimant and the respondent. But not at the same time. Not even an experienced lawyer would be able to formulate the best arguments for both sides if s/he were to submit those arguments at the same time. Instead, the teams submit a memorandum for claimant in early December at which time they receive the memorandum for claimant of one of the other teams. About six weeks later, the teams submit a memorandum for respondent in opposition to the memorandum for claimant they have received. During those six weeks, the students often find that the arguments they were so proud of representing the claimant are not only wrong, but inconceivably wrong. Those students are well on their way to understand the entire business situation and to argue the case for either of the two parties to the dispute.

Those are not the only challenges for the students. The Vis Moot takes place only in English. That means that the majority of the teams must write their memoranda and must argue orally in a language other than their mother tongue. I have always said that this gives the non-Anglophone teams an advantage educationally over the Anglophone teams, at least for those students who think that they might later wish to be engaged in any kind of international dealings whether in a law office, corporation or governmental office. At present, English has become the primary language of international affairs, both commercial and political. The Vis Moot gives the students the opportunity to use English in a professional context without having to worry about the serious consequences to themselves, their employers and the client from making mistakes. Nevertheless, it makes the Vis Moot more of a challenge than a national moot court for many of the participating students.

A challenge for all of the students is to argue in both written and oral form to arbitrators who have a different legal formation from their own. This is particularly true since the Vis Moot always involves a contract of sale and the law of contracts is the heart of the private law in the civil law and the common law legal systems, as well as those that do not fall neatly into either category. The difference in doctrinal approach in the different legal systems is the basis for many misunderstandings between lawyers educated in those different systems.

Aside from the many other difficulties faced by many teams in finding financing and help in understanding what was expected of them, many teams have internal organizational problems. The study of law tends to be an activity one does alone. Unlike some other disciplines (engineering and medicine come to mind), law students rarely work in teams. Law students usually study alone. Even when they study with other law students, it is not a truly joint enterprise. Examinations are taken by oneself. Teamwork is an aptitude that seldom enters into the study of law. However, any sophisticated legal practice is a matter of teamwork. Unfortunately, over the years, there have been several teams that have withdrawn because team members could not work together.

The writers of the chapters in this book have experienced these and other difficulties in the Vis Moot as student participants. Many of them have coached teams in the Moot. A number are now in the practice of law, many doing just the kind of work that the Vis Moot emulates. There is no better group that can advise you on what to look for, how to overcome some of the difficulties, and in general, how to make the most of the opportunities that the Vis Moot offers. Take advantage of their experience by reading the entire book carefully.

Prof. Dr. Eric E. Bergsten

Director of the Vis Moot 1993–2013

Overview

Table of Contents

I. The Vis Moot: A Lifetime Experience

Congratulations! The fact that you hold this book in your hands probably means that you have registered for the Willem C. Vis International Commercial Arbitration Moot.[1] What a wise decision. And if you have not yet registered, you are evidently contemplating to participate in the Moot. Just do it! To participate in the Vis Moot will be a lifetime experience. Yes, that sounds melodramatic but we, the authors of this guide, know it to be true and we do judge from our own experience. Moreover, we are certain that most former Moot participants would agree with us.

This book has a single objective: to assist you in making the best out of this lifetime experience. This book does so by guiding you, step by step, through the course of the Moot; starting well before the first Friday in October when you receive the Vis Moot Problem and ending well after the closing event when you say your goodbyes to newly-made friends. This book tells you how to register for the Moot, how to find and organize your team, how to analyze the case, how to write your memoranda, how to present your case in the oral pleading, how to organize your trip to Vienna or Hong Kong and how to enjoy yourself. At the same time, this book is not a blueprint on how to succeed in the Moot. There is no such blueprint – and even if there was, we would certainly not tell you. Because this would take away most of the unique Moot experience! Ultimately, the Vis Moot is not about taking home a trophy (there is a reason why no such trophy exists), but it is about the so-called "Moot Experience," *i. e.*, something we are not willing to describe at this point but which you will know after having participated in the closing event in the Vienna Congress Center.

So why is the Moot a lifetime experience? Here are five reasons. Pick one, and you will find it confirmed when participating in the Moot.

[1] Hereinafter, "Vis Moot" or "Moot".

1. The Vis Moot Teaches You Invaluable Skills

Law schools teach you certain knowledge of the law, but what matters in real life are skills. If you are going to become the most knowledgeable tax lawyer on this globe but are unable to convince the local tax authority, your future client won't be happy nor will you succeed in your personal career. Participating in the Vis Moot will teach you many of the skills you need. During the Vis Moot, you have the chance to add new skills to your own personal "tool box." You will learn how to work in a team. In the first phase of the Moot, you will strive to convince professional arbitrators with a written piece of work, *i. e.*, your memorandum, and that requires more than simply presenting a sound legal analysis. Most of you will learn to work in a foreign language, *i. e.*, English, and native speakers will learn to adapt their use of language to non-native speakers. During the oral hearing, you must argue and defend your position with vigor, charisma and persuasiveness. In essence, the Moot provides you with a unique opportunity to acquire and apply those skills.

2. The Vis Moot is a Tough Challenge

The Vis Moot requires stamina, *i. e.*, a lot of strength and persistence. The Vis Moot is not the proverbial piece of cake. You are expected (and expect yourself) to perform at your best. Don't be fooled by the parties and festivities that surround the Moot, especially in preparation for and during the oral pleading phase. When you ask former participants to tell you about the Moot, everyone will elaborate on the unique atmosphere in Vienna, describe the tension in the room before the results of the general rounds are announced, and of course, remember the party nights at the Ost Klub (now known as Schwarzberg). What former Mooties might forget to tell you is that participating in the Vis Moot requires five hard months of work prior to the grand finale in Vienna or Hong Kong. There might be moments during your preparations in which you think about quitting. You might think about walking away from the "Project Vis Moot" because you don't get along with the other team members, because you spend less and less time studying for other courses or because you are simply sick of talking about the same Moot problem over and over again. But that's part of the challenge and it is part of the Moot Experience. The Vis Moot would only be half as instructional if everything was a walk in the park. At the end of the day, you will be proud of what you and your colleagues have accomplished.

3. The Vis Moot is a Stepping Stone for Your Career

As a "Mootie," you are probably not one of those students who streamline all their activities to foster a future career. Good! However, even if you were, your participation in the Moot would make perfect sense. Being a "Mootie" is more than a nice add-on to your resume. It demonstrates to your potential employer that you are a hard worker whose goal to work in international arbitration is not the result of a recent trend among fellow students but fed by true interest in the field. The Vis Moot is the event in the annual calendar of everyone working in the area of international commercial arbitration. When you wander the streets of Vienna or Hong Kong during the Vis Moot weeks, you will be amazed by how many eminent arbitrators from all around the world are present and follow the Vis Moot. Talk to them! Participating in the Moot gives you the unique chance to be "up close and personal" with potential future employers. The various events and receptions make it even easier for you to get in contact with attorneys, law professors and arbitrators from all around the world. In a nutshell, the Moot is the perfect nucleus for establishing a professional network in the international arbitration scene.

4. The Vis Moot Will Show You the "Real Life"

The Vis Moot strives to come as close to reality as possible – and it does a great job in this respect. When you receive the Moot Problem in October, endless hours of legal research and legal writing lie ahead of you – like in any real arbitration when you receive your opponent's submission. And when you arrive in Vienna or Hong Kong for the oral pleadings, your Moot problem will come alive even more. Of course, it will not be Mr. Langweiler whom you will meet at the coffee station in the Dachgeschoss. And it will not be Mr. Fasttrack who sits across the table when you present your case in front of the Arbitral Tribunal. But some "cast members" of your Moot problem might cross your path in Vienna or Hong Kong. You might see Gary Born or I. Martin Hunter heading to their next sessions as arbitrators. In fact, you might have cited from Robert Hunter's textbook on international arbitration and then find yourself in a pleading with him – defending your (opposing) position. Or you might engage in a game of table soccer with Dr. Stefan Kröll during a long night at the Schwarzberg (formerly known as Ost Klub). And then you will suddenly realize that there is a life behind the textbooks! The Vis Moot has become the largest, most international and multicultural event in the global arbitration community – and it shows.

5. The Vis Moot is Meeting Nice People from All Over the World and Having Fun

When you finally meet the other participants, either during one of the many pre-moots or in Vienna and Hong Kong, you will soon realize that they are all a bunch of nice people. Why is that so? Why is it that year after year, Moot participants who hardly know each other get along so easily and maintain friendships long after the Vis Moot is over? The answer is easy: you share the same spirit. There is at least one thing all of you have in common: the Moot. Since we all are some kind of a "social animal," making friends with your colleagues from all over the world is a crucial part of the entire undertaking. Combine that feeling with the true Moot challenge you need to master and with the joy of accomplishing something after months of hard work, and you might be close to what is universally (at least in the universe of arbitration) known as the Moot Experience. Some translate it simply to "having fun," but that really is quite a simplification.

Again, dear reader, pick one of those five reasons why the Vis Moot could become a lifetime experience for you and find at least this one reason confirmed during your actual participation in the Moot. We hope and trust that this book will help you enjoy the Moot so that you, in the end, will return from Vienna or Hong Kong with your unique, very personal Moot Experience.

In this book, we can only share with you our own experiences. If you have different experiences (and we hope you will not only follow beaten paths), tell us about them! Just send an e-mail to **vis.moot@bakermckenzie.com** and describe your own personal Moot Experience. As you will see, the last two chapters of this book consist of reports written by arbitration practitioners as well as interviews with former Mooties. We will include the most vivid and telling report in the next edition of this book, and, if we get your permission, that report might as well be yours.

6. Up Close and Personal: Interview with Professor Eric E. Bergsten

On the occasion of the 21st Vis Moot in Vienna in April 2014, Lisa Reiser and Markus Altenkirch had the chance to interview Professor Eric E. Bergsten.

Professor Bergsten is the spiritus rector of the Vis Moot: he knows everyone and everyone knows him. Despite his many commitments during the Vis Moot week in Vienna, Professor Bergsten devoted some of his precious time to us and our questions. We were delighted! And we were thrilled when Professor Bergsten not only talked about well known facts but actually revealed some insights to the history and development of the Vis Moot that you have probably not heard anywhere else before. But read for yourself:

BM Prof. Bergsten thank you very much for agreeing to meet us for this interview. We are very glad to have you here, and we would like to ask a few questions on the Moot – how it has developed over the years and where you see the Moot in the future.

Let us begin with the history of the Moot: How and where did you develop the idea of the Vis Moot?

E.B. Well, the Moot was first suggested at the UNCITRAL Congress on International Commercial Law in 1992. The

Congress took place in the General Assembly hall of the United Nations in New York.

BM Who suggested the Moot?

E.B. It was Michael Sher, a lawyer from New York who had experience with the Jessup Moot. He suggested organizing a Moot in order to promote the CISG, the United Nations Convention on the International Sale of Goods. Back in 1992, there were not as many signatories to the CISG as there are today.

The idea was from the beginning to have an international Moot. And of course, if you're going to have a Moot, you have to have a tribunal. For several reasons, the idea was to have an arbitration Moot. There were no other arbitration Moots in existence at that time.

One of the persons attending the UNCITRAL Congress in New York was Professor Albert Kritzer who had been the head international contract lawyer for General Electric. He had been a big supporter of the CISG from the very beginning. He thought the CISG was the most wonderful thing that had ever been invented – we are talking about legal instruments of course. Upon his retirement, Professor Kritzer was working at Pace Law School.

This is how the Moot got to Pace Law School. At Pace Law School, Professor Willem C. Vis and I worked with Al Kritzer to plan the first Moot and to draft the first problem. When Willem passed away just before the first round of arguments, we decided to name the Moot after him.

BM As far as we understand, Mooting as such has a long history in American legal studies.

E.B. It started in England. It's basically how you train barristers.

BM Did you participate in a Moot when you were a law student?

E.B. When I was a law student in the United States, yes. It must have been during my first year in law school. We had to do a Moot. But this was simply a small competition in our law school.

BM It doesn't sound like you liked it.

E.B. It was worthless. The way it was structured, what we did, basically, I didn't learn anything from it. But at least I knew what Mooting was about, obviously.

BM The Vis Moot has changed. The Moot is a great success story. Where eleven teams participated in the first Moot, today more than 290 teams from 67 countries participate in the Moot and travel to Vienna for the oral arguments. What do you think were the biggest changes over the years?

E.B. Obviously the increase in numbers and geographical spread is a big change. But I don't think that's your question. If you look at the Vis Moot Problems, you can see that they have become more realistic. At the beginning they were "professor's problems" that had good legal issues, but didn't have the flavor of real commercial transactions or real arbitrations. Today, we emulate – to the extent possible – what would happen in a real arbitration. Of course, the Moot does not and cannot cover every phase of a real arbitration. It's not completely realistic, but with regard to the aspects that the Moot covers – we think – that it as much as possible emulates what happens in a real arbitration.

BM Who drafts the Vis Moot Problems?

E.B. Well, for the first 20 years, I wrote the problems. I wrote every one of them. Today, there is a committee with well-known professors who take care of the drafting of the Vis Moot Problems.

BM How did you create the Vis Moot Problems? Where did you get the ideas from? Did practitioners send in their ideas?

E.B. When you ask me where the ideas for the Vis Moot Problems came from, there were two ways: One is that you start with a particular legal issue. The other is that you start with the dispute. Most of the time, it was something that I saw myself, sometimes, it was suggested to me. For example, once, Prof. Peter Schlechtriem presented to me a case which raised very interesting legal questions. Another time the Vis Moot Problem was a real case where a friend had to file a submission. Of course, there were enough changes so that it was anonymous and also some changes that had to be made because a Moot has several constraints. You can't have factual issues where you would have to have testimony.

BM What about the procedural issues? Does the arbitral institution suggest something or did you choose the procedural problems?

E.B. Again, it came both ways. In the later years, in particular, I would ask the institution: "Is there something in your rules that you think might raise some good problems?" Again, these problems had to fit in the context of the Moot. Not every problem that they were facing in their practice permitted that. Usually, the institutions suggested a suitable procedural issue. Sometimes, I came up with the procedural issues myself because I looked at their rules and picked something out.

BM How did the distribution of the memoranda develop over time? I remember that, when we participated in the 11th and 12th Moot, we had to hand in hardcopies of the memoranda. It is probably incredible for students nowadays that memoranda were not sent by e-mail but hardcopies were sent by post.

We heard that back then all hardcopies were stored in your apartment. Is that right?

E.B. At the very beginning, it was in the apartment. But then, it so happened that in the building where we lived, there was a storeroom available and I was able to store the memoranda there.

BM So, you didn't have to use your living room and your wife didn't complain about the memoranda all being sent to your house?

E.B. Well, yes, but she was still complaining because we had to open these packages and put them on the shelves. And then when we sent them out, we had to go and pull them off the shelves. So, yes, when we switched to e-mail, it was a big change. Nowadays, the memoranda are not even submitted by e-mail anymore but are uploaded to the website.

BM One thing that did not change over the years: All students come to Vienna and have fun while participating in the Moot.

E.B. This was deliberate on our part. When we were planning the first Moot, we were discussing: How are we going to structure this competition? When I say "we", I mean in particular Albert Kritzer, Willem C. Vis and me. We all had international experience of one form or another. We were all involved with UNCITRAL, an international organization where the delegates come from different countries with differences in expectations of relationships – hierarchic or collegial – and that was a real issue on a couple of occasions.

We thought that it is very important for law students to understand that people from other countries – who have the same background insofar as they have all studied law – have different social habits, ways of talking to one another, different expectations of how the legal system works – whether on the substantive law or on the dispute resolution side. Even if the students in the Moot don't understand in-depth how all these are different in India, Germany, Brazil or China, the Vis Moot teaches them that there is a difference. To us that was part of the educational function of this Moot.

Of course, we also wanted the Moot to be fun for the students. They were supposed to work hard when drafting the memoranda or preparing for the oral rounds. The fact that they come to Vienna or now also go to Hong Kong and have fun is part of the pay-off for them at that stage of their career. And I think, it's been a big part of the success of the Moot – both educationally and in terms of kind of bringing people together.

BM Are you aware that many Mooties met their life partner – wives and husbands – at the Moot?

E.B. Of course, I am.

BM Have you ever been invited to a wedding?

E.B. No, I haven't been invited to the weddings, but yeah, sometimes I receive cards. I know of Germans in Dubai, in Korea, in Australia. You know, there is one negative aspect to that. Oftentimes, one set of grandparents will not be close to their grandchildren…

BM Have you ever met a Moot baby?

E.B. Ah yes, I have met more than one.

BM How do you feel when you imagine that you are responsible for this?

E.B. For the babies? I disclaim any responsibility.

BM Where do you see the Moot in ten years from now? I mean, 20 years have passed so far. What will change in the future?

E.B. Well, first of all, I hope, there is no fundamental change in the Moot. Right now, I cannot imagine how it would get any better. The three who have taken over the organization of the Vis Moot from me are very experienced and have been involved in the Moot for many years. They certainly have the right attitude towards what the Vis Moot should accomplish. So I don't see any deliberate changes.

The only changes which will certainly occur are changes in the administration of the Moot – similar to moving from paper to e-mail.

One might wonder whether the Moot will get even bigger in Vienna? I really hope that there is never any serious thought to having any kind of regionals that would limit the number of teams participating in Vienna. As said before, the Moot is not strictly about the legal issues. The Moot is about the personal, the cultural experience in Vienna or Hong Kong. Also, I have the feeling that the students, who get the most out of it, are the ones who are not very serious, but come from places which are not really into arbitration yet. In the Moot, they don't necessarily do that well, but may get more out of the Moot educationally than the Americans or the Germans or the ones from so many other countries who have good support – both in terms of research facilities and in regard to the general atmosphere. Vienna happens to have facilities that from a logistical point of view can accommodate many more teams yet. There is, of course, a downside to the huge number of teams: the arguments are not just in the Juridicum but in several law firms nearby.

BM Professor Bergsten, our last question is one that you have probably been asked many times before: Why is participating in the Vis Moot so invaluable?

E.B. Okay, there are many reasons but I'm going to pick up on just one. I think the Vis Moot is a unique educational experience because you do not participate alone. During legal studies, law students usually study alone. Law students are not working in teams. Engineering students, medical students, yes. Law students, no. Some might study with friends, but it's still self-studying. In the examination you are only graded on your own performance. But when you practice law and you do international work or commercial work in general, you're working in teams and you have to learn how to work in a team. The Vis Moot teaches you exactly this. I think, for some participants this is the hardest thing to learn – how to work in a team – that your colleagues count on you and you have to be able to count on your colleagues.

BM This is true! From our own experience we strongly agree with your last point. We learned for the first time during the Vis Moot what it means to work in a team.

Thank you very much for this interview, Professor Bergsten. We hope that you will stay with the Vis Moot and its participants for many more years to come!

II. The Vis Moot: Facts and Figures

1. What is a "Moot Court"?

A moot court (or simply a moot) is a mock trial for law students. It is characterized by five features:

- At the core of the moot lies a fictitious case. This case usually poses several legal questions that need to be addressed by participating students. There are many moot courts involving many different substantive laws, *e. g.*, the Sir Manfred Lachs Moot on Space Law,[1] the Jean-Pictet Moot on International Humanitarian Law[2] and the oldest and largest international moot court – the Philip C. Jessup International Law Moot Court Competition[3] – on Public International Law.[4]
- A moot court has a practical element. In contrast to lectures and seminars at law school, a moot court is a practical role-playing exercise and thus excellent preparation for professional life. Law students act as a team of lawyers in a simulated court proceeding or arbitration. They are expected to prepare written briefs as well as oral arguments for both parties to the dispute, *i. e.*, claimant and respondent (usually in English).[5]
- Further, a moot court has a competitive element. At the end of the day, one team wins. The students present their arguments in front of a panel of judges/arbitrators who make their decision on the basis of various criteria, *e. g.*, persuasiveness of the arguments and lawyering skills. Many moot courts award a prize to the best team, the best advocate or the best memoranda. There are inter-university competitions as well as national and international competitions where a team represents its home university.
- In addition, a moot court has an educational element. The idea behind the moot is learning by doing. Primarily, the students deepen their understanding of the substantive law applicable to the case at hand. Over the course of the moot, the participants

---

[1] http://www.iislweb.org/lachsmoot/.

[2] http://www.concourspictet.org/index_en.htm.

[3] In the following "Jessup Moot."

[4] http://www.ilsa.org/jessuphome. The first Jessup Moot was held in 1960. Today, more than 500 teams from more than 80 countries participate.

[5] Some Moot Courts only require oral arguments.

have to conduct in-depth legal research and apply their theoretical knowledge to a practical case. Moreover, the students learn a lot about procedural law which, in many law schools, plays a somewhat subordinate role. Some moot courts are subject to the English Civil Procedure Rules,[6] while others portray criminal proceedings according to United States law,[7] and again others are arbitrations pursuant to the Rules of the International Centre for the Settlement of Investment Disputes.[8] What is more, beyond "hard" legal skills, students, through their participation in a moot, acquire legal writing and presentation skills.

- Last but not least, a moot court has a social element. Students cannot participate individually, but only as part of a team. Furthermore, the highlight of each (international) competition is the oral round. As described in detail below, the Vis Moot is unique in this regard. For one week in March or April, more than 300 teams from more than 70 countries meet in Vienna, Austria for the oral rounds. Even the Vis Moot's "sister," the Vis Moot (East) in Hong Kong, has recently attracted 125 teams from 32 jurisdictions.

2. What is the Vis Moot?

The Vis Moot is a fascinating experience. Participants have the chance to meet their peers from around the globe and to socialize at the Moot Alumni Association's Welcome Party, Goulash Dinner, Farewell Party and at the official Moot Bar. In addition, the Vis Moot is one of the most prestigious moots. Participants of the Vis Moot and the Jessup Moot often discuss which moot is bigger. If one looks at the number of participating teams, the Jessup Moot is ahead. However, in the Vis Moot, all participating teams are invited to the international rounds in Vienna and Hong Kong. There are no national elimination rounds as are in the Jessup Moot. As a consequence, there are more teams in Vienna for the Vis Moot than in Washington D.C. for the Jessup Moot.

---

[6] See, e.g., the ICLR Annual Mooting Competition (http://www.iclr.co.uk/learning-zone/mooting) (ended, however, in 2014).

[7] See, e.g., the Annual Herbert Wechsler National Criminal Law Moot Court Competition (http://wings.buffalo.edu/law/bcls/).

[8] See, e.g., the Frankfurt Investment Arbitration Moot (http://investment-moot.org).

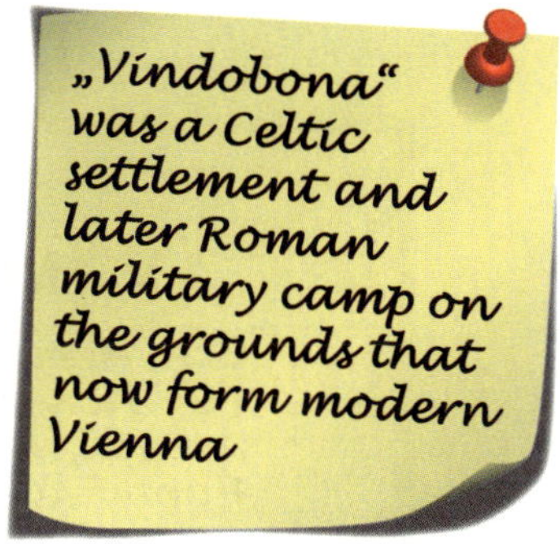

The fictitious case for the Vis Moot always has the same features: claimant and respondent are parties to an international sales agreement. The dispute settlement mechanism of their choice is International Commercial Arbitration. The parties are usually from Equatoriana and Mediterraneo, two fictitious countries who are both member states to the United Nations Convention on the International Sale of Goods (CISG). The CISG is thus the substantive law governing the dispute. The seat of arbitration is always Vindobona in Danubia.

Danubia has adopted the United Nations Commission on International Trade Law (UNCITRAL) Model Law on International Commercial Arbitration (UNCITRAL Model Law). The UNCITRAL Model Law is thus the law governing the arbitral procedure. The case is always fictitiously handled by a real arbitration institution (so no ad-hoc arbitration). The institution differs from year to year so that different rules apply.

It is often said that "it's not the winning but it is taking part that counts." This may be true but at the same time the Vis Moot is a competition. And it is good that the Vis Moot is a competition because the ambition to win an award in this highly-reputable competition makes students work harder and strive for an excellent memorandum or an excellent oral presentation as they hopefully will do in their professional life.

There are five awards in the Vis Moot: two awards for the best memoranda, one for the best speaker and one for the best team. In addition, the best ten percent of the participating universities and students receive an Honorable Mention. Finally, there is the"Spirit of the Moot Award" which may be, for example, be bestowed to the team that had to overcome the most obstacles to participate in the Moot.

VIS MOOT AWARDS

- Best Memorandum for Claimant (in Vienna "Pieter Sanders Award", in Hong Kong "David Hunter Award")
- Best Memorandum for Respondent (in Vienna "Werner Melis Award", in Hong Kong "Fali Nariman Award")
- Best Individual Oralist during the General Rounds (in Vienna "Martin Domke Award", in Hong Kong "Neil Kaplan Award")
- Best Team in the Oral Rounds - "Winner of the Moot" (in Vienna "Eric E. Bergsten Award", in Hong Kong "Eric Bergsten Award")

3. Why Apply for the Vis Moot

"The Vis Moot was my best experience in law school." This is certainly a quote that could come from almost all Vis Moot participants for a number of reasons discussed below.

The Vis Moot is an excellent preparation for professional life. First of all, students have to work on a practical case instead of a theoretical legal question. Second, the students learn how to work in a team, which fairly reflects the everyday life in an international law firm. Third, the Vis Moot introduces many students to the law of international arbitration. Even though arbitration is the number one dispute settlement mechanism in cross-border contracts, it is rarely taught at universities. Fourth, since the students write two memoranda, they improve their legal writing skills. The participants learn how to convince the reader within 35 pages that their client is right. Finally, the students have to present their arguments orally in front of an arbitral tribunal in Vienna or Hong Kong. Thus, they improve their presentation skills – another asset for professional life.

In addition, through the Vis Moot, students get a good grasp of international commercial law and the law of arbitration. It is impressive to see how the students in Vienna and Hong Kong handle the CISG. By way of example, they know the *force majeure* provision of Article 79 by heart, they quote relevant cases on the duty to mitigate in Article 77 and explain how good faith has to be considered under the CISG. The same applies to the students' knowledge of the law of arbitration. The students often know the New York Convention inside out and can address any concern the tribunal might have concerning the enforceability of the award.

It might be added that the participation in the Vis Moot is a major asset on one's CV. Future employers know the Vis Moot and specifically hire former Mooties. Many law firms sponsor Vis Moot teams, and many even send delegations to Vienna and Hong Kong in order to get to know the students and to advertise their law firms as attractive employers.

Last but not least, the Vis Moot is a huge social event. It has been said that no Moot Court can top the Vis Moot in that regard. The Moot enables the participants to have a lot of fun and to establish an international network. The social character of the Vis Moot becomes apparent even before the oral rounds start in Vienna and Hong Kong. In many countries, there are so-called Pre-Moots, *i. e.*, practice rounds as preparation for the actual competition. Aside from providing students important opportunities to practice, these Pre-Moots have a great side effect: there are usually parties organized in the evenings so that the teams get to know each other before everyone travels to Vienna or Hong Kong. At the actual Vis Moot, the Moot Alumni Association (MAA) is responsible for the best social events. And they do their job very well.

The first chance to meet and greet fellow Mooties is the opening party the day before the official Moot reception. Furthermore, there is a Moot Bar in Hong Kong and Vienna where teams are supposed to spend their evenings – and many do. Moreover, it is highly recommended to go for the Goulash dinner in Vienna and the seafood dinner in Hong Kong – not so much for the food but for meeting Mooties. The biggest party generally is the farewell party, which is also

organized by the MAA. At that point in time, the day before the final argument, almost all teams do not need to worry about the next morning.

4. History of the Vis Moot

The idea for the Moot was presented at an UNCITRAL Congress in 1992. Mr. Michael Sher, a representative of the Association of the Bar of the City of New York, suggested an international Moot Court as a means to promote the acceptance and use of the CISG. The idea was picked up by the Institute of International Commercial Law at Pace University Law School (White Plains, N.Y.). Why? The team of the newly-founded institute included Professor Eric E. Bergsten and Professor Willem C. Vis, both former Secretaries of UNCITRAL, as well as Mr. Albert Kritzer, a strong advocate for the CISG. They developed a concept for the Moot and chose Vienna, home of the UNCITRAL Secretariat, as the venue for the oral arguments.

The first Moot was held during the 1993–1994 academic year. A couple of months before the oral arguments, Professor Vis passed away. His co-founders decided to name the Moot in his honor. Pace University Law School organized the Moot during the first 14 years. In July 2007, the "Association for the Organization and Promotion of the Willem C. Vis International Commercial Arbitration Moot" (of which Pace University is a member) took over.

The Vis Moot started with teams from eleven law schools in nine countries. In the following years, it grew tremendously. The 24th Moot in the 2016–2017 academic year saw 338 registered teams from more than 70 countries.

Pictures say more than a thousand words. We have gathered all the information on participating law schools from the first Vis Moot in 1993–1994 to the 21st Vis Moot in 2013–2014. Have a look at the following charts to see how the Vis Moot has rapidly taken over the world.

Inaugural Willem C. Vis
International Commercial Arbitration Moot | 1993-1994

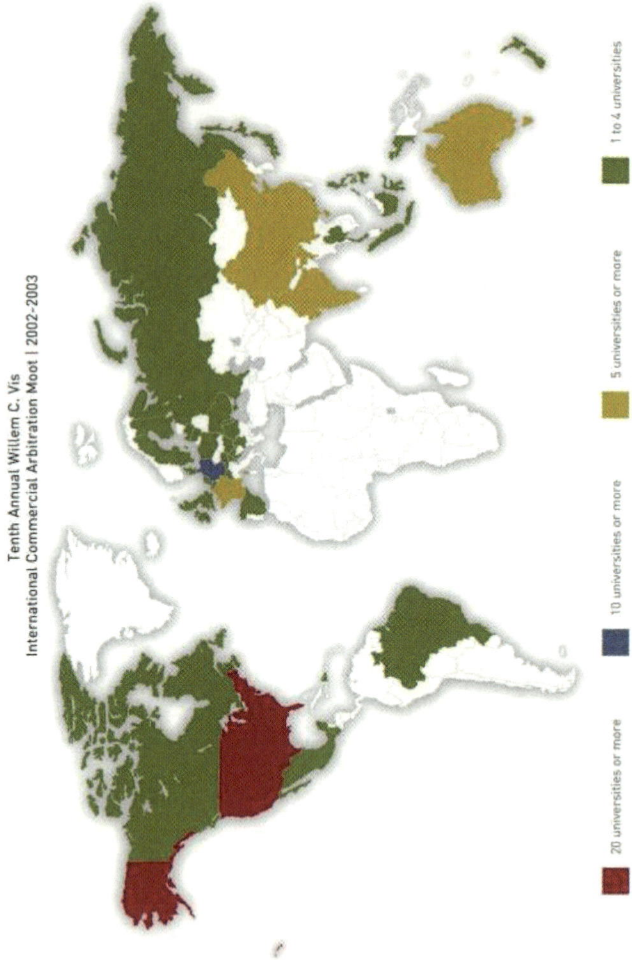
Tenth Annual Willem C. Vis
International Commercial Arbitration Moot | 2002-2003
20 universities or more
10 universities or more
5 universities or more
1 to 4 universities

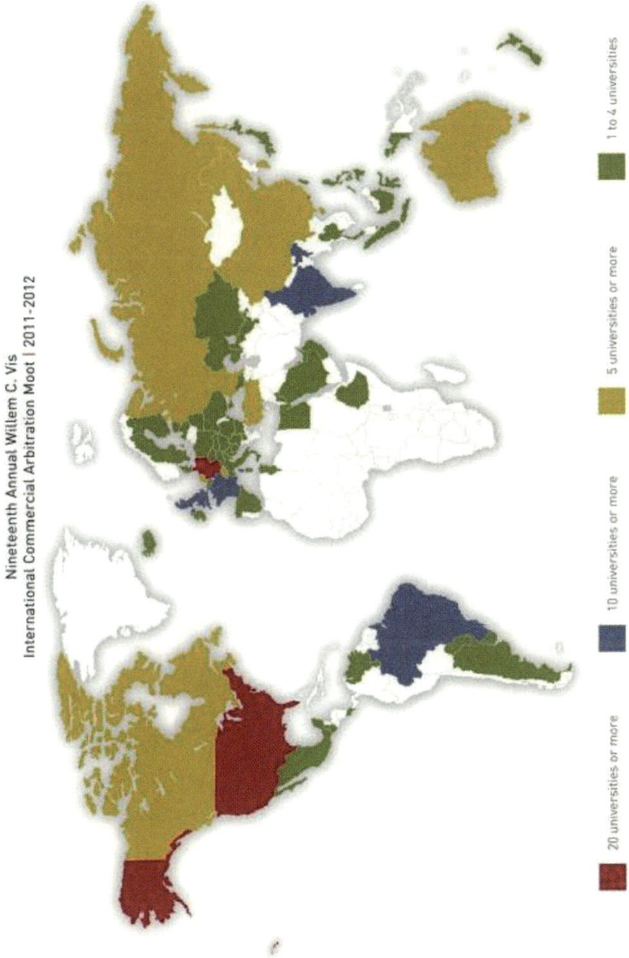
Nineteenth Annual Willem C. Vis
International Commercial Arbitration Moot | 2011-2012
20 universities or more
10 universities or more
5 universities or more
1 to 4 universities

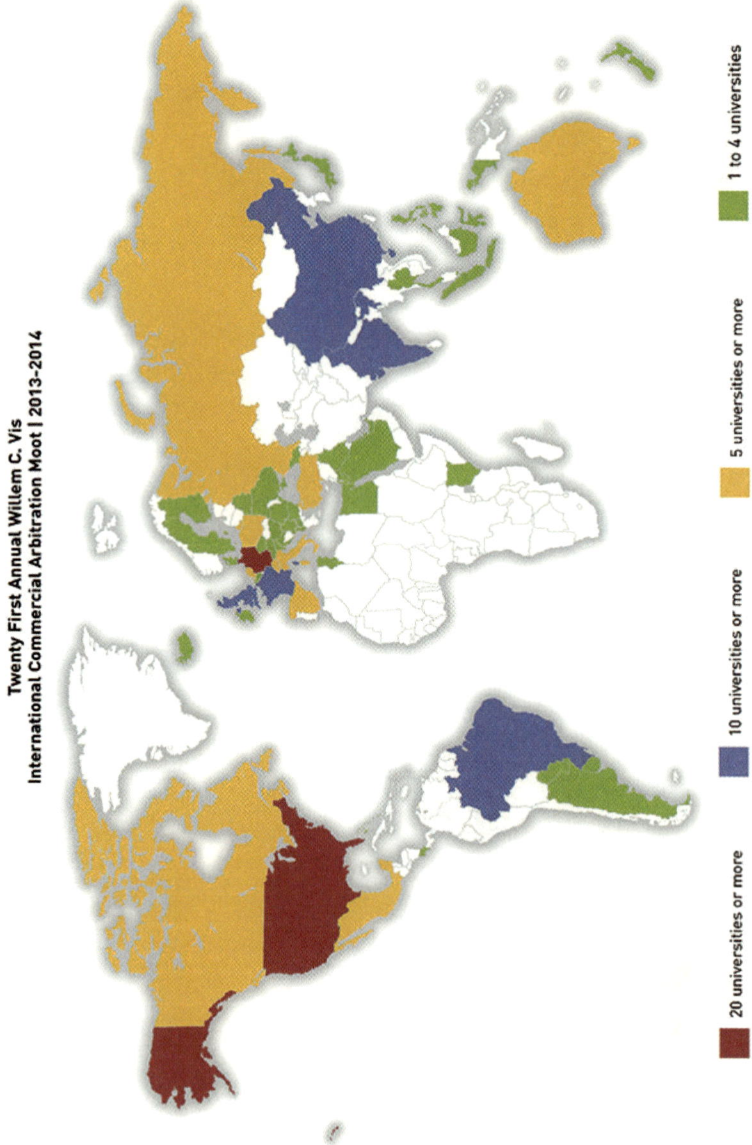
Twenty First Annual Willem C. Vis
International Commercial Arbitration Moot | 2013-2014
20 universities or more
10 universities or more
5 universities or more
1 to 4 universities

5. The Timeframe of the Vis Moot

The Vis Moot kicks off on the first Friday of October. On that day, the Vis Moot Problem is posted on the official websites https://vismoot.pace.edu/ and http://www.cisgmoot.org. From that day on, hundreds of students around the world dig into the CISG and the law of international arbitration. The participants will take a deep breath at the beginning of December and at the end of January once the memoranda for claimant and respondent have been submitted. The Vis Moot West closes on Thursday before Easter (usually at the beginning of April) and the Vis Moot (East) ends eleven days before that. Overall, the entire Vis Moot process consumes the better part of a six-month period, and most Mooties do not know what to do with themselves when it is over.

The following was the timeline for the 24th Moot in Vienna. It is representative for every Vis Moot:

Friday, 7 October 2016	Distribution of the Problem
Thursday, 27 October 2016	Deadline for requests for clarification
Wednesday, 30 November 2016	Closing date for submission of registration form.
Thursday, 8 December 2016	Memorandum for claimant due
Friday, 9 December 2016	Payment of registration fee due
Thursday, 26 January 2017	Memorandum for respondent due
Thursday, 6 April 2017	Moot Alumni Association Welcoming Party
Friday, 7 April 2017	Official Welcome and reception
Saturday – Tuesday, 8–11 April 2017	General Rounds of argument
Tuesday evening – Wednesday – Thursday, 11–13 April 2017	Elimination Rounds of argument
Thursday, 13 April 2017	Awards Banquet

5.1 The Distribution of the Vis Moot Problem

Give me the facts!

The first documents in a real arbitration as well as in the Vis Moot Problem are the Request for Arbitration and the Answer to the Request for Arbitration. Both documents offer an overview of the facts of the case, present a short legal argument and are accompanied by supporting exhibits. The Vis Moot Problem also contains correspondence between the parties and the arbitral institution concerning the first procedural steps such as the appointment of arbitrators. The Vis Moot Problem comprises approximately 60 pages.

On the last pages of the Vis Moot Problem, in Procedural Order No. 1, the arbitral tribunal sets out the procedural guidelines, the due date for the memoranda and, most importantly, the issues to be addressed in the briefs and oral arguments. Each Moot Problem deals with procedural as well as substantive issues. The procedural issue usually is whether the tribunal has jurisdiction. An example of a common substantive issue is whether the seller's breach of contract is a fundamental breach under Article 25 CISG.

The 16th Vis Moot, for example, was about two procedural and two substantive issues (paragraphs 12 and 13 of Procedural Order No. 1, respectively):

> *"12. The memoranda should discuss the following issues. In regard to jurisdiction of the Tribunal:*
> *– Whether or not Universal was ever bound by the arbitration agreement in the contract between Mr. Tisk and UAM; and*
> *– Whether the insolvency law of Oceania by which the arbitration clause became void in Oceania upon the commencement of insolvency proceedings in regard to UAM affects the jurisdiction of the tribunal proceedings in Danubia.*
> *13. In regard to the merits, the memoranda should discuss:*
> *– Whether Universal should be held liable for the breach of the contract by UAM; and*
> *– Whether there was fundamental breach of the sales contract authorizing Mr. Tisk to avoid the contract."*

5.2 Deadline for Requests for Clarification

Why?

Unlike in real life, in the Vis Moot, counsel cannot meet with their clients to gather further information concerning the facts of the case. What is more, in the Vis Moot, both parties are from fictitious countries (usually Equatoriana and Mediterraneo). If a question concerning the national law of one of these countries arises, there is no commentary or textbook that could be consulted.

Unlike in real life, the Vis Moot therefore provides for a clarification phase. The participants are invited to request clarifications from the Moot Administrator.[9] If the questions are relevant and material in the context of the Vis Moot Problem, they will be answered in Procedural Order No. 2. This compilation of questions and answers is distributed amongst all participating teams irrespective of whether a team has actually made a request for clarification. Statements in Procedural Order No. 2 become part of the Vis Moot Problem and can be used for arguments.

5.3 Closing Date for Submission of Registration Form, Payment of Registration Fee Due

I am on board!

According to the Vis Moot Rules, registration is a three-step procedure. It consists of (1) submission of the registration form, (2) payment of the registration fee, and (3) submission of the memorandum for claimant by the set date. Over the last years, the registration fee amounted to EUR 700 for the Vis Moot in Vienna and USD 1,120 for the Vis Moot (East) in Hong Kong. Of course, the Vis Moot organizers do not make a profit from the Moot. In return for the registration fee, the teams are invited to the Opening Reception and the Awards Banquet.

There are special rules on registration for the Vis Moot (East) because the number of teams is limited.[10] Thus, registration may be completed even before the Vis Moot Problem is distributed (*e. g.*, in the 13th Vis Moot East, all places had been allocated by the end of the first week in October). Admission to the Vis Moot (East) is given on a "first come first served" basis. Chapter III 2.2 describes the registration process for the Vis Moot (East).

---

[9] *Cf. para.* 27 Vis Moot Rules.
[10] *Para.* 10 Vis Moot Rules (East).

5.4 Memorandum for Claimant Due

The claimant is right!

During the first months, the participating teams represent the claimant. They must write a memorandum of no more than 35 pages on the issues determined by the tribunal in Procedural Order No. 1 (see above at II.5.1). The due date generally is in early December. The memorandum has to be sent to the Vis Moot administration by midnight of the respective day.[11] According to the present Vis Moot Rules, the memorandum must be submitted by midnight Vienna time. For the Vis Moot (East) teams can submit their memorandum by 24:00 h local time. There have been years, however, in which also the Rules of the Vis Moot (East) required the teams to send the memorandum by 24:00 h Hong Kong time. What seems like an unimportant question now – midnight in Hong Kong or midnight in Greenwich or elsewhere – will certainly be of utmost importance on the due date. We have seen many memoranda being sent at 23:59 h.

The drafting of the memoranda is the subject of chapter IV.

5.5 Memorandum for Respondent Due

The respondent is right!

After the memorandum for claimant is submitted, the students usually take a few days off. They deserve it. One week after the submission of the memorandum for claimant, at the latest, the teams receive a memorandum for claimant from another university. Teams from a civil law country usually receive a memorandum from a common law country and vice versa. The teams change allegiance and continue working as counsel for respondent. Their job during the second phase of the Moot is to rebut the memorandum for claimant they have received. The memorandum for respondent is usually due at the end of January.

5.6 Official Welcome and Reception

I know my pleading by heart.

After the written phase is over, the teams prepare for the oral arguments. The oral hearing takes place in Vienna (Vis Moot [West])

[11] *Para.* 40 Vis Moot Rules.

and Hong Kong (Vis Moot [East]). By the time the students get there, they will have practiced their oral pleading day and night. Some teams take part in the so-called Pre-Moots, *i. e.,* practice rounds with several other teams. Of course, this book dedicates a separate chapter to the oral pleadings (see below chapter V).

The night before the oral rounds finally start, the students are invited to the Official Welcome and Reception. In Hong Kong, this event takes place at the City University. In Vienna, the official reception is hosted in the Wiener Konzerthaus, an impressive concert hall with more than 1,000 seats. Details as to these events can be found in chapter VI.

5.7 General Rounds of Argument

Now it really counts.

The day after the official opening ceremony, the first pleadings commence. Every team has four pleadings in the General Rounds of argument. Every team will represent the claimant and the respondent twice.

5.8 Elimination Rounds of Argument

The best of the best.

After the fourth pleading, the organisers will announce the best teams that will proceed to the Elimination Rounds. In Vienna, 64 teams make it to the next round; in Hong Kong, only 32 teams go on to the sixteenth Round. How do you qualify for the Elimination Rounds? Each speaker is scored during the General Rounds on a scale from 50–100 points (This is a change introduced for the 24th Vis Moot in Vienna in April 2017. The 14th Vis Moot East still used the old scoring system with a scale from 25–50 points.). The teams with the highest cumulated score will proceed. Thus, it does not matter whether your team does better in the General Rounds than your "opponents" as long as you collect enough points (for further details, see below V.1.6).

5.9 Awards Banquets

It's time to say "goodbye."

On the last day of the Moot in Vienna, everyone is invited to the Awards Banquet. This is a festive event and the appropriate setting for a look-back at the events of the last six months. Most students, however, while eager for the good food or drinks, impatiently await the announcement of the awards.

In Hong Kong, this festive event is the Gala Awards Banquet.

However, the winners of the awards are not the only ones who have a reason to cheer. There will be several honorable mentions in each category.

6. Up Close and Personal: Interview with the Moot-Organizers

On the occasion of the 24th Vis Moot, Max Oehm and Fabian Römer had the chance to meet the persons responsible for the Moot: Patrizia Netal (PN), Christopher Kee (CK) and Stefan Kröll (SK). This trio took over the role as Moot-Organizers from Eric Bergsten in 2012 and have done an amazing job preserving the values of the Moot while implementing some important changes. Find out how they come up with interesting and challenging problems each year, why they changed the scoring system and read about their personal Moot highlights over the years.

BM Thank you very much for taking time out of your extremely busy schedule to do this interview with us. You are the persons behind the Moot. But before we start talking about the Moot and its organization, maybe you could tell us a bit about yourselves. What do you do besides the Moot?

PN If I am not at the Moot, I am a Partner in an Austrian Dispute Resolution Firm, doing mostly commercial arbitration work as Counsel and Arbitrator.

CK When I am not doing the Moot, I am a Professor of Law at the University of Aberdeen in Scotland. I am involved in both teaching Arbitration and Sales and Commercial Law generally within the Law School. But I also hold senior management positions within the University as a whole.

SK When I am not working for the Moot, I am either sitting as an Arbitrator or teaching at Bucerius Law School in Hamburg, where I am an honorary professor, or for some other institutions or universities. I am a Sole Practitioner in Cologne, Germany and a part-time academic. BM

PN All three of us grew up with the Moot. We did not step in just a few years ago, rather more than 20 years ago. I started to work for the Moot while I was a student here at the University of Vienna. The work intensified from year to year and in 2012 we became the Directors of the Moot.

BM What are the individual tasks each of you have as Directors of the Moot?

CK We each have different but overlapping portfolios. My portfolio takes in the teams, the arbitrators and the logistics of the competition, as well as pedagogic and educational aspects.

PN My principal responsibilities are the logistics here in Vienna. Since I am located in Vienna it is much easier for me than for my colleagues. Additionally, I take care of the financial, business and legal aspects of the Moot. Policy decisions are taken by the three of us.

SK I primarily deal with everything related to the problem, i. e. write it, answer the requests for clarifications and prepare the arbitrators' brief. In addition, I deal with the sponsors and the educational side. But actually all three of us have regular discussions about in principle everything; the admission of students or whether certain things are acceptable or not. It would not be possible to have one person doing everything with a full time career on the side.

BM Is there something that rewards you for all your effort?

CK Just seeing the opportunity that the Moot presents for all the students who participate is rewarding. That opportunity, the excitement amongst the students, the whole feel of the place, that is a constant reward for us and I think this is what particularly keeps us all interested in doing these roles as organizers.

BM On the financial aspect of the Moot, how does the Moot finance itself?

PN The Moot is financed by the registration fees mostly. It is also financed by sponsorship contributions from many arbitral institutions around the world as well as the publishers who come to Vienna. We have a certain policy: We encourage only institutions and the publishers to become sponsors of the Moot. We want to maintain the Moot being a non-commercial event.

One of the reasons why we do not approach law firms as sponsors is because law firms actually sponsor teams or support them in coaching. We hope that law firms continue to make this important contribution to the teams. One exception to this rule are some law firms here in Vienna, who provide their rooms for the hearings. We are constantly struggling with the room situation due to the continuous growth of the Moot.

BM How many teams participated this year in comparison to last year?

CK We now have 338 teams. There had originally been 344, but a few teams dropped out last minute. Last year we had 311 team. So, there is substantial increase again this year.

BM How did you develop the idea for this year's problem which at least 338 teams pondered about?

SK Whenever I read something which might be interesting for a problem, I jot down notes. I ask colleagues working in arbitration to talk about their cases which always gives me ideas. And then, I usually meet up with Petra Butler for two or three days to basically exchange ideas. The result is always a mixture of my own experiences as arbitrator, and something which I read while publishing as well as the discussions with Petra and other colleagues.

Sometimes we include certain aspects which we think the students should learn about but that have no real relevance to the outcome of the case. The Moot is an educational experience. For example, this year's problem included the UNCITRAL Transparency Rules. These rules had no real relevance to the case but now a lot of students have looked at them and know now about them. In particular, regarding the discussion here in Europe about arbitration taking place only behind closed doors, the students now have the necessary knowledge to hopefully defend the concept of arbitration.

BM So, in the Moot problem you react to the real world. Has it ever worked the other way around?

SK Funny enough, yes! After last year's problem, for example, there were many conferences where we discussed costs in arbitration which was one issue in the case. I was amazed to see a completely different perception during these conferences than during the Moot.

That was the reason why we have, for the first time, started to ask students questions about the Moot. We want to generate some statistics that will give insights into how the next generation of arbitrators and international commercial lawyers see certain problems; and whether that is perhaps influenced by presenting respondent or claimant in a certain case.

The Moot problem is also an interesting opportunity for arbitral institutions. Institutions regularly publish revisions in their rules. It might be useful to them to test how their revisions are applied by more than 2,000 students and 1,000 arbitrators.

BM Generating statistics is not the only new thing. You have changed the scoring system of the Moot this year. How did it come to this change and what do you expect to improve?

CK When the scoring system was originally developed, Eric Bergsten chose a scale of 25 to 50 because he felt that was a scale that was not used in any university institutions or national systems. Professor Bergsten chose this scale to avoid any "national baggage" – much like the intent of the terminology used in the CISG. While 25 to 50 in reality is a 26 point scale, over the years it was relatively rare to see scores that were in the lower part of the scale. And increasingly, we were finding that teams were ending up on the same score after the general rounds. This is understandable because there are only so many numbers that you could end up on. But one of the aims of the broader scale is to give greater "granularity" to the scoring scale. There are more points and it allows arbitrators to be a bit more discerning in the way they do their math. We hope to see that reflected in the scores coming through.

BM Another hot topic we would like to talk about is "Women in the Moot and in International Arbitration". What is your take on the issue of diversity and how do you see the role of the Moot here?

PN I think that the Moot has a great impact in the development of gender diversity. In practice, there is substantial underrepresentation of female arbitrators but also counsel. I think that will change over the next years. We can see that significantly in the number of student participants in the Moot. For the last two years a majority of female students participated in the Moot. This is certainly not reflecting the real arbitral practice.

Real arbitral practice, however, is reflected when it comes to Moot arbitrators. While a third of the arbitrators in the Moot are female arbitrators. Only a minority of them are highly experienced arbitrators. Most of the female arbitrators are young coaches or associates of law firms; former Moot participants that now act as arbitrators. Their participation is important. But what we miss are a critical mass of the female role models for the students. There are high-profile female arbitrators who come to the Moot, but they are relatively few in number. If you look at the male arbitrator participation, you have the entire range from less experienced to high profile arbitrators. If you now look at female arbitrator participation, you have a lot of less experienced arbitrators and fewer experienced arbitrators. I am also quite active in certain women networks and what I try is to invite high-profile female arbitrators to come to Vienna. I really hope, and try to promote, that we have more experienced female arbitrators coming to the Moot because in practice they exist and it would be beneficial for the students to also learn from them.

BM Could you give us an outlook, what are your dreams for Moot?

CK We hope that the Moot continues to grow.

BM Is there any specific region you believe that is yet underrepresented at the Moot?

SK Absolutely. We do not have many teams from Africa. The problem is always that they have to find sponsors. By sponsors, we particularly mean they have to find dedicated people helping them for the first two Moots getting started. There is the Pittsburgh consortium which has done a lot of great work in Eastern Europe first and now in the Arab world. It would be great to have comparable initiatives for Africa.

We know there is a very promising initiative of two former Mooties which brought a team from Ethiopia to Vienna this year. But it is just two people. We would like to see more initiatives so that we have more African teams in the future. Hopefully, there will be an increase participation of countries coming from Africa soon.

BM Now, maybe some more personal questions: One thing that appears as a theme in any opening reception are the Moot babies and the Moot relationships on a personal level. Have you ever met any Moot couples or even Moot babies?

CK There are genuinely lots. And there is probably one around at the moment. Proof can be found on YouTube. There is a video the Moot Alumni Association did a couple of years ago as a tribute to Eric Bergsten. In this video, there was a couple who met through the Moot. He is American, she is German. Both participated and met during the Moot. They got married. It was very nice that they shared their story as a tribute to Professor Bergsten.

BM Are there any special moments you would like to share from your personal Moot experiences?

SK There are a lot: One of them relates to an Iranian team. Three years ago I got an email from an Iranian student who was very enthusiastic. He wanted to bring the first Iranian team to Vienna. I was very happy about that. But the team did not have any support. So, we contacted an American colleague and long-time supporter of the Moot, Phil Ray. He then got together a number of other people and they basically coached the Iranian team via Skype. Imagine that: We had Americans coaching Iranians via Skype. That is what the Moot is about: peaceful resolution of disputes.

CK This happened also to the Iraq teams. There are American professors teaching teams from Iraq via Skype. And I think this is so special about the Moot. The borders that we know do not necessarily exist in the Moot.

BM We have a final set of questions. In one sentence: What is the Vis Moot about? What does the Moot mean to you? And how does the Moot benefit the students most?

PN The Moot is about team building; it means to promote students from all over the world, to help them starting their career in an international environment, which goes beyond the competitive aspect of the Moot.

CK The Moot benefits the students the most by the experience it provides; they get the chance to make an experience completely separate from any substantive law issues.

SK The Moot is about meeting interesting people, discussing an interesting problem and learning that peaceful resolution of disputes is possible.

BM This was very interesting. Thank you very much for your time.

III. How to Start

1. Composition of the Teams

If you are already on a team, you might decide to jump to the next section. If, however, you are planning to put together a team at your university for the next year's Moot, you may consider the following advice.

Three questions need to be addressed: 1) who is eligible for the team, 2) how do you select a team, and 3) how many students shall be in a team.

1.1 Eligibility

The Vis Moot is a competition for students. Therefore, no one who has been licensed to practice law is eligible to participate.[1] Furthermore, the participants need to be registered at the university that they represent.

There are complicated rules on the eligibility of former participants. No restriction applies to the written phase of the Vis Moot, *i. e.*, a student may participate several times. If a student has participated in any elimination in Hong Kong or Vienna, he/she is not eligible to participate in the oral arguments of either Moot in the future. This rule, of course, intends to prevent universities from sending the same students into the competition each year. It is important that as many students of a university as possible get the unique opportunity to participate in the Vis Moot.

1.2 The Selection Process

The selection process varies between universities. Some universities provide for a written application followed by a short interview. The students simply need to prove their interest in the subject as well as their proficiency in English. Other universities invite the students to assessment center-like exercises. Lastly, some American universities choose the team after an intra-university Moot competition. That means all students may enroll in a law school course that

---

[1] *Para.* 31 Vis Moot Rules.

revolves around the Vis Moot Problem. As a coursework, the students write the Memorandum for Claimant. The students who write the best briefs are selected for the team in Vienna and/or Hong Kong.

The "perfect" Mootie understands international commercial law, finds persuasive arguments and presents his/her case convincingly. Anyone who selects a team is therefore well-advised to test these three skills. Our suggestion is to ask the students to carry out a short case study. Choose a judgment on the CISG or one issue in last year's Vis Moot Problem and ask the students to present their solution in an interview in English.

1.3 The Number of Students in a Team

The size of the team is important. For one thing, there are certain official rules that need to be observed. For another, the success in the Vis Moot to a certain extent depends on the number of team members.

The two most important official rules concerning team size are:

- ➢ A Vis Moot team comprises at least two students.
- ➢ If a university intends to participate in both the Vis Moot (East) and the Vis Moot in Vienna, the minimum team size is four students because "*no student may argue orally in both Moots in the same year.*"[2]

It is advisable to have more than two team members because the Vis Moot entails a lot of work that is best divided amongst many people. The numerical average of team members is 6.5.[3] From our experience, however, it is not advisable to have more than six students in a team unless a team participates in both the Vis Moot in Vienna and the Vis Moot (East) in Hong Kong. Why is this?

There is rarely a team with more than six students that makes it into the Final Rounds/Elimination Rounds in the Vis Moot. The main reason for this is that if a team consists of eight students and each student participates in the oral arguments, each student has one pleading during the General Rounds (as there are four pleadings for the team). If a team consists of six students and each student participates in the oral arguments, each student has at least one pleading and the two best speakers have two pleadings. Since the seventh and eighth best students are never as good as the best and second best students, the team's overall score is much higher in the second scenario. Since the level of competition in Vienna as well as

---

[2] *Para.* 32 Vis Moot Rules.

[3] http://www.cisg.law.pace.edu/cisg/moot/questions.html.

Hong Kong is very high, every point is needed to get into the next round.

A further reason for having a six-member team instead of an eight-member team are the Martin Domke and the Neil Kaplan Awards. These are the awards for the best oralists in Vienna and Hong Kong. To be eligible for the awards, a student must have argued at least twice during the General Rounds, once for the claimant and once for the respondent.

Many large teams have a policy that only the best four students may participate in the oral arguments. This solves the problem described above. However, it may impede team spirit. The oral arguments are the highlight of the Vis Moot and every student who has worked for six months on the Vis Moot Problem deserves this reward. In addition, it is honorable if you follow the traditional Olympic principle and concentrate on the participation itself rather than on the competitive element. If that holds true for your team, nothing prevents all eight team members from participating in the oral argument.

2. What Must Be Done to Register?

The rules for registration are subject to change each year. Each team is thus advised to check carefully the Vis Moot Rules as well as the websites of the Vis Moot in Vienna and the Vis Moot (East).

2.1 Registration Process for the Vis Moot in Vienna

Registration is a three-step process. It requires completion of the registration form, payment of the registration fee (in 2016, it was EUR 700) and submission of claimant's memorandum.[4] Please note the deadlines: the registration form must be submitted before the memorandum for claimant. In the 24th Moot, it was 30 November 2016. The deadline for the memorandum for claimant is usually at the beginning of December. In the 24th Vis Moot, the deadline was 8 December 2016. Payment of the registration fee is due one day later.

2.2 Registration Process for the Vis Moot (East)

Registration for the Vis Moot (East) is also a three-step process. There is, however, a significant difference because the number of

[4] *Para.* 11 Vis Moot Rules.

teams that are able to participate in the Vis Moot (East) is limited. Admission to the Vis Moot (East) is offered on a "first come first served" basis, possibly with some exceptions. In some years, 50 % of the spots were reserved for Asian teams, and no country was allowed to fill more than 25 % of the available spots. Therefore, the submission of the team registration form on time or rather as soon as registration opens is of utmost importance.

The registration fee in Hong Kong has recently been USD 1,120.

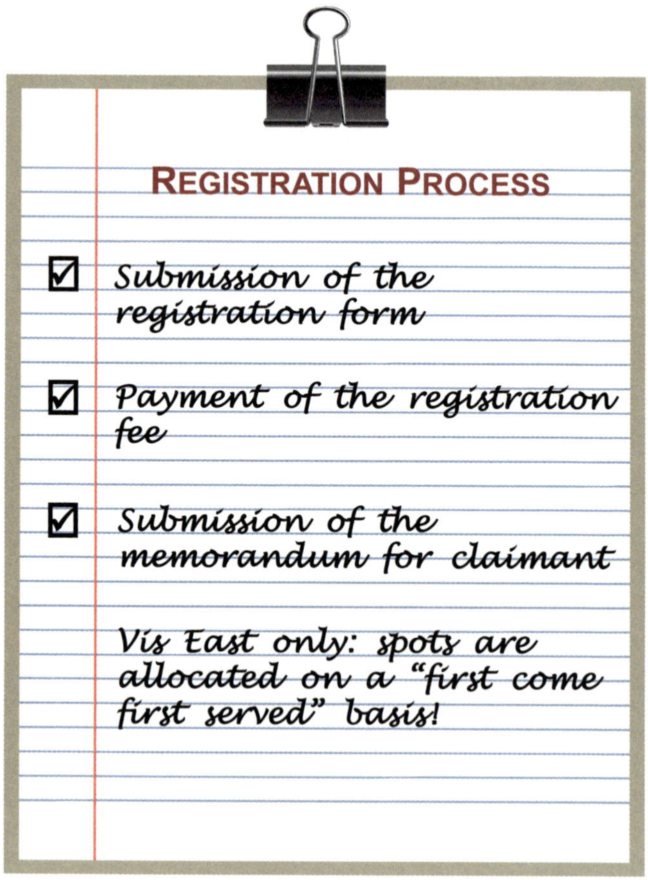

3. Team Building

Team building is the key to successful mooting. Thus, a complete chapter is dedicated to this topic.

3.1 Why Is Team Building so Important?

There are five reasons for attaching importance to team building:

- You can only win the Vis Moot as a team. This is for two reasons: It would be too much work for one person alone to write both memoranda and prepare for the oral hearings. Furthermore, it would simply be against the Vis Moot Rules to participate in the Moot as a "lone ranger."
- You can only win the Vis Moot as a team that functions well. If team spirit is missing and the students do not like each other, they do not enjoy spending time together and they lose interest in their common goal to be successful in the Moot. As in real life, negative team spirit affects the work product.
- Law students are often good individual workers but rarely good team players. Perhaps the stiff competition within legal education is to be blamed for this. It does not come as a surprise if you find a law student in the library late at night, alone, hunched over books and case law. As a law student, you do not necessarily need to be a good team player. Hence, Vis Moot participants are in great need of team building.
- Usually, you do not choose your team members yourself. Rather, you have to work with students who you might know from your class but who are not your best friends (yet).
- Finally, team building is of such high importance because you will spend a lot of time together. You will meet almost every day, you will travel to practice Moots, and eventually to Vienna or Hong Kong.

So, do yourself a huge favor and do not neglect team building!

3.2 Some Suggestions for Team Building

- Team building should start well before the Vis Moot starts in October. If you are a coach, once the new team is selected, invite the students and all other coaches for drinks. The students will have the opportunity to get to know each other in an informal atmosphere. Furthermore, you, as a coach, can brief the students on what they can expect from the Vis Moot. If you are not a coach but a member of the new team, try to find out who is on your team and how you can contact them. Then, organize an informal get-together on your own initiative.
- Spend some free time together before and during the Vis Moot. Plan activities that foster team spirit. We know of teams that went bowling and trekking together. One team decided to cook dinner

together. All these activities helped facilitate bonding and created a pleasant working atmosphere.

➢ Have Moot drinks every Thursday evening. Meet weekly after work in a bar/café/restaurant once the Moot has started. Experience shows that sometimes the best ideas/arguments for the memorandum or the oral pleading are sparked while having an informal discussion with colleagues over a drink.

➢ Invite the Vis Moot alumni from your university to all the abovementioned events. This has several benefits. First, if your team does not have a coach, the Vis Moot alumni can teach you the basics of the Vis Moot, of the CISG and international arbitration (for more comments on Coaching, see below at III.4). Second, even if your team has a coach, it is good to get first-hand experience in how the Vis Moot works at your university. To give a few examples: Where did last year's team meet? Which books did they use? Which professor agreed to support them? Where did the team find the funds to finance the Vis Moot? Where did last year's team stay in Vienna or Hong Kong? Third, Vis Moot alumni usually offer to help during the written and oral phase of the Moot. They can read and comment on the draft memoranda. Moreover, they can serve as arbitrators in internal practice rounds.

4. The Benefits of Having a Coach and How to Find One

The benefits of having a coach as a leader of the team are manifold. Below is a non-exhaustive list of reasons:

➢ A coach can take care of the administrative work, *e. g.*, the registration of the team.

➢ A coach can organize practice Moots at your university or at other universities in your country/region. A coach can also organize the trip to Vienna or Hong Kong.

➢ A coach can give an introduction to the CISG and international arbitration, two topics rarely taught at universities.

➢ A coach is a first contact point with relevant experience. The team members thus have a good chance to find answers to their questions or at least an educated opinion concerning international commercial law and international arbitration.

➢ A coach gives constant feedback on the memorandum or the oral presentations. This distinguishes a coach from a Vis Moot alumnus who helps out once or twice during the Moot. A coach should be deeply involved and know the Vis Moot Problem almost as well as the students.

At most universities, the team does not need to worry about how to find a coach because the university or a professor designates someone. At some universities, the coach is even paid for his or her job. In all other cases, the current team members should try to convince someone to support them. The most obvious choice for a coach is a Vis Moot alumnus from last year's team. Sometimes, alumni have to be persuaded to do the job because even coaching is a time-consuming exercise. However, it pays off in the end. Amongst other things, a coach learns how to lead a team, how to teach, how to organize, how to give feedback, how to motivate and how to get things done. All these are important skills for professional life.

5. Getting to Know the Subject Matter

The subject matter of the Vis Moot is new for most students. The dispute that forms the Moot Problem is an arbitration arising out of an international commercial contract governed by the CISG. Neither international commercial law nor international commercial arbitration is part of the regular curriculum at law schools. We do, however, recommend getting to know the basics of both areas of law before the Vis Moot starts. A basic understanding will help you direct your research and your focus on the right questions from the outset.

The ideal preparation for the Vis Moot would be a tailored introductory lecture or workshop that prepares the students for the Vis Moot. Maybe a professor at your university can offer such course. Alternatively, last year's team members or your coach might be happy to give a short presentation on what they have learned about international commercial arbitration and the CISG.

Finally, there are freely available articles that offer a good overview. Consider reading:

- On the CISG:
  - P. Huber "Some introductory remarks on the CISG" IHR 2006, p. 228–238[5]
  - P. Huber "CISG – The Structure of remedies" 71 Rabels Zeitschrift für ausländisches und internationales Privatrecht (2007) p. 13–34[6]

---

[5] Available at http://www.cisg.law.pace.edu/cisg/biblio/huber.html.

[6] Available at http://www.cisg.law.pace.edu/cisg/biblio/huber1.html.

➢ On International Commercial Arbitration:
  - The UNCTAD Project on Dispute Settlement in International Trade, Investment and Intellectual Property[7]
  - E. Bergsten, Module 5.1, Overview International Commercial Arbitration[8]

If you can answer the following basic questions, you are ready for the **Vis Moot:**

QUESTIONS ON THE CISG

- *When does the CISG apply?*
- *What are the buyer's legal remedies under the CISG in case of defective performance?*
- *What are the requirements for avoidance of the contract?*
- *What are the requirements of a fundamental breach?*
- *What are the requirements for an exemption of the seller for force majeure?*
- *What are the general rules on the interpretation of contracts?*
- *What law applies if a gap in the CISG needs to be filled?*

---

[7] Available at http://unctad.org/en/Pages/DITC/DisputeSettlement/Project-on-Dispute-Settlement-in-International-Trade,-Investment-and-Intellectual-Property.aspx.

[8] Available at http://unctad.org/en/docs/edmmisc232add38_en.pdf.

Questions on International Commercial Arbitration

- Name five differences between state court litigation and International Commercial Arbitration
- What is the purpose of the New York Convention on the Recognition and Enforcement of Foreign Awards? What are the grounds for rejecting the enforcement of an award?
- What is the purpose of the law at the seat of arbitration and the arbitral rules?
- Name three instances where state courts get involved even though the parties agreed on an arbitration clause

6. Kick-Off Meeting

As mentioned above, the Vis Moot Problem is distributed on the first Friday in October. It is very helpful if the team members read the Vis Moot Problem carefully over the weekend and schedule the kick-off meeting with the coach as soon as the following Monday. The following may serve as an agenda for the kick-off meeting:

6.1 A Timetable

It is highly advisable to agree with your teammates and your coach on a timetable for the next months – at least through the day in January when the memorandum for respondent is due. According to our experience, it is very important to provide in your timetable for a weekly deadline on which the draft memorandum is to be sent to the coach and a weekly meeting during which the draft is discussed and revised.

Second, it helps a lot if the timetable displays at which times of the week the team members cannot work on the memorandum or the oral pleadings. We therefore recommend that each team member discloses the following: does a team member have to attend mandatory lectures at law school? When are the lecture times? When are the exam dates? Does a team member have a job? When does he/she work? Does a team member play in a sports team? When are the training hours? What days shall be reserved for free time?

What seems like an intrusion into the privacy of the team members is of utmost importance. The Vis Moot is time-consuming. This should also be communicated by the coach and the alumni. Experience shows that differing attitudes towards time commitment are the most frequent point of conflict. It can be very irritating if two team members spend ten hours a day working on the memoranda while the other team members consider the Vis Moot a part-time activity.

Drafting a timetable will not change the fact that – as in every team in real life – some people do more work than others. However, if a timetable is drafted at the kick-off meeting, the absence of a teammate will not come as a surprise. Further, drafting the timetable helps to ensure, at an early point in time, that everybody becomes aware of the expected workload. If a team member is unable or unwilling to commit himself or herself to fully participate, you might consider replacing that team member rather than knowingly running into conflicts.

6.2 The Resources

The coach should show you the resources on the CISG and on arbitration at your university. Where do you find the relevant books in your library? Which books did last year's team use most? Is there anything you can do if the book you need is not available in your library?

If there is one book you need, it is *Schlechtriem & Schwenzer*, Commentary on the UN Convention on the International Sale of Goods (CISG), 4th Edition, Oxford University Press, 2016. It is the most elaborate work on the CISG and it is THE authority to use in the memoranda and the oral arguments. As you will see in Vienna and Hong Kong, most teams take along the commentary and have it on their desk during the pleadings. If your university lacks the resources on the CISG, there is a very good substitute: the Online

CISG Database at Pace Law School.[9] It provides case law, commentary and scholarly writing (more than 1,600 texts) for free.

On the topic of international arbitration a key database is certainly Kluwer Arbitration.[10] Unfortunately, this database is quite expensive and thus available at a few law schools only. Trial subscriptions are available, though. Experience shows that many articles on arbitration can also be found on the internet. Many authors put their publications on their website. Moreover, if you are lucky, Google Books may have the book and the pages that you are searching for.

6.3 The Assignment of the Issues

At the kick-off meeting, the coach or the students need to decide how to assign the issues. As pointed out above, there are always procedural as well as substantive issues in the Moot Problem. Thus, some students have to start reading the textbooks on international commercial arbitration while others have to read through the Schlechtriem & Schwenzer commentary (and other resources on the CISG). After two or three weeks, a question arises: change the assignment or stick to it? There seems to be a split opinion on this question. Half of the teams and coaches argue as follows: If you change the assignment, the work that has been done during the preceding weeks will be in vain. If you change the assignment, the new team has to re-read the same books that the former team has already read.

The other half argues that it is reasonable to change the assignment every two or three weeks in order to allow the input from the entire team on a certain issue. The students who were dealing with international commercial arbitration during the first three weeks might come up with new ideas if assigned to the CISG issues and vice versa. Our recommendation is to change the assignments every three weeks.

6.4 The Introduction to the Vis Moot Memoranda Writing Style

The first phase of the Vis Moot is the written phase. Drafting the memoranda for claimant and respondent sets the agenda. The problems the students face are twofold. First of all, they are not used to writing a lawyer's brief. Second, a Vis Moot memorandum follows a particular style (for further details on formalities and style, see below, chapter IV).

---

[9] http://www.iicl.law.pace.edu/cisg/cisg.

[10] http://www.kluwerarbitration.com.

Our recommendation is to read and compare several memoranda of last year's Vis Moot. Ask your Moot alumni. They will be able to provide you with several memoranda. Then, download the winning memoranda from the Vis Moot website.[11] Every team member should read and annotate five different memoranda. Have a group discussion at the end of the kick-off meeting and discuss the following questions: Which memorandum did you like best and why? What do all memoranda have in common? Do you recognize a certain Vis Moot style? What formalities seem to be important?

The advantages of this exercise are the following: the students get a first impression of how a Vis Moot memorandum has to look like and the students gain the perspective of the reader of a Vis Moot memorandum. As to the latter point, it is our experience that you become a better writer if you put yourself into the shoes of the reader. Of course this is only one of many rules on how to write an effective memorandum (see separate chapter IV below).

7. The Costs of the Vis Moot and the Possible Ways of Funding

The Vis Moot is worth every dollar, euro, renminbi, rupee and all the currencies of the world. Nevertheless, you should think about the costs and funding from the very beginning.

7.1 The Costs

Obviously, the costs greatly depend on the number of team members for which transportation, meals and room and board have to be provided. There is an obvious but important advice: keep costs to a minimum by booking flights and hotels early. Do not wait until February.

The following lists serve as a rough guide on the various cost items in Vienna and Hong Kong.

---

[11] The winning memoranda of the 24th Vis Moot in Vienna are available at https://vismoot.pace.edu/site/24th-vis-moot/programme.

Willem C. Vis International Commercial Arbitration Moot

Vienna

Registration Fee	800 USD
Flights to Vienna	**** USD
Double room in a hotel per person (8 nights)	350 USD
Three bedroom apartment per person (8 nights)	250 USD
Public transportation per person (8 days)	45 USD
1 Schnitzel dinner per person (incl. beer)	25 USD
1 piece of Sachertorte, (an Austrian cake specialty)	6 USD
1 Viennese Coffee	4 USD
1 beer at Schwarzberg	5 USD
1 Hot Dog at the Sausage Shop in front of university	4 USD

Willem C. Vis International Commercial Arbitration Moot

Willem C. Vis International Commercial Arbitration Moot

Hong Kong

Registration Fee	1,120 USD
Flights to Hong Kong	**** USD
Double room in a hotel per person (7 nights)	400 USD
Public transportation per person (7 days)	35 USD
Sunset boat trip and Seafood Dinner	48 USD
MAA Farewell Party	25 USD
MAA Antique Open-Deck Party Tram Tour	13 USD
1 beer at Rula Bula	8 USD
Dinner at Temple Street Night Market (incl. soft drink)	8 USD
1 Big Mac	2 USD

Willem C. Vis International Commercial Arbitration Moot

7.2 The Possible Funding Sources

Most students receive at least some financial support from their universities. Many, however, need to rely on sponsors. The good news is that a number of law firms sponsor Vis Moot teams. And rightfully so! It was already stated that the Vis Moot is an excellent preparation for professional life and that students acquire many skills that employers are looking for. Therefore, many international law firms are very keen to recruit their future lawyers from the pool of Vis Moot participants.

In order to win a law firm as a sponsor, your application should have a professional appearance. Add CVs of all team members. Dedicate one or two pages to an explanation and a short history of the Vis Moot. Explain why a law firm benefits from sponsorship. You should be able to, after making use of this very book (see above at I.1.–5. for the features of the Vis Moot and on the reasons for applying).

8. "New Media" and the Vis Moot

When the first Vis Moot took place in 1993, personal computers and the internet were still in their infancy. In those "good old days", the memoranda were sent through the post and Professor Bergsten stored them at home in a separate room. In 1995, one Mr. Bill Gates framed the famous sentence: "*The internet is just a hype!*" – it's reassuring to learn that even the pioneers of our time are sometimes (horribly) wrong.

Of course, you can say that "*everything was better in the old days*". However, you certainly cannot deny that many things have changed since then. Today, we all have computers, laptops, tablets and smartphones in our pockets, ready to access the internet wherever we go. We communicate via E-mail, Facebook or Twitter (the so-called "new media"). This has become a natural part of our day-to-day life. How can these new media be used for the purposes of the Vis Moot? Here are some thoughts for you:

8.1 Use New Media for Research!

You can use new media for research. In the first years of the Vis Moot, teams were usually limited to research arbitration and CISG books available at their university or would need to travel to other universities. Today, the internet has made research work much easier. There are several online databases that will help you when writing your memoranda. In the free *CISG-online* database, for example, you can find (nearly) all court decisions from around the world dealing with the CISG. Additionally, Pace University offers a free online database including both case law and scholarly materials regarding the CISG:

- http://www.cisg-online.ch/index.cfm?pageID=28
- http://www.iicl.law.pace.edu/cisg/cisg

In addition, there are several fee-based databases that some universities have access to:

- http://www.kluwerarbitration.com/
- http://www.lexisnexis.com/
- http://www.westlaw.com/

8.2 Use New Media for Promotion!

You can use new media for promotion. Depending on where your team is located, travelling to Vienna or Hong Kong and participating in Pre-Moot events can be expensive. Most teams receive at least some financial support from their universities. Many, however, need to rely on sponsors. The good news is that a number of law firms sponsor Vis Moot teams. And rightfully so! As noted above, the Vis Moot is an excellent preparation for professional life, and participating students acquire many skills that employers are looking for. Many international law firms, therefore, are keen to recruit their future lawyers from the pool of Vis Moot participants.

The new media can offer you great ways to promote your team when applying for sponsorships. Why not set up your own homepage or create a Facebook page? This is an easy way to present your team and regularly blog about the different stages of the moot. If you can refer potential sponsors to your own web presence, you will give your application a modern and more professional touch. Plus, sponsors will probably show more interest in supporting your team if, in return, you can place their firm's logo at a prominent position on your homepage. The ancient Romans already knew that "*one hand washes the other*"!

Similarly, new media can be a great tool if you plan to host (and – again – find sponsors for) a Pre-Moot event at your university. In fact, most of the Pre-Moots held in recent years had their own web presence where interested participants could find the general program of the event, the number of teams participating, the registration procedure and fees. Some organizers also posted pictures and videos to promote their events. This is a perfect opportunity for interested teams to catch a first impression of different Pre-Moots and to find their way "through the jungle" (see below at V.8.6).

8.3 Use New Media for Getting Together!

You can use new media for getting together with other teams during all phases of the moot. It's easy for you to get in touch with a team that has its own homepage or Facebook-page.

For example, when you're preparing for the oral arguments and you want to arrange a practice round with a team located near your university, this team might only be a few mouse-clicks away! And for the more adventurous Mooties: in times of *Skype*, you can also organize video-conferences and hold practice rounds with teams from distant countries or continents.

Furthermore, the new media can be useful for getting together during your days in Vienna or Hong Kong. In Vienna, even though it will always be possible to meet other Mooties in the legendary "Dachgeschoss" during the day and the "Schwarzberg"-club at night, Facebook-messenger or Whatsapp can help you make more specific plans to meet up. Free Wi-Fi is regularly available in most of the universities' and law firms' rooms both in Vienna and Hong Kong, so you don't need to fear expensive roaming charges.

Finally, social media makes it very easy to stay in touch with the friends you made once your days in Vienna and Hong Kong have passed. Use that opportunity! Apart from networking reasons, having friends around the globe can be a really great thing when travelling.

8.4 Use New Media for your Supporters at Home!

Finally, you can use new media for your supporters at home. Supporters at home? That's right! Many universities have a large number of moot alumni that support the current team, be it in the preparation of memoranda or in improving the team's pleadings. Although some supporters are physically present in Vienna or Hong Kong to cheer for their team, those who couldn't make it have a hard time at home, full of excitement for their teammates and desperate to know if they are doing well. Have a heart for these invisible supporters! With a little help from new media you can keep them connected.

One option is creating a blog for your team's time in Vienna or Hong Kong. Each day, one of your team members can update supporters with a short blog post, describing (for example) how the pleading went, what other experiences the team had and so on. You can make it even more authentic if you also post pictures. A daily blog is a nice thing for your supporters at home – but it can also be a great souvenir for you, just like a diary, that will always remind you of your unique time in Vienna or Hong Kong.

Another option is setting up a "live ticker". For example, you can use Twitter or (if you don't want the shared information to be shown publicly) a closed Facebook group to which you invite only team members and supporters. For example, one of your teammates can post about the final seconds before a pleading begins or, directly afterwards, about how your team did. "Before and after" pictures can be a nice thing – and, again, a great memory! Furthermore, you can use the live ticker not only for the pleadings, but also for other crucial events like the announcement of the finalists. As noted above, free Wi-Fi is available in most of the universities' and law firms' rooms in Vienna and Hong Kong.

8.5 A Note of Caution

Once upon a time there was a world without the internet and without social media. The Vis Moot already existed in those long-ago days; and Vis Moot teams had fun and success (in that order of priority). You can have fun and succeed in the Vis Moot with the internet, without the internet, and with a little bit of internet. Choose wisely.

The internet makes information accessible to everybody, creating equality among participants. That is good. But equal access to information also tends to create uniformity, because everybody has the same information and it is easy to literally copy-paste arguments from well-known authors or even from competing teams. This tendency is *not* good. It kills creativity. Don't limit yourself to understanding and repeating the thoughts of somebody else. Think for yourself.

The use of electronic media may also reduce your chances to succeed in the Vis Moot if that is what matters for you. Consider the following: if everybody raises the same arguments, found in some database or tweeted to team members by a friend listening to another team's compelling oral pleading, how can the arbitrators distinguish your team from others? "*Be daring, be different, be first*", an advocacy principle explained elsewhere in this book, is always worth bearing in mind.

In the long run, you want to go for the real thing, that is, becoming an arbitration lawyer. In the real world, there are not 300 teams dealing with the same case at the same time, creating immense opportunities for (to use a euphemism) "knowledge sharing". There are just you and your "*learned friend*", as the English often put it – your opposing counsel. Here, being a copycat will not help you prevail for your client; you must be yourself. Especially if you have a bad case, you sometimes must find new and innovative arguments, those which nobody has thought of before. Use the Vis Moot to train for this situation and find out whether or not you are good at it.

There is no way that you won't use the internet, databases and social media when participating in the Vis Moot. And we don't need a crystal ball to see that the influence of the internet will be even bigger five or ten years from now. But don't allow the internet or social media to take decisions you should make yourself. It's your choice alone. Choose wisely.

9. Start Visa Application on Time

Many students need a visa for Vienna or Hong Kong. Check whether your passport is valid for another six months after the Moot and start your visa application on time. The organizers of the Vis Moot will assist you and information concerning the visa application will be sent to all teams at the beginning of December. The Austrian Europe Integration Foreign Affairs Federal Ministry provides visa information in English. Check their website: https://www.bmeia.gv.at/en/travel-stay/entry-and-residence-in-austria/entry-and-visa/. If you are travelling to Hong Kong, check the website of the Chinese embassy in the United Kingdom: http://www.chinese-embassy.org.uk/eng/visa. Check the Vis Moot website and the frequently asked questions for further guidance.

Following these guidelines all at once will be a little too much. We therefore recommend you to already manage some issues once you have selected your team, so that you can fully focus on the memoranda once the problem is out (the funding for the registration fee should not quicken your pulse as the due date for the memorandum for claimant gets closer). This is our suggestion:

Once You Have a Team You should…

- Focus on team building
- Get to know the subject matter
- Check the resources on arbitration and the CISG at your university
- Look for ways of funding
- Check whether team members need a visa for Vienna or Hong Kong
- Keep an eye on the registration process

ONCE THE PROBLEM IS OUT YOU SHOULD…

- Organize the team with a timetable
- Assign the issues of the problem
- Get familiar with the writing style of the Vis Moot Memoranda
- Have a weekly meeting during which the current draft is discussed and revised
- (Buy a coffee machine)

IV. How to Write Effective Memoranda

1. The Moot's "Written" Phase

You have formed a formidable team. You have invested in team building. You have the best coach possible. You have already studied the basics of the key legal areas relevant in the Moot, namely international arbitration law and the CISG. You are ready. Then, regularly on the first Friday in October, your team receives this year's Moot case,[1] typically consisting of the Request for Arbitration, the Answer to the Request for Arbitration and correspondence between the parties and the arbitral institution concerning the first procedural steps such as the appointment of arbitrators. The Moot has ultimately started. And it starts, as in every real arbitration, with the "written phase," *i. e.,* submissions by both parties.

1.1 Course of the "Written" Phase

The course of the Moot, including the "written" phase, has already been described above, but a brief recapitulation does no harm. Your team receives the Moot case on the first Friday in October. Then, you have about two months to draft your first submission, namely the one where you represent claimant. Another six weeks later, the memorandum for respondent is due. The memoranda must be submitted through the Moot website in PDF as a single computer file so that the memoranda can be printed complete with cover page.[2]

1.2 The Basic Structure of Your Memorandum

"How should we structure our submission?" is among the first questions asked by Mooties. Well, there are few formal, mandatory requirements under the Moot Rules but over time, a certain "practice" has been developed which is nowadays widely followed. Our

---

[1] The Moot Problem is the same for the Vis Moot (East) and the Moot that takes place in Vienna.

[2] Care should be taken that the PDF file does not exceed one megabyte. Memoranda that exceed one megabyte will be returned with a request that they be reconverted to a smaller file (see *paras.* 53 *et seq.* Vis Moot Rules for further details).

recommendation is: do not only study the Vis Moot Rules but match them with last year's winning memoranda, which you will find on the Vis Moot's website.[3] This way, you will acquaint yourself with both the hard and soft rules as to how you should structure your submissions. If you scroll through the memoranda of last year's winning teams, you will probably notice the following:

➢ *Start with a professionally-looking cover page*: The cover page usually contains the name of the university, the university's emblem, the names of the team members, the names of the parties to the arbitration and the brief's title, *i. e.,* memorandum for claimant or memorandum for respondent. Here is an example:

TWENTY SECOND ANNUAL

WILLEM C. VIS INTERNATIONAL COMMERCIAL ARBITRATION MOOT

Vienna, Austria 27 March - 2 April 2015

MEMORANDUM FOR CLAIMANT

University of Erion

UNIVERSITY OF ERION

On behalf of	Against
Mediterraneo Elite Conferences Services, Ltd	**Equatoriana Control Systems, Inc**
45 Conference Place	286 Second Avenue
Capital City, Mediterraneo	Oceanside, Equatoriana
CLAIMANT	**RESPONDENT**

TEAM MEMBER 1 TEAM MEMBER 2 TEAM MEMBER 3 TEAM MEMBER 4

[3] https://vismoot.pace.edu/site/24th-vis-moot/programme.

- *Page 2 is a meaningful table of contents*: On the second page, you should insert a table of contents. Even though the Vis Moot Rules do not require a table of contents, a table of contents is an (informal) must. This has several compelling reasons. First, every seasoned arbitrator evaluating your memoranda is used to finding a table of contents as the introductory part of any brief in real world arbitrations. If you disregard that custom, you are perceived as unprofessional. Second, your arbitrator = evaluator wants to understand the basic structure of your memorandum before getting into details. Third, if your arbitrator later decides to re-read certain parts of your memorandum, *e. g.*, for comparing it with other memoranda, you will want him/her to find the relevant part on the spot. Finally, and perhaps most importantly, a professionally written table of contents provides the crucial first impression, that your memorandum is well-structured, organized and not leaving out any key argument. Actually, the table of contents and the corresponding titles in your memoranda are so important, that we have devoted a separate chapter on this issue which you will find below. For the time being, and as a first step, review the table of contents of last year's winning memorandum to get an idea of how a good table of contents should look like.
- *Continue with a concise and accurate statement of facts*: Your arbitrator will expect to read a statement of facts next because that is what he or she encounters in real arbitrations. Don't confuse the arbitrator by choosing a different structure that you might find preferable – but not your arbitrator. And in accordance with the old Roman Law doctrine "*Da mihi facta, dabo tibi ius*,"[4] that established practice makes eminent sense because the arbitrator will always need to know on which facts he or she is expected to apply the law. Consequently, in real arbitrations, the statement of facts section of your memorandum easily covers 70 % of the entire brief and it is written with a certain "twist," *i. e.*, presented in a subjective manner emphasizing the facts in support of your client's position, and downplaying (or even omitting) facts that might be seen as harmful to your client's case.
- *Be aware that the Moot is different in this respect*: When your arbitrator = evaluator of your brief starts reading, he or she will already have read the analysis of the Vis Moot Problem and thus knows the facts. In addition, your arbitrator might have read and evaluated other memoranda, including the presentation of facts provided therein. Hence, your arbitrator is not that interested into this part of your brief and might even skip it. The conse-

[4] Translated: 'Give me the facts, and I give you the law (on those facts)."

quence is clear: keep the statement of facts short, as short as possible, in order to gain more space for your substantive arguments. It is here where the art of writing in a concise manner, discussed in more detail below, unfolds its true relevance. Resist the temptation to present the facts with a "twist" in support of your party's position. In the Vis Moot, we have seen many memoranda that were marked down by an arbitrator who found the statement of facts to be too one-sided. Thus, keep the factual part of your memorandum concise and objective.

- ➢ *Summary of Argument*: Although you cannot find it in the Vis Moot Rules, you are expected to include a short summary or introduction in your brief. This is usually about one page long and contains a concise summary of your position.
- ➢ *Arguments as key part of your submission*: All the abovementioned components of your memorandum are just a prelude to what ultimately matters – you arguing the merits of the case, be that in terms of procedural questions related to arbitral law or to substantive questions related to the CISG. In the Moot, you receive some guidance with regard to the order you should present those issues. To this end, Procedural Order No. 1 determines four or five issues to be discussed in your memorandum. Do not try to be creative by changing this pre-determined high-level structure of arguments. Otherwise, your arbitrator will be confused and it is somewhat unlikely that he or she will consider your structure preferable to the suggestion of the Moot Court organizers.
- ➢ *Conclude with a request for relief and your signatures*: Since the Moot aims at coming as close to reality as possible, you must conclude your memorandum with a formal request for relief and your signatures. It is true that in many civil law jurisdictions and corresponding state court proceedings, the request for relief precedes any other statement and thus forms part of the beginning of a submission. However, in international arbitration, the common law practice prevails, *i. e.*, a request for relief at the end of the memorandum, and you would be ill-advised to challenge that practice. Finally, conclude your memorandum with your (legible, if at all possible) signatures confirming that you accept full responsibility for your submission, as counsel to the parties in real arbitral proceedings do.
- ➢ *Add the table of authorities and the table of abbreviations*: Many teams put the table of authorities and the table of abbreviations at the beginning of the memorandum right after the table of contents. However, this common practice is neither required under the Vis Moot Rules nor recommended. Put yourself into the

shoes of your arbitrator: how interested are you in the books and articles that the team has used in preparing the memorandum? And are you truly eager to read the abbreviations used in the memorandum before you encounter those abbreviations in the text itself – and disregard the fact that you already know two-thirds of those short forms without any need for further explanations? Asking those questions already provides the answer. It compels putting those pages at the very end of your memorandum even if this is not mirrored by the award-winning memoranda to date. If enough teams read this book and follow our advice, Moot practice will undergo a swift change and will bring the Moot memorandum in this regard closer to a real legal brief.

STRUCTURE OF MEMORANDUM

- *Cover page*
- *Table of contents*
- *Statement of facts*
- *Summary of argument*
- *Argument*
- *Request for relief*
- *Signatures*
- *Table of authorities*
- *Table of arbitral awards*
- *Table of court decisions*
- *Table of abbreviations*

1.3 Formalities and Tips for Brushing Up Your Memorandum

The Moot will (probably) be the largest enjoyable event you will encounter during your studies, but it is still a competition. Competitions need rules to permit a fair evaluation of all competitors. The Moot and its written phase form no exception. Hence, you must make yourself familiar with those rules, printed also in the back of this book, and you then must adhere to those rules meticulously. Bending and stretching those rules are not only unfair to your fellow participants from other universities, if discovered, it will eliminate your chances to do well in the written phase. Here are some key rules to remember:

➢ *The length of the memoranda*: According to the Vis Moot Rules, the memoranda must not exceed 35 pages.[5] These include any statement of facts, argument or discussion and any conclusion. Usually, the statement of facts and the summary of argument will account for two pages. This leaves 33 pages for the actual arguments, the request for relief and your signatures. Note that the cover page, the table of authorities, and the table of abbreviations do not count against this page limit.

➢ *Formatting requirements*: Yes, you will almost certainly find yourself in the dilemma that you have more to say about the Moot Problem than what fits into the meager 35 page limit. What are you going to do to solve the problem? Shorten and streamline your arguments! Drop the less compelling ones! You have no alternative to this approach because the Moot Rules put forward stringent formatting requirements: the statement of facts and the actual arguments must not exceed 35 pages; paragraphs must be numbered; type style shall be no smaller than 12 points; line spacing should be 1.5; and all margins must be at least one inch or 2.5 cm.[6]

➢ *Footnotes and citations*: No footnotes are permitted, and citations and references must rather be in the text of the memorandum.[7] Hence, you are deprived of the "chance" to shorten your text by "outsourcing" less important arguments to footnotes using space-saving fine print.

---

[5] *Para.* 50 Vis Moot Rules.

[6] *Cf. paras.* 45 and 50 Vis Moot Rules.

[7] For details, see *para.* 47 Vis Moot Rules. Footnotes were once admitted. The students, however, tended to compose academic writings instead of lawyer's briefs.

➢ *Other rules*: Paragraphs must be numbered and references to statements in the own memorandum or the opponent's memorandum must be to the paragraph number.[8] Pursuant to the Vis Moot Rules, the table of authorities should be in a form that is intelligible to all the readers of your memorandum,[9] *i. e.*, arbitrators and other students. Since they are from many countries around the world, particular care has to be given to the respective style of citation. Try to use a citation that enables your readers to find the authority that you are quoting. A further important rule concerning the table of authorities is the following: the teams must refer to each paragraph in the memorandum where the case or doctrinal authority is cited.[10]

Those formal requirements leave you with little leeway as to the formatting of your submission and, consequently, the outer appearance of your memorandum. However, there are still a few things you can do to improve the first visual impression created by your memorandum. Consider the following:

- The Moot Rules are silent on the font style you use. True, Times New Roman and Arial are by far the most common fonts, and you surely make no mistake using them. But you may find one which is easier to read, looks better or at least distinguishes your memorandum from all the rest.
- The Moot Rules require you to insert paragraph numbers, but it is your choice whether you put those numbers in front of each paragraph or insert margin numbers on the right hand side of each paragraph. The latter requires some efforts as to formatting but it certainly looks better.
- You may well consider not making full use of the writing space permitted under the Moot Rules. "But that means raising fewer arguments or not exploring those arguments in depth," which you may counter. That is true, but rest assured that the arbitrators = evaluators of your memorandum neither give bonus points for exhausting the permitted page limit nor do they add up words or arguments for translating the total number into the score your memorandum deserves. Instead, an arbitrator might be more impressed by how easy-to-read your memorandum is – be that due to generous margins or due to citations not pressed into brackets but set forth in a separate, indented paragraph.

---

[8] *Para.* 45 Vis Moot Rules.
[9] *Para.* 48 Vis Moot Rules.
[10] *Para.* 46 Vis Moot Rules.

You will have probably figured out by now that the rationale of the preceding recommendations is to invest time and effort in improving the outer appearance of your memorandum. Few arbitrators will love your arguments if your submission looks shady. If you are lucky, your submission will be reviewed by an arbitrator who is easily impressed by the submission's "visuals." Don't miss that chance.

1.4 Special Rules for the Memorandum for Respondent

What happens after the memorandum for claimant is submitted? Approximately one week after the due date for the memorandum for claimant, your team receives the memorandum for claimant from another university. If you are from a civil law country, you will probably receive a memorandum from a common law country and vice versa.

The most important rule for the memorandum for respondent is: be responsive! As the Vis Moot Rules state: "*When judging the memorandum for respondent, account will be taken whether it is responsive to the arguments raised by the claimant.*"[11] You should be aware that the four arbitrators who read your memorandum for respondent are the ones who have already read the memorandum for claimant to which you are responding. While being responsive is the most important rule, your memorandum must at the same time be coherent in itself and must not be a list of disconnected answers to the allegations made by claimant.

In a real arbitration, you are lucky if you receive a weak memorandum for claimant because it will be easy to respond to and convince the tribunal of your position. In the Vis Moot, however, you are lucky if you receive a strong memorandum for claimant because it is easier to write a strong memorandum for respondent if claimant has raised the relevant arguments. What do you do if the memorandum for claimant that you received does not raise an important argument? It would be a mistake not to address it. The arbitrators might otherwise mark your memorandum down for lack of substance. The Vis Moot Rules explicitly deal with this problem: a team shall respond to those arguments that should have been made by a claimant[12] – at least in the team's opinion. If a response to such possible argument is made, the team should identify it in an appropriate manner. We recommend the following:

---

[11] *Para.* 61 Vis Moot Rules.
[12] *Para.* 42 Vis Moot Rules.

"Claimant might argue in the oral hearing that ... Such argument, however, would be without merit."

1.5 The Grading of Your Submission

Vis Moot memoranda are assessed in two rounds. In the first round, each arbitrator receives four memoranda. The Vis Moot organizers ask the arbitrators to do two things: first, read and comment on the memoranda and second, rank the four memoranda. The first task is mainly for educational purposes. Arbitrators are expressly encouraged to give feedback so that the students who drafted the brief can improve their legal writing. The comments, however, also serve as a justification for the ranking. If an arbitrator ranks a team's memorandum poorly, he/she should give a short explanation. Each memorandum will be read and judged by four arbitrators.

One-fourth of the memoranda that have – on average – the best ranking, make it to the second round of evaluation. Although there are no statistics, we would say that your memorandum needs to achieve at least two first places and two second places in order to be among the best 25 %.

In the second round, a separate jury determines the winners of the awards for best memorandum in each category. The best memoranda will receive the Pieter Sanders and Werner Melis Awards in Vienna or the David Hunter and Fali Nariman Awards in Hong Kong. The winners are announced on the last day of the oral phase of the Moot at the Awards Banquet in Vienna and the Gala Awards Banquet in Hong Kong. By the way, the written phase is scored separately from the oral phase. Thus, even if your memoranda are not amongst the best, you may still be the winner of the oral phase.

If the Vis Moot administrators do not change the instruction to the arbitrators, your memorandum will be judged on the basis of five criteria[13]:

- *The substance of the memorandum ("quality of the analysis").* The arbitrators will evaluate whether you have presented good arguments and addressed all relevant issues of the Vis Moot Problem. Does your memorandum evidence that you have done thorough research? Did you stick to the facts as stated in the Vis Moot Problem?
- *The effectiveness of the memorandum ("persuasiveness of argument").* How persuasive are your arguments? How well are they presented and are they easily comprehensible? If you follow the

[13] *Para.* 61 Vis Moot Rules.

rules on persuasive legal writing as described in this chapter, you will have a fair chance to get high marks for the effectiveness of your memorandum.

- *Use of authorities ("thoroughness of research")*. The arbitrators will evaluate your use of authorities. Is the number of authorities that you use reasonable? Is the citation intelligible even for foreign students and arbitrators?
- *Presentation ("adherence to the elements of style")*. Your memorandum should have a professional appearance and should come as closely to a brief in a real arbitration as possible. The Vis Moot organizers remind the arbitrators to ensure compliance with the formatting rules and the formalities as explained above (at IV.1.3, 1.4).
- *Use of language ("clarity of the writing")*. Of course, your memorandum should be free of spelling errors. Arbitrators will praise clear language and formal English style. The Vis Moot Rules expressly remind the participants that slang or contractions (aren't, didn't) should not be used.[14]

2. Reality Check: Submissions in International Arbitration

A principal objective of the Moot is to come as close to real arbitration as possible. With regard to the written submission phase, the Vis Moot accomplishes this goal to a remarkable extent as the following comparison demonstrates.

2.1 The Course of Written Submissions in International Arbitrations

Most international arbitrations nowadays, at least the major ones, start with a relatively short request for arbitration, containing only mandatory requirements stipulated in the applicable arbitration law and arbitration rules. Those key requirements are, *inter alia*:

- the name in full, description, address and other contact details of each of the parties;
- the name in full, address and other contact details of any person(s) representing the claimant in the arbitration;
- a description of the nature and circumstances of the dispute giving rise to the claims and of the basis upon which the claims are made;

[14] *Para.* 49 Vis Moot Rules.

- a statement of the relief sought, together with the amounts of any quantified claims and, to the extent possible, an estimate of the monetary value of any other claims;
- any relevant agreements and, in particular, the arbitration agreement(s);
- where claims are made under more than one arbitration agreement, an indication of the arbitration agreement under which each claim is made;
- all relevant particulars and any observations or proposals concerning the number of arbitrators and their choice (see, *e. g.*, Articles 12 and 13 of the ICC Arbitration Rules (2012) ("ICC Rules")), and any nomination of an arbitrator required thereby; and
- all relevant particulars and any observations or proposals as to the place of the arbitration, the applicable rules of law and the language of the arbitration.

Compare, for example, Article 4 ICC Rules for further guidance. This short request for arbitration is answered by an equally short "Answer," also only containing some basic information about the dispute to be arbitrated, cf. Article 5 ICC Rules.

Once the arbitral tribunal is established, it will summon a procedural conference. Therein, the tribunal will discuss with the parties the procedural rules to be applied (subsequently ordered to be applicable by a formal procedural order) and a provisional timetable. In addition, the tribunal might determine, on a preliminary basis, the issues to be decided (cf. Articles 23 and 24 ICC Rules). Such provisional timetable regularly foresees two full rounds of submissions. The first round of submissions consists of a statement of claim and, subsequently, a statement of defense. In a standard case, each party has three months to submit the respective brief. In many international arbitrations, this first phase is followed by an intermediary phase that is devoted to document production, and that phase may last six weeks. The second full round of submissions consists of the so-called reply (claimant) and the rejoinder (respondent). It is customary that roughly two months are scheduled for each phase.

The hearing follows two months after receipt of the rejoinder, lasting one to three days, depending on the scope of evidence taking, *i. e.*, the testimony of witnesses and experts. Finally, the parties are granted two months for filing post-hearing briefs in which they are asked to comment on the evidence and to summarize their arguments. A further three months later, the arbitral tribunal will render its award. While every seasoned arbitrator can raise countless examples where this schedule was shortened (relatively rare) or grossly extended (frequently), we consider this timeline somewhat representative or – at least – of exemplary value.

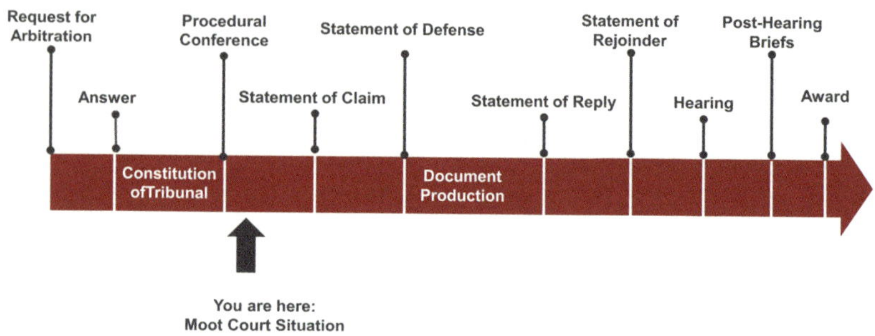

In the timeline above, we have indicated the situation you find yourself in when receiving the Moot Problem in October. You may well assume that the procedural hearing has taken place, procedural rules have been established (Vis Moot Rules) and a procedural calendar has been fixed. In addition, the issues to be decided have been determined on a preliminary basis. You find those in Procedural Order No. 1. Hence, the situation you encounter is a very realistic one.

2.2 The Typical Content and Format of Written Submissions

The typical structure of written submissions resembles the structure proposed above for your memorandum – actually that is the very reason why we proposed that structure. However, there is one major difference: In real life, a convincing brief focuses on the presentation of the facts and the corresponding evidence. An intense discussion of legal problems often is not required because the legal consequences are easy to draw once the facts are established and proven.

In a disputed construction project, for example, responsibility for project delay might be a major issue but that question is "factually" decided by a proper delay analysis outlining the single reasons for the delays accompanied by a cause and effect analysis. Few legal issues may need to be discussed. Similarly, in a post-M&A dispute, the parties might fight over the correctness of the target company's balance sheets. Once the (in)accuracy of the accounting is established, the application of the corresponding contractual guarantee "the past annual statements are correct in all material respects" creates no problems. If legal problems need to be discussed in depth, that discussion complements the factual allegations.

All this is different in the Moot where the facts are usually concise and legal issues play the key role. However, this does not mean that working with the facts of the Problem is less important. The purpose of the memoranda in the Moot is more than "just" discussing legal problems in an abstract way. Rather, the task is to apply the law to the particular case, as in real life. Thus, your memorandum will be more convincing if – in your argument – you work as intensely as possible with the given facts. In the end, the people assessing your memoranda are mostly arbitration practitioners, and they will be more impressed the more your memorandum resembles a real brief.

The format of written submissions again comes close to what you are expected to file in the Moot, except that in our experience in most civil law countries, rarely are the parties required to abide by a page limit such as the one in the Moot. Many arbitrators are reluctant to impose a page limit without the parties' consent fearing that such restriction might violate the parties' right to be heard.

Numbering paragraphs is the rule. Typically, a broad side margin is employed to (1) allow the arbitrators to take notes on the page, and (2) to make reading easier for the arbitrators (a page fully covered by words and letters is difficult to read). The submission is always complemented by a table of exhibits and sometimes also by a timeline (chronological order of events) and a *dramatis personae*, *i. e.*, a list of all persons involved in the dispute indicating their relation to the parties and their role/function in the dispute.

In the Moot, those additional exhibits are for obvious reasons not needed. Finally, the trend in international arbitration is towards electronic briefs. Not only are submissions exchanged electronically via e-mail, but some top-notch submissions are also electronically "linked" to relevant exhibits, *i. e.*, the arbitrator must only "click" on the cited reference or the documentary evidence to have immediate electronic access to the original document.

2.3 The Cultural Divide Revisited: Different Styles of Briefs

There is a lot of talk about "common law style" arbitrations and "civil law style" arbitrations, and you will also hear such discussions during your time at the Vis Moot. But be aware that arguably there is no such divide anymore in arbitration. Yes, there are domestic arbitrations in which only practitioners of one jurisdiction come together; in this case, the arbitration will be very much like proceedings before the national courts. For international arbitration, however, one often finds a hybrid, including elements of common law and civil law. As a very broad generalization, one can say that the phase of an arbitration concerning the taking of evidence has borrowed quite a few elements from the common law tradition,[15] even in arbitrations where no common law practitioners participate, one will often have elements such as witness statements, cross examination and disclosure. The written phase drifts more towards the civil law tradition. Traditionally, in civil law countries, the focus of the proceedings lies on written briefs that fully set out the facts of the case. Unless those facts are evidenced by witnesses, it may be that witnesses do not play a role in an oral hearing at all. Also in international arbitration, briefs tend to become more and more voluminous, covering all the facts of the case in detail.

3. Ground Rules for Writing Effective Submissions

Most law schools – at least outside the US – teach you to think like a lawyer, but not how to write effectively. You only write effectively if your reader likes your writing and understands the thoughts you are putting down on paper. If the reader does not understand your writing, your arguments remain unpersuasive. If the reader must invest a lot of effort in understanding your writing, *e. g.*, by reading every sentence twice, he will perceive your line of argument as "complicated" and "twisted," albeit only your writing is. If the reader is bored by your writing, his attention will decrease and his thoughts will drift away from your arguments. Hence, when you are writing your memoranda for the Vis Moot, you should know and apply basic writing rules. Here is why:

Whenever you start writing, either you already know what you are going to write or you are developing your ideas while you are writing. In both cases, you will have no difficulties in understanding your own text once you read it on paper. But that is not because your writing is crystal clear. It is because you had already understood or thought through what you want to express before you have finished your last sentence. Reading your text only serves as a prompter, the text reminds you of what you have thought through and understood.[16] Hence, for you as a writer, understanding comes first, and putting your "understanding" down on paper second. Consequently, you always "understand" your own text without

---

[15] The IBA Rules on the Taking of Evidence in International Arbitration are intended to be a common denominator for arbitrations in which parties and practitioners from both common and civil law traditions come together.

[16] If you do not believe that, do the following: Read a text you have written a couple of months or a year ago. You once understood that text well but because the text's "prompting" effect has already faded away, you will suddenly encounter difficulty understanding your own text.

any difficulties. For your reader, the sequence of understanding is reverse: When your reader starts reading your text, he has no idea what you are going to say. Reading comes first, (hopefully) followed by understanding. Why does all this pose a problem? Because few writers realize that understanding their text is not a given. Even fewer writers know how to write in order to be understood by their readers. And hardly any writer is prepared to invest time and efforts in improving his text and making it more readable.

The German poet Goethe (1749–1832) once started a letter as follows:

> *"I apologize for this long letter. I simply had no time for writing a short one."*

Goethe knew that writing in a succinct and understandable manner requires extra energy. Nobody can put down a complicated thought on paper and – at the same time – concentrate on writing in an understandable way. Doing both at the same time would require multitasking – and our brain is not wired for multitasking. Goethe had also realized that writing well is more a question of hard work and time than a question of talent. So our initial, and perhaps most important advice to you is: Separate the process of putting your thoughts on paper (first step) from rephrasing your text in order to make it readable (second step). You should tackle the second step only sometime after you have finished the first step. Think of tasking a different team member with reviewing your text's readability. And do so with a formal approach, *i. e.,* by strictly applying a predetermined set of "writing rules." This two-step approach is by far the most effective way to avoid the described "prompting" effect.

3.1 Rule 1: KISS – Use Short Sentences

KISS stands for "Keep it short and simple". A similar advice is the "One idea per sentence" rule or, more simply, "use short sentences." Like most writers, you have heard of this rule. Still it is amazing how many lawyers simply ignore this rule, even though its importance cannot be overstated. What is wrong with sentences that are too long? The reader has to save all the information contained in the sentence until he or she arrives at the end of the sentence. Only then can the reader put the saved information into context and digest its meaning. The longer the sentence, the more demanding this exercise becomes. Look at the following random example from an English House of Lords judgment:

> *"My Lords, I have come to the clear conclusion in the present case that the legislative intendment in relation to sections 555 and 556, and their statutory predecessors in the 1986 Act, was that foreign entertainers and sportsmen who, or whose controlled companies, receive payments in connection with their commercial activities in the United Kingdom should be subject to the section 18(1)(a)(iii) charge to tax and that the territorial principle cannot be implied so as to limit the effect of the clear language of section 555(2)." Agassi v Robinson [2006] UKHL 23*

Reading a sentence like this takes a lot of effort. Readers need to maintain their concentration and save the sentence's component parts in their short term memory, until they get to the last bit of important information (here: the territorial principle cannot be implied into section 18(1)(a)(iii)). This is fine for one sentence, but will cost the reader effort if this is the author's general style of writing. This is particularly true considering that in practice, you will often not have a hundred percent of the reader's attention. Rather, readers are distracted by incoming calls and e-mails, and by interaction with colleagues, assistants and the like. If you are lucky, you will have half of the reader's attention. Reading a text consisting of sentences such as the one above is frustrating. Your reader has to re-read the sentence, and maybe the following sentences if they are phrased similarly. After a while, your reader starts skimming, and may finally give up reading. This is the worst that can happen to a lawyer. If you lose your reader, you may lose your case, your client, your business.

Compare the above example to the following text by Lord Denning:

> *"The plaintiffs, Fielding and Platt Ltd are manufacturers of machinery. Their business is in Gloucester. In the middle of 1965 they entered into a contract with a Lebanese company called SCIALE Aluminium of Lebanon. They agreed to make and sell to the Lebanese company an aluminium extrusion press for a total sum of \$L 235,000. The plant and equipment was to be delivered free on board at a British port. The time for delivery was 10 1/2 months from 19 June 1965. Payment was to be made by six promissory notes given by the defendant, the managing director of the Lebanese company, Mr Selim Najjar, personally." (Fielding and Platt Ltd v Najjar, 1969) 2 All E.R. 150.*

Lord Denning was famous for his comprehensible writing and his short sentences. This paragraph has about the same number of words as the quote from the House of Lords judgment; but this time, we have seven sentences instead of one. The effect is the following: whenever you arrive at a full stop, you can virtually feel the break, a break that gives you time to breathe. You can easily digest the information from the sentence you have just read, and move on to the next short sentence. You thereby get into a certain pace, a certain reading rhythm. As a result, you can read the work product quickly, and you have to read it only once to understand it.

Our recommendation to you is as follows: Agree on the maximum length of a sentence, *e. g.*, "two lines" or "20 words." Once you have finished your text, start counting. Circle each sentence which is longer than the limit agreed upon. Then shorten the sentence by deleting any word not necessary for understanding the sentence. Or simply split the sentence into two sentences. If neither measure leads to the desired result, rethink your argument. Apparently it is too complicated to be understood.

3.2 Rule 2: What Matters Most – Subject + Verb

Research shows that readers look for an answer to a simple question: Who does what? Readers find texts easier to understand if the subject is presented early in the sentence, and if the verb is close to the subject. "Early" does not mean that the subject has to be the first word, and "close" does not mean that subject and verb ought to be adjacent. You do not want to write "Tarzan loves Jane" style, as your writing would become dull. But avoid sentences like this one:

> *"As a preliminary remark, it must be noted that unlike Claimant repeatedly attempted to make the court believe, Respondent, who has more than 20 years of experience in the construction industry and who carried out foundation works in no less than ten similar projects, at no time failed to afford adequate protection to the foundation works against temperatures lower than 10 degrees Celsius."*

There are 18 words before the reader arrives at the subject, and another 28 words before the reader gets to the verb. How can one repair the sentence? Taking a closer look, the first remarks ("as a preliminary remark, it must be noted that") are just clutter and can be safely deleted. For the remaining bit, we recommend to follow Rule 1 and break down the sentence in two sentences. Automatically, the subject and the verb move closer together:

> *"**Respondent** has more than 20 years of experience in the construction industry and carried out foundation works in ten*

similar projects. At no time ***did Respondent fail to protect*** *the foundation works adequately against temperatures lower than 10 degrees Celsius."*

To back that up by some science: Our ultra-short term memory has a storage capacity of roughly three seconds. Average reading speed is three to four syllables per second, hence a maximum of 12 syllables in three seconds. Twelve syllables translate into roughly six words. Consequently, if you insert more than six words between your subject and the verb, chances are high that your reader will have forgotten the subject when arriving at the verb. And if the reader does not remember the subject, he fails to understand the sentence. Got it?

You probably anticipate our recommendation for tackling this problem. Yes, take a formal approach: Once you have finished your text, assign somebody to count the words between your subject and the verb. If the result exceeds six words, highlight that sentence and rephrase it. That may sound somewhat formalistic, but it works.

3.3 Rule 3: Choose the Right Subject and Apply That Subject Consistently

Research shows that the readers love stories, they expect stories and are most interested in learning about the main character. Do not disappoint your reader, answer that question quickly by presenting the subject of the sentence quickly. But which subject? Research demonstrates that we best understand texts in which individual characters are acting, *e. g.*, "Julius, Karoline and Björn." If we do not designate a certain person, *e. g.*, by talking about "the children", the attention decreases. If the subject gets more abstract, attention slips away further. Tangible objects, *e. g.*, "the ship," are still better subjects than abstract nouns such as "the law." The worst subject you can choose is an abstract noun in a technical language understood by insiders only, *e. g.*, "consideration" or "arbitrability." One can even talk about a pyramid of understandable subjects, which would look like as follows:

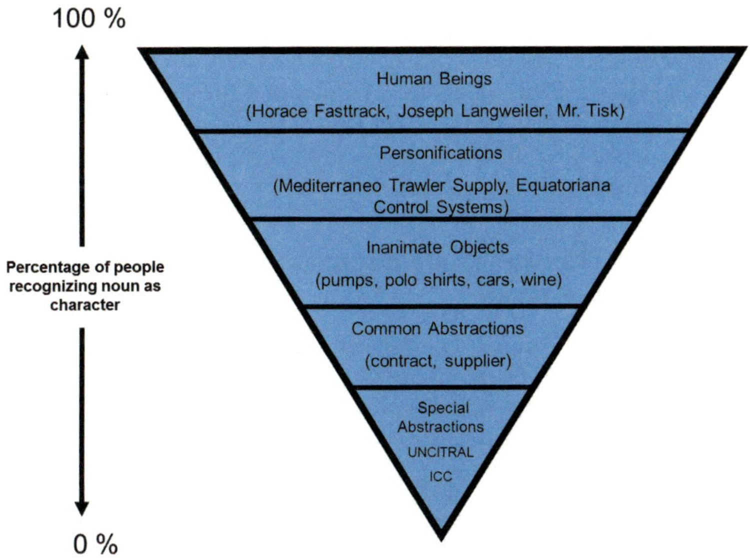

For illustration, compare the following sentences:

> *"Judge Jennings has ruled that the 14-year old Julius must not buy tobacco."*
> *"A Missouri Court has held that persons under the age of 18 must not buy tobacco."*

and

> *"The law says that minors must not buy tobacco."*

Which sentence do you understand immediately?

When using a subject numerous times, avoid the use of substitutes for the subject. That includes the use of personal pronouns. Why is that? Whenever you use a substitute term or a personal pronoun, you require your reader to work. The reader must invest time and effort because the reader needs to translate the substitute term or the personal pronoun into the subject itself. This translation exercise is slowing down your reader and, in the worst case, even annoying him to a degree that he stops reading.

That may sound rather abstract, so look at the following example: Imagine, the German Siemens AG is a party in your case. Instead of Siemens, you can now write about "*the company*," the "*German multinational*," the "*Claimant and Counter-Respondent in this case*," the "*world-market leader in the power-generating sector*" or simply "*it*." You, as a writer, may take pride in having an extensive vocabulary (even in a foreign language such as English) allowing you to vary your expressions; however, your reader is not thrilled because he must embark on detective work to find out who "the company" "the claimant" or "it" refers to. That is not a fun exercise, it does not please the reader and chances are high that the *unpleasant* translation exercise will reflect badly on the overall comprehension of your text – and ultimately on the grading of your memorandum.

3.4 Rule 4: Choose Wisely Between Active Voice vs. Passive Voice

Which one is better: "*The hunter shot the bear (with a clean shot in the head)*" or "*The bear was shot by a hunter*"?

The correct answer is the typical lawyer's answer: It depends. It is a common myth that active voice is "better" than passive voice. At this point, some grammar is useful. Passive voice is used when the focus is on the recipient of the action, or the patient as it is called in grammar. In active voice, the focus is on the subject acting, or the so-called agent. So to give the right answer to the introductory question, it depends on whether the statement is made to an audience of hunters or animal lovers and why. Hunters would prefer the focus to be on their colleague, and animal lovers on the poor bear. So it is active voice for hunters, and passive voice for animal lovers.

Similarly, a caring parent finding his daughter in tears when picking her up in kindergarten does not want to hear the following sentence: "*The ball hit Jenny.*" The kindergarten teacher's correct sentence is "*Jenny was hit by the ball*" even though it is a passive voice construction. The parent is not interested in the ball, but in Jenny.

To put it differently, the reader focuses on the subject and if you want to evoke the right emotions in the reader, you must choose your subject wisely. Compared to the "focus on the subject" rule, the choice of active or passive voice is of secondary importance. Imagine, you need to inform a client about the outcome of an arbitral proceeding. If you have been successful, you want the focus on your firm: "*Baker McKenzie has prevailed with the argument that…*" (reader's emotion: great law firm!); in the very rare case of an unfortunate outcome, you better write "*The Arbitral Tribunal was not convinced by the argument that…*" (reader's emotion: damned Arbitral Tribunal) instead of conceding "*Baker McKenzie did not convince the Arbitral Tribunal by arguing…*" (reader's emotion: why the heck did they fail…).

Here are some further examples of situations where the passive voice is useful:

➢ The acting person is not known, or the author does not want to reveal the agent:
  - "*Mistakes were made.*" (typical politician's talk, and most likely the agent and the writer are members of the same party)
  - "*In yesterday's riots, five cars were incinerated.*" (the wrong-doers are unknown, using "unknown perpetrators" as the subject does not add any useful information)

➢ The author wants or needs to sound formal and authoritative:
  - "*Smoking is strictly prohibited*" is more formal than "*You must not smoke here.*"

➢ Avoid unwieldy gender neutral language ("her or she"):
  - "*Your objective should be a work product that your reader can read quickly, and that he or she* only needs to read once to understand it" can be turned into "*Your objective should be a work product that can be read quickly, and that needs to be read only once to be understood.*"[17]

The above examples go to show that the active voice is not generally 'better' than the passive voice. However, you should have sound reason for writing a sentence in the passive voice. It seems to us that quite a few writers simply use a mix of passive voice and active voice more or less arbitrarily. Our advice is to use language, in all respects, consciously. If you have sound reason to write a sentence in the passive voice, then do so. Otherwise, write in the active voice. If you do so, you will find that the majority of your writing will be in the active voice.

3.5 Rule 5: Put the Power into the Verb, Avoid Nominalizations

Readers analyze texts by looking for actions. Who does what to whom, and what happens thereafter? In essence, there are two ways of expressing actions, namely verbs and nominalizations. We can say "*an agreement was reached*" or "*the parties agreed.*" We can make "an assumption" or we can "assume." There is no difference in meaning, but a marked difference in terms of clarity: Research shows that readers tend to look for verbs rather than nouns when seeking the action. Texts in which the action is buried in nominalizations,

[17] Another useful way of avoiding the awkward his or her is the plural "*… a work product that your readers can read quickly, and need only read once to understand it.*"

rather than presented openly in verbs, are more difficult to understand. Look at the following example:

> *"The Court's **dismissal** of Claimant's argument that Mr. Jones did not have sufficient **authority** to sign the contract was predicated on Claimant's **failure to substantiate** the allegation."*

Various actions are buried in nouns here, but the sentence can easily be converted into a leaner, more accessible statement:

> *"The Court **dismissed** Claimant's argument that Mr. Jones was not **authorized** to sign the agreement because Claimant **had failed to substantiate** the allegation."*

The word "dismissal" becomes "dismissed," "authority" becomes "authorized" and "failure" becomes "failed." As a result, the sentence is more readable. Some may say that the first version sounds more authoritative, more lawyer-like. But lawyers are backing the wrong horse when trying to derive authority from turgid language. Authority should follow from content, not form.

Once again, the best cure for the "nominalization-disease" is a formal approach: After finishing your text, grab a pencil and circle all nouns that do not refer directly to a person. Then try to transform the noun into a verb. You will be surprised how often you succeed.

3.6 Rule 6: Delete Adjectives and Adverbs

Georges Clemenceau (1841–1929), first a newspaper publisher before becoming the prime minister of France, is said to have instructed the journalists working for him:

> *"Whenever you want to use an adjective, come to my office in the third floor and ask for my permission."*

That is a drastic order but it underlines a rule of good writing: Strip your sentence of all words not necessary to convey the idea you intend to convey. Many of those unnecessary words will be adjectives or adverbs. Have a look at the following examples:

> *"Claimant raised the ~~very interesting~~ argument that …."*
> *"Claimant runs a ~~extremely profitable and~~ successful business."*

"Respondent protested vehemently ~~and forcefully~~."
"The victim screamed ~~loudly~~."
"The ~~huge~~ elephant."

The writer who uses many adjectives and adverbs has not searched hard enough for the proper noun or verb indicating precisely what the writer wants to express. Compare the following examples:

"state precisely" = "accentuate"
"say loudly" = "scream"
"huge, extinct animal" = "dinosaur"
"evidently correct argument" = "no-brainer"
"valid, binding agreement" = "contract"

Hence, double-check whether you improve your text by adding an adjective or adverb. The easiest way to do so is again the formal approach: After finishing your text, go through it and circle all adjectives and adverbs. Then, as a second step, explain how the adjective or adverb improves your text. If you can't find an explanation within three seconds, delete the adjective or adverb.

3.7 Rule 7: Do Not Overuse Legalese and Lawyerisms

Mooties often commit the mistake of trying to give more "legal" weight to a submission by using lawyerisms. By lawyerisms, we mean the jargon that laymen typically associate with lawyers, and usually not in a good way. For the beginner, it often seems as if words such as *aforesaid, hereinafter* and *henceforth* add credibility to the writing and indicate professionalism. Those words do have a certain sense of precision, but this is usually a false sense.

Here are examples of legal jargon, and the better alternatives:

Adequate number of	sufficient	**Is able to**	can
At the present time	now	**Notwithstanding the fact that**	Even though
At the time when	when	**On the ground that**	because
On a daily basis	daily	**Prior to**	before
Due to the fact that	because	**During such time as**	while
Excessive number of	Too many	**At this point in time**	Now/ presently

For the reason that	because	**During the course of**	during
In the event that	if	**Henceforth**	From now on
In the near future	soon	**Upon the expiration**	At the end
Subsequent to	after	**It is important to note**	*Don't use it!*

The strategy to power up your submission by using lawyerisms usually fails, and has the same effect as "pimping" an underpowered car.

Experienced arbitrators such as the ones marking your submissions in the Moot will not fall for such strategy. If the content is not convincing, lawyerisms will not blind the arbitrators to this fact. And if the content is convincing, it shines for itself, without legalese.

3.8 Rule 8: Use Headings Effectively

What your reader sees first is the heading of the paragraph to follow: A good heading identifies a point, not a topic. Look at the following two headings:

Limitation of Liability

The limitation of liability clause in No. 10.4 of the Agreement is invalid

The first heading just identifies a topic. It informs the reader that the next section will deal with the subject matter of "limitation of liability." It is still better than no heading, but a good heading identifies your point, *i. e.,* "The limitation of liability is invalid." The advantage of a heading identifying the point is that it gives your reader an early indication about the outcome of your analysis. The reader is therefore not forced to anticipate the result of your arguments and can fully focus on your line of thought. Moreover, if your reader reads the memorial for a second time, your heading serves as an effective prompter, reminding the reader of what he has read and hopefully understood during his first reading.

Do also avoid amateurish introductory lines for each paragraph, again only identifying (or even worse, repeating) the topic. Look at the following (bad) example:

> *"Limitation of Liability*
>
> *In the next section, Respondent will analyze whether the Limitation of Liability clause contained in Clause 10.4 is applicable. Clause 10.4 is invalid for the following reasons..."*

Not only is this style of writing repetitive, and therefore boring. You are also wasting precious space. Compare this to the following introduction:

> *"The Limitation of Liability provided in Clause 10.4 is invalid.*
>
> *The limitation of liability clause in 10.4 is invalid for the following reasons..."*

A good way to check your headings is the following: Look at the table of contents. By simply reading the headings, the reader should have a good idea of your arguments and their direction, even without reading the text itself.

3.9 Rule 9: Avoid Spelling Errors

If, in the reader's impression, your brief does not look professional (*i. e.*, in line with the perceived standard), the reader will intuitively conclude that the contents are also not professional. If the brief looks good from the outside, the reader will anticipate that the content is "good".

Deficient formatting and spelling is among the first things an arbitrator who reads the memorandum notes. It is – of course – a banality that spelling errors must be avoided. However, our experience shows that some Moot teams still do not pay sufficient attention to this banality, perhaps because they focus on content rather than form. Spelling errors create the impression that the writer has not invested a lot of care into the brief and if that is true, the impression is that the writer may not have invested a lot of care in presenting the facts and/or legal arguments adequately.

3.10 Rule 10: Always Start by Indicating the Issue

This rule is of paramount importance. You may therefore wonder why this rule is enumerated in this section. One reason is that you intuitively attach more importance to Rule No. 10 than to Rule No. 5 or 6 – you find the underlying logic if you study the recommendations for advanced writers below. The other reason is that the most suitable time for phrasing the "issue" is after you have completed your content. It is now that you are in the best position to identify and summarize the issue you have been writing about.

But back to the content of Rule No. 10:

It is essential to start each section of your work product by indicating the issue or your conclusion. In other words, you must avoid work product that provokes the question: "What is your point?" In a legal submission, you will generally pursue a number of "points" in a structured manner. Below you will find a random example.

Point 1: Claimant's claim must be dismissed.
Point 1.1: Claimant is wrong on the merits.
Point 1.1.1: Claimant is incorrect on the facts, because…
Point 1.1.2: Claimant is incorrect on the law, because…
Point 1.1.2.1: Argument No. 1 is incorrect, because…
Point 1.1.2.2: Argument No. 2 is incorrect, because…

The structure of your conclusions will generally resemble your table of contents. And for each of these sections, you must remember to state your conclusion clearly and comprehensibly.

In order to take this rule in review newspaper articles, academic papers, e-mails or anything else. Look out for the issue, the conclusion, the message, or whatever you may want to call it. Once you have identified the author's main message or conclusion, circle it. In a good work product, it should not take you too long to identify the main message; in a bad work product, after a while you will ask the very question, "what is your point"? You will further notice that in a good (*i. e.*, comprehensible and well structured) work product, the conclusion appears towards the beginning of the work product. Generally speaking, one can distinguish *conclusion first* from *conclusion last* structures. In a conclusion first structure, the author presents his conclusion first ("Respondent's argument is incorrect") followed by the supporting argument ("because first… second… third"). In a *conclusion last* structure, the author starts off with his or her arguments ("First… second… third") and then presents his or her conclusion ("Therefore, Respondent's argument that… is incorrect"). For many junior academic writers, writing *conclusion last* comes naturally, simply because it is deductive and resembles the way we think. But for most forms of professional writing, including legal submissions, *conclusion first* is the required style of writing. Otherwise, your reader is distracted by attempts to anticipate your conclusion, or the direction of your writing. Always remember that your reader's attention is a scarce resource that you should handle with care. If you present your conclusion first, your reader can fully concentrate on your reasoning, and on determining whether your reasons support your conclusion.

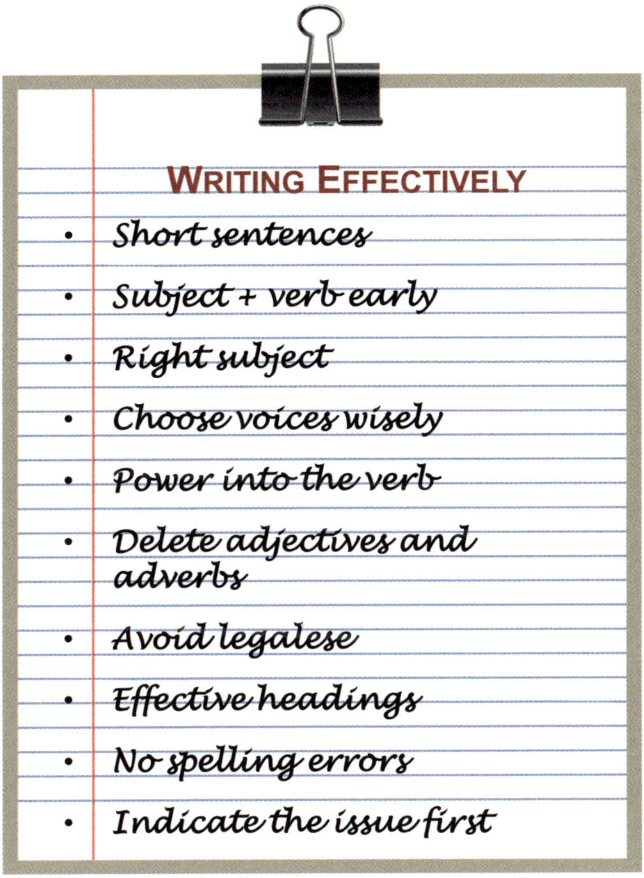

4. Recommendations for Advanced Writing (Or: Rules For Winning)

As far as your writing style is concerned, you will submit an excellent memorandum if you adhere to the ten basic writing rules stated above. However, for a truly outstanding memorandum, you need to do more. Here are some recommendations:

4.1 Recommendation 1: Persuasion Triggers – The Hidden Power of the Word "Because"

We have said that you should avoid legalese and lawyerisms, and rather go for plain language. For example, quite a few lawyers seem to be afraid of using the plain and simple word "because." Instead, they will use turgid phrases such as "for the reason that" or "due to the fact that." Not only is such wording less elegant, in our view, it also deprives you of the opportunity to benefit from what is called *persuasion trigger* such as the word "because." So what is a persuasion trigger?

There are two modes of persuasion. Conscious or mindful persuasion on the one hand, and subconscious or thoughtless persuasion on the other. In the mode of conscious or mindful persuasion, the addressee decides based on reason, *e. g.*, by listening to and evaluating the pros and cons of a certain issue. In the mode of thoughtless persuasion, your addressee is persuaded on a superficial level, *e. g.*, by things like outward appearance, simple clues and persuasion triggers. Think of yourself doing grocery shopping. You have to stock up on cereals, and you see a brand that you rather like with a huge red sign next to it saying:

"Today only $2.99!"

This is a simple sales pitch. In the mode of mindful persuasion, you would now visit several grocery stores in order to compare prices for the brand to find out whether $2.99 really is a good deal (or today, you would pull out your iPhone and search for the price online). But chances are you will simply buy the product. This is because for relatively unimportant decisions such as buying cereal, you are in the mode of mindless persuasion, making decisions based on persuasion triggers such as a flashy advertisement. The deal is most likely not that bad, and even if it is, it won't ruin you. (On the other hand, you would not buy a car simply because of a sales pitch saying, "Today only $29,999.00!") So if your addressee is in the mode of mindless persuasion, use persuasion triggers.

We expect one counterargument here: If the use of persuasion triggers only works in the mode of mindless persuasion, than it has no place in arbitration, because surely, arbitrators will always decide based on a thorough evaluation of arguments, *i. e.*, they are invariably in the mode of thoughtful persuasion. Here, we must disappoint you. Also in real life arbitration, you will come across decision makers who are prone to be persuaded mindlessly. Research has shown that the mode of mindless persuasion is also active when your addressee does not have sufficient time or motivation to listen and decide thoroughly. And occasionally, arbitrators will fall into this category, and so may your arbitrators in the Moot.

Coming back to where we started: Why is the word "because" a persuasion trigger? In his book "Influence – The Psychology of Persuasion," the psychologist Robert Cialdini describes the following experiment by sociologist Ellen Langer.[18] In the experiment, a test person in a university is queuing in front of a copy machine where there is a long line. In the first scenario, the test person asked: "*Excuse me, I have five pages. May I use the Xerox machine because I'm in a rush?*" The success rate of this request was very high (94 %) because the test person provided a good reason – lack of time. In the second scenario, the test person asked: "*Excuse me, I have five pages. May I use the Xerox machine?*" The success rate this time was only 60 %. It appears that the difference in success rates occurred because scenario 1 provided a convincing argument – lack of time. But then, scenario 3 was tested. This time, the test person asked: "*Excuse me, I have five pages. May I use the copy machine because I have to make some copies?*" Obviously, the reason provided this time is not persuasive; all people in line needed to make copies. Still, the success rate here was 93 %. What we learn from this is that the persuasion trigger was not the good reason (lack of time), but simply the word "because." We imagine that the success rate would have been less had the test person been a law student asking: "*May I use the copy machine for the reason that I have to make some copies?*"

4.2 Recommendation 2: Use Enumerations to Become More Persuasive

Enumerations are a useful tool to structure your writing. Take the following passage for example: It stands to reason that Claimant's claim must be dismissed. The delivered products were fit for purpose and Claimant failed to notify the alleged defects within the contractual notification period. What is more, the claim has become time-barred.

Compare that to the following:

Claimant's claim must be dismissed because:

(1) the delivered products were fit for purpose;
(2) the alleged defects were not notified within the contractual notification period; and
(3) any claim would have become time-barred.

[18] Robert B. Cialdini, "*Influence, The Psychology of Persuasion,*" Chapter 1.

In the example above, the structure of your arguments is clear at first sight. You identify the number of your arguments, and they can be easily remembered.

Enumerations are powerful because they render your writing more authoritative. They demonstrate that your arguments are thought through, that you have a structure, and that you know what you are writing about. As a result, your reader will be more willing to accept you as a guide and to follow you through your line of argument.

There are various ways of using enumerations:

(1) *External Enumerations* are used outside the text, such as in the example above. These are usually used for the big picture, your "Level 1" arguments.

(2) *Internal Enumerations* are used within the text itself: "The claim fails because (i) the goods sold are fit for purpose and (ii) any claim would be time-barred." Internal enumerations may also include the use of "First, ... Second, ... etc.". We would recommend using internal enumerations for subordinate arguments.

(3) *Bullet Points*: In most instances, we would recommend against bullet points. When exchanging submissions in an arbitration, you will often have to make cross-references to the other side's submissions or your own previous submissions. This is more difficult with bullet points ("*cf.* Statement of Claim, Section 5, third bullet point").

Sometimes, one sees enumerations, external or internal, that run up to "Fifteenth... Sixteenth...Seventeenth..." Our clear advice is: Less is more. A list of too many arguments (*i. e.,* more than five) is counterproductive. A long list of arguments is rather daunting for your reader. Once confronted with enumerated arguments, your reader will want to complete the list and feel frustrated if the list continues for countless pages. Reward your reader by presenting only lists than can be handled without too much effort. More importantly, such lists tend to dilute the strength of your winning arguments; they will be lost in the flood of weaker ones. Finally, it is unlikely that you found 17 equally strong arguments that merit being enumerated in this manner. In most instances, it will easily be possible to group various aspects of one argument in one point and thus reduce the list considerably.

Let us back this recommendation with some science: In his bestselling book "Paradox of Choice – Why More is Less", Barry Schwartz demonstrates that potential buyers are confused by a large variety of products and as a consequence, tend to become "inactive", *i. e.,* not to buy anything. A supermarket offering 36 kinds of strawberry marmalade sells fewer jars than a shop concentrating on four kinds. In addition, buyer's remorse increases if the buyer had a lot of options: "Did I make the right choice or would one of the products have been better?"

How do products such as strawberry marmalade relate to the arguments raised in your memorandum? Well, if you want to succeed in the Moot, you better want your arbitrator buy your argument.

4.3 Recommendation 3: Use Evidence and Exhibits Effectively

As explained above (at IV.1.3), it is highly recommendable to follow the formatting rules and to clearly address in the memorandum the issues laid out in Procedural Order No. 1.

Many briefs in real arbitration consist of the brief itself and voluminous attachments/exhibits. If the respective brief is only 50 pages long, it may be accompanied by no less than 10 folders consisting of exhibits that are referenced in the brief. The reasoning behind this presentation structure (if there is a reasoning at all) may be the following: The attachments ensure that the brief itself is not overly long. The counsel offers the choice to the arbitrators to read the attachments or simply to believe its originator. By presenting a lot of paper (numerous files) the counsel demonstrates to the arbitrators that his or her case has some weight.

All these assumptions are hardly convincing.

The truth is that arbitrators rarely read exhibits, especially those exhibits that are stored in files separate from the brief. It is simply burdensome to stop reading when the text is interrupted by a reference to some exhibit, then to find the exhibit in one of the voluminous files and then to allocate within that exhibit the passage in the text to which it refers before – finally – resuming the interrupted reading again without having forgotten what might have been said.

There are only two ways out of this dilemma:

- ➢ Quote the passage from the exhibit in the brief itself. If that is done, in 90 % of all cases, the arbitrator will take for granted that the quoted passage is indeed contained in the referenced exhibit. In the remaining 10 % of cases, the arbitrator might double-check and that is harmless.
- ➢ In appropriate cases, it is advisable not only to quote the passage, but also to copy/photocopy that passage directly into the brief. For example, instead of quoting an e-mail, it is more convincing to show the email itself since the typical e-mail format and

spelling errors often contained in e-mails add to the credibility of the offered evidence. In a nutshell: We believe more in what we see than in what we read. Hence, seeing an email is more convincing than reading a quote from an e-mail.

In the Moot Problem, there are much less exhibits than would usually be in real arbitration. Nevertheless, you may follow these recommendations in some instances to create a professional brief.

4.4 Recommendation 4: "First Impressions Count, Last Impressions Stay"

An area of some debate is the ranking of arguments. Let us assume that you found five arguments to support your case, which are ranked as follows on your scale of persuasiveness (10: extremely persuasive, 0: not persuasive at all):

Argument No. 1: 9
Argument No. 2: 7
Argument No. 3: 5
Argument No. 4: 3
Argument No. 5: 1

In which sequence do you present these arguments? It is (almost) common ground that you must present your best argument first.

Sometimes, it is suggested to save one of the better arguments for the ending, and to present arguments of average persuasiveness in the middle. This strategy is usually linked to the results of the so-called free recall exercises that are performed in psychological research. In these experiments, test persons are shown a limited list of words, each of the words only for a short moment. The word disappears, and the next word is shown. After all words have been shown, the test persons are asked to write down all the words they could remember (in any order, which is why the exercise is called "free recall").

Such exercises show that test persons can usually recall a higher number of words that appeared in the beginning (the so-called primacy effect), and still a high number of words appearing towards the end of the list, even though the number is smaller than for the words appearing at the beginning (the so-called recency effect). Lower values are achieved for those words appearing in the middle.

The curve appears as follows:

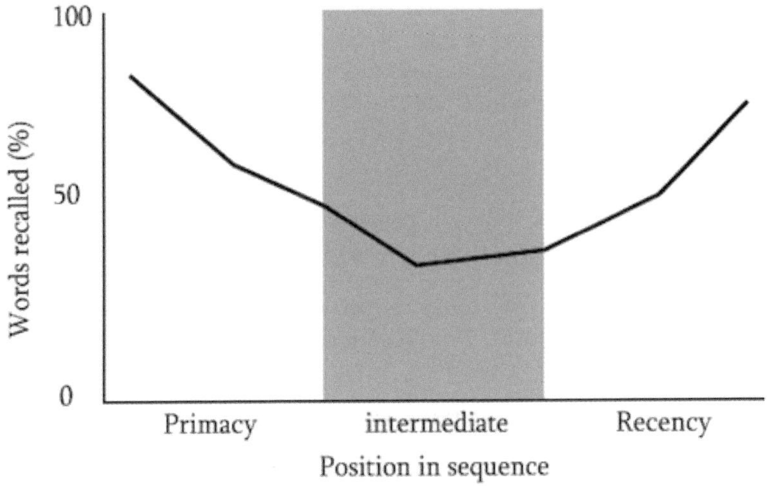

The position of your arguments is therefore a relevant factor on how well your audience will remember them.

So if you want to play it by the book, you should rank your arguments as follows:

1 2 5 4 3
Or
1 2 4 5 3

Having said that, you should not be a slave to the scientific research produced in free recall exercises. These are based on lists in which each word is equally prominent or distinctive. If you place your best argument in the middle, it will not be forgotten, because it is more persuasive and therefore more prominent than the others; but still, this would be a mistake. A professional legal audience expects you to present your best argument first; if you present your best shot only as the second or third argument, automatically it will lose persuasiveness in the minds of your reader, because your reader assumes that you yourself do not find the argument convincing. The flip side is that you can increase the persuasiveness of a weaker argument by presenting it early in the sequence of your argument.

One word of warning concerning weak arguments, such as Argument 5 in the above scale. Once you have assembled your list of arguments, you will find it difficult to simply omit one or more of the arguments. But be aware that weak arguments can also weaken your case. They tend to evoke the impression that you do not consider your case strong enough if you have to present such a weak argument. By the same token, the more arguments you present, the more you run the risk of diluting the effect of your better arguments (see above at IV.4.4). Consider therefore to leave out your less convincing arguments, because less is often more in this respect. We would therefore recommend the following sequence:

1 2 4 3

4.5 Recommendation 5: Quote Powerfully

Pay attention to meaningful introductory and exit sentences for any of your quotes. Frequently, one reads sentences like the following:

> *"The Court of Appeal decided as follows:"*

This is an empty sentence, simply wasting space. Choose a sentence that smoothly leads your reader into the quote, and prepares him or her for its content:

> *"The Court of Appeal decided that limitation of liability clauses such as the one found in Clause 10.4 of the Contract are invalid:"*

After the quote, insert a sentence that leads your reader back into the main text, such as the following:

> *"Given that the limitation in Clause 10.4 is invalid, Claimant is not prevented from claiming damages in an amount higher than..."*

If you use proper introductory and exit sentences, your reader may read the quote, but does not have to understand the submission. A good way to check is to read the two sentences before and after the quote to see whether they form a meaningful unit without the quote.

For the quote itself, only quote as much of the document as necessary. It is frustrating and tiresome to read through various unnecessary paragraphs of quotation until the relevant part is finally reached. It is fine to highlight the part of the quote on which you intend to focus.[19] But quite often, you will find that this is only second best to shortening the quote. As a result, you can often do without emphasizing parts of the quote.

[19] In which case you indicate "*emphasis added*" or a similar wording at the end of the quote.

If you have found a significant quote, truly to the point in your case, make sure that you do not waste the effect. Assuming that you are quoting a court decision that concerned a similar case as the one in issue, take some lines to explain the setting of the case in order to demonstrate the similarities. Otherwise, the effect may be lost on the arbitrators.

> *"In Smith v Vade, the Court of Appeal had to decide on the validity of a limitation of liability clause in a sale and purchase agreement. Like in this case, the Respondent had employed standard terms of contract in the sales agreement, terms that were discussed during the contract negotiations but eventually not changed. The Court of Appeal decided that the limitation of liability clause was invalid."*

4.6 Recommendation 6: Create Images in Your Readers' Minds

It can be a very powerful tool to devise a theme, or a picture that captions the soul of your case.

Think of the following example. Your case concerns a dispute between partners of a partnership with regard to the distribution of profit. The partners have contributed to the profits of the company to varying degrees – some less, some more. Now, the profit is distributed according to a certain formula that is attacked by some of the partners. In essence, theses partners believe that the formula makes it possible for some of the less productive partners to eventually earn higher than the more productive ones.

As their attorney, you will do various things. Obviously, you will have to find a legal line of argument why the formula, by law, has to be changed. You will also present to the judge various calculations in order to demonstrate that the formula favors less productive partners.

But you can also endeavor to sum up the dispute 'in a nutshell' by creating an image. Think of a revolving door, like the one shown on the next page.

Your image could be the following: In essence, the formula works like a revolving door wherein one person enters after another, but comes out first!

Obviously, there is no such revolving door, and there shouldn't be. If you are successful, the arbitrators will read all further submissions with a picture of your magic revolving door in their heads.

The key to success in a court case or an arbitration is to convince the judge that the formula is unjust. You will have a hard time winning a case unless the judge has a certain gut feeling that the equities of the case lie with your client.

A powerful tool to create this gut feeling is the use of such mental images, or a theme, that will stick in the arbitrators' mind. Such images work as a shortcut: rather than having to memorize a complex factual background and evaluate it, the arbitrators may consciously, or subconsciously, be influenced or even convinced by such images. There is a further advantage: an image that is planted at an early stage of a dispute will work as a so-called anchor. Anchoring describes the common human tendency to rely heavily on the first piece of information when making decisions. If you are successful in anchoring a powerful image in the arbitrators' head, like the magic revolving door, you made a big step towards winning the case.

A few words of warning: Such images are *always* an add-on; they must never replace thorough factual presentation and legal lines of argument. Otherwise, your decision maker will get the impression that your reliance on such image is no more than a cover-up for a lack of arguments. Further, your image must be powerful. If you are not fully convinced that your image works, leave it. A lame, unconvincing comparison is rather counter-productive.

V. How to Present Your Case Before the Arbitral Tribunal

This chapter goes to the heart of the Moot: The Oral Pleadings.

1. The Setting of the Oral Pleadings

This is the general setting you will encounter in the oral pleadings:

1.1 The Venue

The majority of the oral hearings are held at the Vienna Faculty of Law (Juridicum), Schottenbastei 10–16, A-1010 Vienna.

However, due to the high number of participating teams, some of the pleadings are held at another faculty building of the University of Vienna (Schenkenstraße 8–10), the University of Vienna Main building (Universitätsring 1) and offices of nearby law firms including Baker McKenzie's offices.

For the Vis Moot (East), the majority of the Oral Hearings take place at the City University of Hong Kong.

The tables in the hearing room are arranged in a U formation. The three arbitrators are seated in the middle, the counsel on the two sides – counsel for Claimant on the left, counsel for Respondent on the right as seen from the arbitrator's perspective. Everyone is seated during the pleadings. Usually, there are a few seat rows reserved for spectators such as the other team members.

1.2 The Arbitrators

There are several hundreds of arbitrators participating in the Moot. These range from eminent professors and famous arbitration practitioners to recent law graduates who may have participated in last year's Moot as team members or coaches. Further, the arbitrators come from different legal systems. The Moot organizers try to ensure that each panel will include at least one lawyer with a civil law background and one with a common law background.

As a matter of course, each arbitrator is acquainted with the case but the level of knowledge about the factual setting of the dispute and the resulting legal issues varies quite a bit: Every arbitrator will have read the case summary and concise analysis which the moot court organizers send to the arbitrators shortly before the oral pleadings take place. Some arbitrators will also have graded written submissions and are thus more familiar with details of the case and the arguments typically raised by the parties. Also keep in mind that most arbitrators participate in three or four oral pleadings so that the arbitrators' familiarity with the case and the arguments made increases over time – as does the danger that the arbitrator will have read or heard the same arguments the umpteenth time and thus be a bit bored, triggering the need for the participants to become more innovative as the Moot proceeds.

1.3 The Number of Oral Hearings and the Number of Team Members Involved

The oral hearings start with General Rounds: Each team will argue four times, usually once per day, from Saturday through Tuesday. Two team members – without any support from other members of the team – will present the argument. The teams are free to choose the oralists for each hearing. Note, however, that in order to be eligible for the Martin Domke Award for Best Individual Oralist, a participant must have argued at least once for the Claimant and once for the Respondent.

In the first two oral hearings – once acting for Claimant and once for Respondent – the teams are expected, according to the Vis Moot Rules, to rely on the arguments given in their written memoranda or at least be prepared to justify why that position has been abandoned.[1] In the next two oral hearings – again once as Claimant and once as Respondent – the teams are expected to act more freely and

[1] See *para.* 68 Vis Moot Rules.

to advance further arguments. However, experience shows that the difference between the first two oral hearings and the following ones is rather small since the distinction requested in the Vis Moot Rules is rarely observed in practice.

The 64 teams that have argued the most successfully (*cf.* below at V.1.6 regarding the grading system used) enter into the Elimination Rounds, which start on Tuesday evening in Vienna. In Hong Kong, only 32 teams enter into the Elimination Rounds. In the Elimination Rounds, the arbitrators do not score the individual team members, they only determine the winning team that proceeds to the next round. The final between the best two teams takes place right before the Awards Banquet at the Vienna Fair and the Gala Awards Banquet in Hong Kong, allowing a huge audience to follow the arguments. Typically, the arbitral tribunal for the semi-finals and the finals is composed of the most famous arbitration practitioners in the world.

1.4 The Available Time

Thirty minutes, in principle, is the time allocated to each team for the oral presentation, including the time required for answering questions by the tribunal. The arbitral tribunal may, however, extend the time to up to 45 minutes (ensuring that the teams are treated fairly, of course).

Members of a team can divide the 30 minutes between each other as they prefer. Yet, it is advisable to allocate the time evenly. It would make a bad impression if one counsel was to speak for five minutes while the other one speaks for twenty-five minutes. Also, you should always reserve one or two minutes for rebuttal. The rebuttal is your last chance to convince the tribunal.

Note, however, that the rebuttal is not designed for repeating oneself. Rather, the idea is to respond to a weak point of your opponents or to counter their argument by a really strong argument in favor of your party. A good rebuttal will remain in the arbitrator's mind when it comes to the scores or to the decision as to which team proceeds to the next round. An arbitrator might not remember all the details of the pleading that was presented almost 30 minutes earlier, but the arbitrator will certainly remember the rebuttal, *i. e.*, the counsel's last words.

Exceeding the time limit would be a serious transgression. We have seen many arbitrators who have marked a team down because it exceeded the time limit, so make sure you stay within the time allocated.

We recommend, first, that you ask your co-counsel to make notes indicating how much time is left. This has a great added benefit: the arbitrators will most likely praise your team work, and team work is an evaluation criterion.

Second, if you run out of time, do not simply continue with your arguments but signal to the tribunal that you have an eye on the time:

> *"I see my time is running short. May I thus restrict my arguments to one last important point ..."*
>
> *"I see my time is running short. May I ask the Tribunal to grant me another two minutes to finish my arguments ..."*

1.5 The Typical Course of the Oral Pleading

The arbitrators are asked to act as they would do in a real arbitration. Taking into consideration the different legal backgrounds and the arbitrators' personal style, the teams thus need to be flexible. According to the Vis Moot Rules, the course of the oral pleadings lies within the discretion of the tribunal. The arbitrators may decide on (i) the order of presentation, (ii) whether to permit rebuttal arguments, and (iii) whether and to what extent to ask questions.[2]

The practice of the Vis Moot, however, is somewhat different from what the Vis Moot Rules provide. Even though the arbitrators may determine the course of the oral pleadings, they usually leave it to the teams to do so. It is absolutely normal for the teams to talk to each other before the opening of the proceedings. Usually, the teams divide the hearing into a first part dealing with the procedural problems of the case and a second part designated to the substantive issues.

From our experience, it is highly advisable to split up the pleading in such manner because it makes the whole proceeding more lively and allows the teams to counter the arguments raised after a few minutes only. On the procedural issue, it is usually the Respondent who argues first because it is the Respondent who objects to the jurisdiction of the tribunal. The arguments on the procedural issue are then followed by a rebuttal and possibly a short reply. On the merits, the Claimant argues first and Respondent answers, again followed by a rebuttal and possibly a reaction.

With regard to questions from the tribunal, the practice corresponds to what the Vis Moot Rules provide. There are big differences between the arbitrators; some will interrupt counsel frequently, others will only ask a few questions at the end of the pleading.

---

[2] See *paras.* 69–71 Vis Moot Rules for further details.

1.6 The Grading System Used

Since the 24th Vis Moot in 2016–2017, both oralists will be scored on a scale of 50 to 100 by each of the three arbitrators.[3] The scores for the two oralists will be added. Thus, for one argument, a team could score a maximum of 600 (3*100*2) points. The theoretical maximum for the four arguments in the General Rounds is thus 2400 points. Experience from the past (when the old scoring system applied which ranged from 25 to 50) has shown that usually, teams need about 1050 points, *i. e.*, 43.75 out of 50 per oralist per pleading, to enter into the Elimination Rounds in Vienna. In Hong Kong, we do not have any numbers from the last years. However, teams will probably need the same score in order to reach the final round of 32.

When scoring, the arbitrators will take into consideration the following criteria:

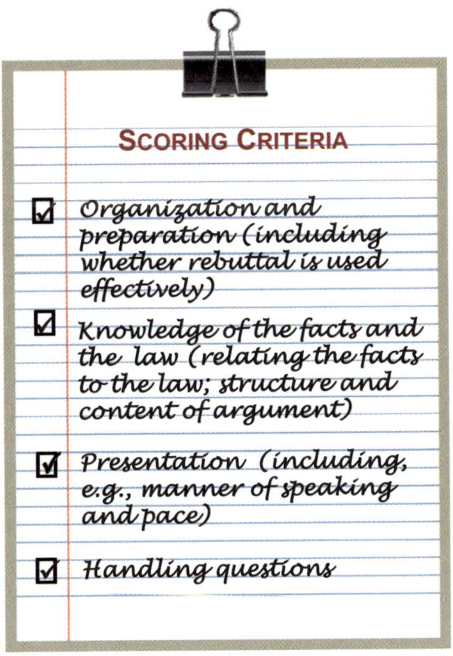

[3] The 14th Vis Moot East still used the old scoring system with a scale from 25 to 50 points.

2. Reality Check: Oral Pleadings in International Arbitration

The Vis Moot is designed to be as close to reality as possible – and it does a great job in coming close to this objective. However, the Vis Moot remains a student competition. It is illustrative to briefly outline what role oral pleadings have in the real world of international arbitration.

2.1 Civil Law Style vs. Common Law Approach

Traditionally, arbitrators with a common law background attach much more importance to oral hearings than to written pleadings. In the United Kingdom or the United States, the judge expects that everything that matters is introduced orally into the hearing. This may be because the roots of the common law go back to times where parties and jurors were mostly illiterate.[4] The civil law systems, in contrast, are to a great extent based on the written Roman law which placed a greater emphasis on written proceedings.[5]

In state court proceedings in civil law countries, the oral hearing usually is comparatively short, and it may happen in civil cases that the counsels do not hold a pleading at all. This is also due to the different role of the judge. The traditional civil law approach is often called "inquisitorial." This means that the judge plays an active role: he or she directs the proceedings, frequently asks questions and conducts the witness examination. The lawyers may add further questions, but there is no such thing as cross-examination as found in common law proceedings. In contrast, under the common law system, it is the parties and their counsel who mainly drive the proceedings. The judge's main function in the hearing is to monitor the oral arguments and to ensure that the procedural rules are complied with.[6]

---

[4] *See Demeyere*, An Essay on Differing Approaches to Procedures under Common Law and Civil Law, in: SchiedsVZ 2008, p. 279 *et seq.*, at p. 281; *Elsing*, Procedural Efficiency in International Arbitration: Choosing the Best of Both Legal Worlds, in: SchiedsVZ 2011, p. 114 *et seq.*, at p. 119.

[5] *Elsing*, in: SchiedsVZ 2011, p. 114 *et seq.*, at p. 119.

[6] *Elsing*, in: SchiedsVZ 2011, p. 114 *et seq.*, at p. 117.

2.2 Importance of Oral Pleadings

In international commercial arbitration nowadays, there is a tendency towards limiting oral pleadings. Frequently, there is either a strict time limit (*e. g.*, 30 minutes) or there is no oral pleading of counsel at all. One argument for that is to save time. Further, written submissions are usually very voluminous and are designed to cover all the facts and arguments of the case. However, this does not render oral pleadings superfluous.

To the contrary, where the briefs are complex and the facts are spread across hundreds of exhibits, there is great value in oral pleadings directing the tribunal to the crucial issues of the dispute. And a seasoned counsel will try to insist on starting the evidentiary hearing with oral pleadings if only to ensure that the arbitrator is familiar with the case and the disputed issues before listening to the witnesses' testimony. Experience shows that once in a while, an arbitrator will have not yet read the written submissions thoroughly and thus would hardly understand the witness testimonies without an introduction by oral pleadings.

In some instances, it can, for example, be very effective to lead the arbitrators through the 10 or 20 most important documents or provisions that make up the party's case. The way to do that is to prepare an opening bundle (which, of course, only contains documents that are already on the record), to highlight the relevant passages and to read through the documents together with the arbitrators. An opening statement by counsel – to a much greater extent than a written submission – gives the opportunity to put the really decisive factors on the tribunal's agenda. If – and it frequently occurs in practice – an arbitrator is undecided after studying the briefs, oral argument becomes crucial.[7]

All this underlines the importance of oral pleadings in practice – and this is why the oral pleading phase in the Moot deserves so much attention.

3. Before You Start

The oral pleadings begin before you have spoken your first word. This is ignored by many and has a rather devastating effect on a team's success in the Moot.

---

[7] *Scalia/Garner*, in: Making your Case. The Art of Persuading Judges, 2008, p. 139.

3.1 You Never Get a Second Chance …

… to make a first impression. It is common ground in psychology that people decide within seconds whether or not they like a person who they meet for the first time. They base their decision (which is more of a gut feeling than a balanced decision) on the person's outer appearance and on the first words spoken by that person. Thus, in any event, do not spoil the first impression even before you get started, *e. g.*, by coming late, by not being attentive, by forgetting the names of the arbitrators, by not being dressed properly or by having an unorganized desk in front of you. These recommendations are self-evident.

However, in addition, we have a tricky recommendation: Look attractive and likeable. This is a tricky one for two reasons: First, how does one manage to look likeable? Second, why does it matter, because in the end, the Moot is not a beauty competition but a serious legal event (though a highly enjoyable one), isn't it? Nevertheless, psychological research has shown that persons who are considered attractive are more successful.[8] Sad, but true. Psychologists explain that we tend to assume that people who are physically attractive also possess other socially desirable personality traits such as intelligence or competence. This may – for good reasons – be considered unfair. However, the good thing is that you can influence whether you are perceived as attractive and likeable.

3.2 How You Look – It Matters

Aiming at attractiveness does not only mean to dress smartly. Rather, psychological studies show that we like persons who are similar to ourselves.[9] Therefore, it is advisable to dress similar to the arbitrators. This means: no sweater and no tuxedo either. A conservative suit (and tie for males) will probably be a good choice although the Moot might be a little less formal than real arbitration. It goes without saying that the aim is to look professional, not to be dressed up as if attending an evening event. For women, wearing mini-skirts or low-cut necklines hardly increases the kind of attractiveness that counts in the Moot.

Over and above that, there are more subtle ways to help the arbitrators like you. This is by mirroring the arbitrator's behavior, if possible and appropriate. This may include copying a gesture he or she frequently uses or taking the same seating position. If you

[8] *See, e. g., Cialdini*, Chapter 5.
[9] *See, e. g., Cialdini*, Chapter 5.

observe that the arbitrator speaks slowly you should mirror that by speaking slowly yourself. In a real arbitration where you might know a bit more about the arbitrators, you could even go further and try to establish some common personal ground with the arbitrator (*e. g.*, slipping in a remark that you graduated from the same law school). We will elaborate in more detail on this issue below at V.5.5.

3.3 Make the Life of the Arbitrators Easy

The arbitrators need to know who they are dealing with in order to be able to score each speaker. That is why it is very important that you introduce yourself and your team colleague to the arbitrators. Experience shows that there are two rounds of introduction; let us call them the informal introduction and the official introduction. For the informal introduction, counsel are usually the first ones in the hearing room. They greet each other and discuss the course of the proceedings. When the arbitrators enter and take their seats on the bench, counsel get up, shake hands and exchange business cards. Note that the use of business cards is highly recommendable because the arbitrators must fill in a scoring sheet and need to know the names (and their correct spelling) of counsel. Note that when you exchange business cards with Asian arbitrators, hold your business card with both hands, accept their card with both hands and examine the cards before putting them into your pocket. It is a sign of respect.

Once all participants are present, the official introduction takes place. This is necessary and expected in the Moot, and it is even an evaluation criterion. Nevertheless, keep the official introduction short: "I am Robert Johnson and this is my colleague Mary Smith. We are from XY Law School, representing the Claimant, [name of Claimant]. My colleague Mary will address the merits of the case. I will deal with the procedural issue." If you did not provide the tribunal with business cards, make sure that you pronounce your names clearly so that they are understood.

3.4 Your Desk (Should Look Organized)

The desk in front of you is easily perceived as mirroring your state of mind: Mess on the table means mess in your head. Thus, if your desk looks as if you had no idea how to organize your file, the arbitrators will most likely suspect that you do not master your case either. It is practical to have with you a copy of the file containing the Problem. And this should be the only thing lying on the table apart from your notes and a note pad.

All other materials that you need for your presentation should be on your co-counsel's desk. Most teams bring along a big folder containing all the authorities that they rely on and all the authorities that might be quoted by the opposing counsel. If appropriate, think about bringing along the Schlechtriem/Schwenzer commentary on the CISG. It simply is *the* authority on the CISG. The mere presence of the book on your desk might give the tribunal the impression that your arguments are supported by Professors Schlechtriem and Schwenzer. When making reference to authorities, ask your co-counsel to hand over to you the relevant copies, or open the Schlechtriem/Schwenzer commentary on the right page. This will yield team work points (see below at V.4.8).

However, be aware that you should only quote and refer to cases and authorities that support your main arguments. Quoting cases in support of minor points will look artificial.

In sum, a clean and organized desk makes a good first impression. If the appearance is not professional, the arbitrator will intuitively conclude that the presentation of the case is also not professional, and worse for the client – the arbitrators may come to the conclusion that the case is weak.

4. Ground Rules

In the following section, you will find a set of basic rules that are the key elements to a solid performance in the Vis Moot.

4.1 Always Start Strong: Cognitive Dissonance and Confirmation Bias

People – and believe it or not arbitrators are people – think and evaluate in a "compared to" modus. Thus, whenever people read or listen to factual statements or a legal argument, they will evaluate that statement by comparing it to something they already know. Psychological research shows a clear tendency on how a newly introduced statement or argument is evaluated: The reader or listener (*i. e.*, arbitrator) has a tendency to uphold a previously formed opinion.

The arbitrator will therefore interpret/understand the newly introduced statement in a way that conforms to what she already knows or believes she knows. In other words: The established standard (or comparison point of the arbitrator) heavily influences the arbitrator's understanding of the newly introduced statement or text. It does so in many cases to a degree that the already established "comparison point" simply overrules a new impression or statement that is not in conformity with the arbitrator's existing understanding. In a nutshell: We make up our mind quickly in order to adapt to new situations. And once we have made up our mind, we rarely change it afterwards but – often unconsciously – look for arguments that support our formed opinion. Psychologists call this phenomenon as "cognitive dissonance," "relational thinking," or "confirmation bias."

You may think that this is all talking in riddles and has no relevance for the Moot. If you think so, you err. That psychological phenomenon results in an immediate consequence for an oral pleading to be effective (*i. e.*, convincing for the arbitrators): If ever possible, start with your strongest argument[10] and do not waste time with formalities. That is why we urge you to limit your introduction to the minimum (compare above at V.3.3). At the beginning, the arbitrators are most attentive and aim at getting a picture of the speaker.

In addition, whatever the arbitrators hear first will establish his/her "compared to" standard and this standard then has a heavy impact on how the arbitrators evaluate your overall performance. Thus, the first sentences establish the "compared to" standard and the arbitrators' gut feeling about the quality of your pleading. The created "thinking standard/gut feeling" will be predominant throughout the whole hearing. This means that if you make a weak point after having started very strong, the arbitrators will very likely think that this slight weakness can happen in the heat of the moment and does not do any harm to the overall excellent quality of the presentation.

4.2 How to Address the Arbitral Tribunal

"Honorable Tribunal," "Messrs. Arbitrators," "Your Honor," *etc.* – all of these are less preferred compared to the actual names of the arbitrators. As Dale Carnegie reminded us:

> *"Remember that a person's name is to that person the sweetest and most important sound in any language."*

Thus, use the actual names of the arbitrators. For doing that, you need to know those names by heart, including their proper pronunciation. About half an hour before the pleadings, the names and

[10] *Scalia/Garner*, p. 14 *et seq.*

origins of the arbitrators are posted at the doors of the hearing rooms. It is highly recommended to learn the names and, if need be, practice the pronunciation. Many people are vain so it does not hurt to use titles such as Doctor, Professor, *etc.*

Further, when addressing the tribunal, look the arbitrators in the eye in order to establish a relationship with them. Do not concentrate on the presiding arbitrator alone. The other members of the panel are dispensing the same number of points to score you and your team. Yet, when you are responding to a question, look at the arbitrator who asked it.[11]

If it is uncomfortable to look at arbitrators from the position of your chair, make adjustments so that you can keep direct eye contact without being in an uncomfortable position.

4.3 Slow Down: Listening Is Difficult

When you start speaking, you know what you are going to say. So your words come after you have already thought through the entire argument. For the listeners, it is the other way round: They first hear and only then are in a position to understand. Further, a reader may read a complicated sentence twice. The listener does not have that opportunity. Finally, some of your arbitrators might not be as fluent in English as you are. All this leads to one important pointer: Slow down when speaking. You will successfully relay your message to the arbitrators only if you allow them the time to digest the information provided. Thus, do not overload the tribunal with information, and speak sufficiently slowly and distinctly. In addition, pauses will help the listener follow your speech. If you are running out of time, slow down even more.

4.4 The Attention Span of the Arbitrators Is Limited – KISS

KISS: If you have already read the chapter on how to write effective memoranda, you know what this acronym stands for (see above at IV.3.1). This principle equally holds true when you present your case orally in front of the arbitral tribunal.

Many teams believe that in order to obtain a good or even excellent score, they are required to present all possible

[11] *Scalia/Garner*, p. 178 *et seq.*

arguments for their position. This is not true. The arbitrators' attention span is limited. So follow the KISS-principle "keep it short and simple." That is one of the golden rhetoric rules. There is an ancient story which is quite illustrative in this respect:

> *The Cretans paid a visit to the city of Sparta. When they arrived, the Cretans gave a speech. When the Cretans concluded their speech, the Spartans said: "That was really an excellent speech; thank you very much. Unfortunately, we have forgotten the beginning and therefore we have not understood the end ..."*

Be careful that you do not fall into the same trap when making your arguments. Arbitrators dislike it if counsel does not get to the point and continue talking without actually saying anything new. The same applies in the Moot. It is recommended to only present three arguments for each issue. Or, as U.S. Supreme Court Justice Antonin Scalia and Bryan A. Garner have put it:

> *"Take pains to select your best arguments. Concentrate your fire."*[12]

For the reasons set out above at V.4.1, start with your strongest argument. The second strongest argument should be placed at the end in order to increase the probability that the arbitrators will remember the "last word."

Psychologists have found an interesting phenomenon: The TMC-trap. TMC stands for "Too Many Choices." If people are offered too many choices, they tend to reject all choices instead of accepting at least one. That finding was confirmed by the following experiments:

- In a first experiment the price for a camera was reduced from EUR 300 to EUR 200. The sale was very successful and many people bought that camera. In a comparative experiment the shop reduced the price of not one but three cameras by EUR100. The result was surprising: Now, the customers could not make up their mind and left the shop without having bought a camera at all.
- Psychologists at Stanford University and Columbia University conducted the following experiment: In a supermarket, they erected a booth and the customers could try and – if so desired – buy jam. In the first booth 24 different kinds of jam were offered. In the second booth (comparative experiment) only 6 types of jam were offered. While 60 % of the customers stopped at the first booth, only 3 % of those customers bought jam. On the second booth, 40 of the customers stopped but 30 % of those bought jam.

---

[12] *Scalia/Garner*, p. 22.

It is at least debatable (though not yet confirmed by psychological research) that the same happens when a listener must choose between different arguments presented by counsel. Less may be more in this context.

Further, you need to keep your argument "simple" in order to make sure that it is understood. If the arbitrators do not understand your argument, you will very likely lose your case in real life – and you will not be successful in the Moot either. Be aware of the fact that you have been dealing intensively with the Moot Problem for months before coming to Vienna or Hong Kong. The arbitrators have not. It can thus be wise to concentrate on the substance of your statement leaving aside a reference to a commentator or a case. If an arbitrator wants to have authority quoted, he or she will probably ask for it. You will then back-up your argument by citing the authority and, in the best case, decide whether to refer to case law or a commentary (based on the arbitrators legal background and presumed preferences).

Many teams – and also many counsel – believe that arbitrators know all documents on the record plus each and every statutory provision and in addition, all leading cases. That is not true. Thus, limit making reference to statutory law to the extent possible. If the case requires quotation of the law, it makes sense to slowly read out the relevant provision. The same applies if you refer to a document. Wait until the arbitrators have found the document in the file and then read out the relevant passage.

Limiting yourself and being brief requires courage. But it shows that you are able to identify the decisive factors. And that is what counts.

4.5 Structure of Presentation Is Vital

The truth is that most people have great difficulty following a complicated speech. We only listen once to a speech and therefore the speech must be structured in a way that a listener understands it the very first time. It is paramount to an immediate understanding that the listener, from the outset:

- ➢ knows what the main issue is; and
- ➢ knows how the speech (*i. e.*, your pleading) is structured.

Listeners (as well as readers of non-fiction text) generally have one key question in mind: "What is the issue?" The reader or listener wants to know what the story is all about and he wants to know right away, and not – as in the case of a best-selling thriller novel – at the end of the brief or speech. Thus, counsel in arbitration is well advised to satisfy the arbitrators' desire by presenting a brief introduction/summary of the case before going into details. Here is a very simple example:

> *"The first issue is: Has the tribunal jurisdiction to decide this dispute? This is questionable because no written arbitration agreement exists..."*

To satisfy the immediate interest of your listeners, *i. e.*, the tribunal, state the issue first before turning to the facts.[13] If you tell the facts first, the arbitrators will not yet know to what they pertain. Under these circumstances, it is hard – if at all possible – to give proper consideration to the facts and to evaluate them. Let us turn to the second issue, the need for a clear structure. Human beings are always looking for order. As a famous arbitrator once put it humorously:

> *"Please present your case in a logical manner. If you can't do that, present it in a chronological manner. And if that fails, do it at least alphabetically."*

Hence, order is important. If you leave it to the audience to search for a pattern in your speech, they will do that – search – and not listen properly. Thus, give the listener a clear structure from the outset:

> *"Respondent has not breached the contract because of the following three reasons ...."*

Now, the listener knows that he has to concentrate on three arguments. In addition, he or she gets the impression that the following arguments are also structured (even if they are not). You can further underline this impression if you terminate the pleading by summarizing the three main arguments in a few words:

> *"To summarize, the following three arguments confirm Claimant's position ...."*

However, resist the temptation to expressly explain the structure of your presentation in detail as in the following negative example:

> *"I will first explain why Respondent has breached the contract and base my position on three arguments. Secondly, I will elaborate on why the breach was material. Afterwards, I will lay out the consequences of the breach which are three-fold ...."*

This proceeding may, to a certain extent, be appropriate to structure a long brief. However, it is not recommended as the beginning of a pleading. In the end, this is talking about formalities and is not a strong opening.

---

[13] *Scalia/Garner*, p. 25 *et seq.*

In addition, giving too many details of the structure renders you inflexible. Imagine that you are running out of time – and may be because of questions by the arbitrators – if you have laid out in detail what you would be talking about, everybody will become aware of your time-problem. Further, you may not get to your closing argument because you feel yourself bound by the structure that you had announced.

It will be much more effective to naturally structure your presentation by:

- ➢ putting things into a logical order (What does the arbitrator need to know first before he or she can properly understand the following issue?);
- ➢ breaking down the presentation in different parts and integrating the outline of the structure of each part in the first sentences of a new part (*e. g.*, "*Let us now turn to why Respondent's breach of contract was fundamental. It was fundamental for two reasons. First, ….*"); and
- ➢ making appropriate pauses between two arguments. This will prepare the listener for the next point.[14]

4.6 Know the Facts of the Case

Abraham Lincoln worked as a lawyer before going into politics. It is said that in his first law firm, he was only assigned cases that everybody considered as lost from the outset. One of those cases was about the defense of a person indicted for murder. Seven witnesses appeared and declared unanimously that they had recognized the accused in the bright moonlight. The case seemed lost. However, at the end of the hearing, Lincoln provided the tribunal with a moon calendar showing that on the night of the murder there was new moon. He won the case.

Although it is very unlikely that the Moot Problem will take a comparably unexpected turn, it goes without saying that intensive preparation is of paramount importance. Knowing the case from every angle, including of course the exhibits, is a prerequisite for a successful oral argument. Only if you master both the file and the law of the case can you have a chance to select the best arguments, react flexibly to questions by the tribunal, and counter the arguments raised by the opposing team.

And even more importantly, only a full command of the case puts you in a position to possibly establish what counsel should be aiming at: A relationship of respectful intellectual equality with the

[14] See also *Scalia/Garner*, p. 146.

tribunal.[15] This is not the relationship of teacher to student, nor a relationship of supplicant to benefactor. Rather, you could compare it to the relationship between an experienced junior partner in a law firm presenting a case to a highly intelligent senior partner. If you manage to be on a par with the arbitrators and, at the same time, display respect for the tribunal, you have done a great job.

A very good tool to master the Moot case is the preparation of speaking notes. By the way, this would also be part of a professional preparation for a pleading in real arbitration. On each speaking note, place the issue in the middle (*e. g.*, "Maximum period for calculation of lost profit"). Underneath, you write – in direct speech – the three arguments that you would like to bring forward in that regard. The more speaking notes you draw up as a team, the better prepared you will become. (For further details on an effective preparation, see below at V.8).

A good way to practice your mastering of the facts is to organize a quiz within your team. To that end, each team member is tasked with preparing five factual questions related to the case. If the other team members are unable to answer the question within 30 seconds, the questioner scores one point. As a consequence, the loser must pick up the bill for the drinks in the post-training session.

4.7 Be Articulate

The purposeful and effective use of language is probably the most important issue when pleading – and it is often neglected. Most people believe they are able to speak accurately in English and that the used "style" is an attorney's individual characteristic and must not be adapted for the arbitrators. To make things worse, few people know what "effective legal language" means because nobody has ever taught them anything about that intricate subject. Some might remember from their high school days that short sentences are better than long sentences and that active voices might be preferable to passive voices. But those "rules" are neither completely correct nor are they applied in practice.

While this is not the place to elaborate in length what "effective legal writing or pleading" stands for, some aspects might be set forth as examples just to create an "aha-effect" and to encourage further study of this topic:

➢ Concentrate on the subject and choose the right one: Research shows that a reader or listener to a speech concentrates on the subject of the sentence (see also above at IV.3.2). It does not

[15] *Scalia/Garner*, p. 33 *et seq.*

matter whether the sentence is phrased in active or passive voice – the subject counts. This is even more true for listeners who only hear a speech once. To please a reader or listener, the subject must appear early in the sentence and it must be the subject the addressee wants to learn more about. Here is an easy example:

- Which of the following two sentences pleases the audience more?

  "The dog chases the cat."

- or

  "The cat is chased by the dog."

- Most persons will, from their high school days, remember that active voice is preferable to passive voice. When it comes to communicating effectively (not to be confused with "writing nicely"), that rule is wrong. As stated, the addressee concentrates on the subject (see also above at IV.3.2). So if you talk to cat lovers you should choose the second alternative in order to create the impression "poor kitty" while if you talk to dog owners you should use the first sentence creating the reaction "yeah, my dog, got it." The proper selection of a subject can increase the effectiveness of your argument as it is shown by the following example:

  "The project was delayed for numerous reasons by Respondent."

- or

  "Respondent delayed the project for the following reasons."

- Clearly, the focus of the two sentences is different. If you are counsel for Claimant you will want to blame Respondent and thus use the second sentence to convey your message clearly.

➢ Use a person as a subject: When listening to a pleading, the addressees look for an answer to the following question: "Who does what?" To please the audience, you should answer that question, at least if you want to be understood. Compare the following sentences:

  "The General Purchase Conditions provide that the liability for product defects …."

- with

  "The Parties agreed that the Seller remains fully liable for product defects …."

- The effectiveness of both sentences cannot be compared. If you want to increase the effectiveness further, you might say:

  "The Parties agreed in paragraph 5 of the Contract – and this is a verbatim quote:

  'The Seller is at all times fully responsible for product defects …'"

➢ Use short sentences: This rule which you might remember from high school is correct for a simple reason: In order to understand the end of a sentence the listener must remember the beginning of that very sentence. Since the memory capacity of our brain is limited and also depends on the addressee's psychic condition at the time of listening, it is hardly advisable to overstrain the arbitrators with long, winded sentences. If that happens, the arbitrator will not blame himself or herself ("Oh, I am really not able to concentrate today.") but he will blame your pleading ("Yeah, this argument is as confusing as is Claimant's entire case.").

- On average, a written sentence that is longer than three lines is too long to be understood or remembered by the arbitrator (while exceptions may apply if the sentence is structured well). For the oral pleading, a sentence should be even shorter. Thus, do not fall into the trap of pre-formulating your pleading or parts of it as if it were a brief. In addition, bear in mind that the arbitrators do not know your thoughts before listening to your argument. Hence, as a rule of thumb, you should not try to convey more than one idea per sentence.

➢ Use direct speech (and do not argue around and around a subject). Begin, for example, like this:

  "There is one question we need to address: Does this tribunal have jurisdiction?"

- If an allegation or argument by the opposing party is wrong, say so, as in the following example:

  "Claimant tells you that he has given proper notice. That is wrong. It is wrong because…."

To sum it up: Communicate clearly and concisely, because, in the words of U.S. Supreme Court Justice Antonin Scalia and Bryan A. Garner:

> *"In an adversary system, it's your job to present clearly the law and the facts favoring your side of the case – it isn't the*

judges' job to piece the elements together from a wordy and confusing brief or argument."[16]

4.8 Team Work – You Count as a Team so Behave as One

Effective interaction with your partner will improve your performance. When your teammate is pleading, make sure that you follow closely in order to be able to assist immediately if required. Before the pleading, agree with your colleague on what kind of assistance you may need. This could include, for example, informing you periodically about the time left or providing you with certain documents from the file and your folder of authorities. Make sure that he or she will find the documents rapidly, by labelling particular documents in the file or marking certain passages in different colors, *etc.* It may also be very helpful if your colleague takes notes in case of long and complicated questions by the tribunal. This is to ensure that while answering the first part of the question, you do not forget the rest of the question.

It frequently occurs in the Moot that after making their arguments, participants fall back into their chair exhausted. This makes a bad impression. Rather, listen attentively to your colleague's and the opposing team's pleadings. Further, it is important that you keep eye contact with the tribunal even if you are not speaking.

This subject takes us to a side note on body language in general. Do not spend too much of your preparation time on that because body language is often somewhat overestimated and – when it comes to details – difficult to change. However, obeying some basic rules will certainly add to a successful oral argument. Those basic rules include the following:

➢ Sit upright and demonstrate attentiveness by looking to the arbitral tribunal when you or your teammate is speaking, and to your opponent if he or she is speaking. Do not hide behind a piece of paper and do not stare into space but maintain eye contact.
➢ Beware of nervous fumbling with a pen or similar behavior.
➢ Keep your hands away from your face (thus, if required, control your hair).

4.9 End on a Strong Note

Listeners are heavily influenced by the first impression they get – and they remember the "famous last words." The latter is the so-

[16] *Scalia/Garner*, p. 23.

called recency effect (for further details see Chapter IV.4.4). For a presentation's effectiveness, it is therefore paramount to end on a strong note. In that context, a very brief summary is recommendable:

> *"To sum it up: Three independent reasons require the dismissal of the claim. First, ... Second, ... Third, ..."*

In the Moot, you are expressly expected to terminate your pleading with an effective conclusion, which usually means a summary. Thus, make sure that sufficient time is left to properly conclude your arguments.

Make sure that from what you say and the way you say it (intonation), it clearly follows that your contribution has come to an end. It would be a pity if your argument trailed off in uncertainty and uncomfortable silence because the tribunal is wondering whether you wanted to add something further.

ISSUES TO REMEMBER

- *Start strong!*
- *Address the tribunal properly*
- *Slow down*
- *KISS*
- *Structure your presentation*
- *Know the facts*
- *Be articulate*
- *Behave as a team*
- *End on a strong note.*

5. Rules for Success

If you follow most of the advice given above in Section 4, you will complete the Moot with a respectable result. That is fine, because after all it is the taking part that counts.

It really is and it would be a shame to spoil the wonderful experience in Vienna or Hong Kong by working doggedly day and night or by getting angry about your performance. However, there may be some among you that are a bit more ambitious, so this chapter is for you. We would like to help you to – over and above having fun – also be successful in the Moot.

5.1 Be Daring, Be Different, Be First

The majority of teams will be very well-prepared for the Moot. Almost all of them will have come across the same legal arguments. It is thus very unlikely that the decisive factor in the Moot will be the presentation of a new argument that is unique among the participating teams. In other words: The factor of success for the oral pleadings is not the legal argument itself but the way in which the arguments are presented.

You may choose between two strategies:

- You line up the arguments as completely as possible and underline the scientific character of your pleading by citing as much case law and references as you can. That is what most teams do.
- You try to stand out and set yourself apart from the other teams by the way of your presentation. That is what very few teams have the heart to do.

Both strategies have their advantages: The first enables you to achieve at least a middle ranking. However, if you just line up the arguments, you will do "ok" but not great. Remember that most of the arbitrators have read and graded submissions and thus will know most of the arguments. At least, they will have read the summary provided by the organizers of the Moot. In addition, they might have listened to oral pleadings the day before. If you follow the "completeness-strategy," it will, to a great extent, be left to chance whether you will make it into the Elimination Rounds.

The second strategy is more risky. It may well happen that a courageous presentation or presentation style is disliked by some arbitrators. However, only those who stand out have a chance to win. As a consequence, we would like to encourage you to think about a saying by Helmut Maucher, the former chairman of the board of Nestlé AG. His motto was:

> *"Be daring, be different, be first!"*

You are invited to reason how you could differ from other teams – accepting the risk involved.

5.2 Opening Bundles and Illustrative Objects

One way to be remembered could be to take into the hearing room something other than just the file. This could be an illustrative object, *e. g.*, a screw if the case is about the delivery of screws which – arguably – were too short. Note, however, that according to the Vis Moot Rules, no exhibits may be used that do not come directly from the Problem.[17] Sometimes, you can even use objects for illustration that are on the table for other reasons. Take, for example, a case involving defective iron bolts. Why not pick up your pencil and address the arbitrators as follows: "Imagine that this is the iron bolt we are talking about. If this iron bolt is exposed to just a little tension it ... breaks." And when saying that, break the pencil.

Another possibility is the preparation of an opening bundle that we have already briefly talked about (above at V.2.2). This is a good option if you want to focus on the evidence on file. In such case, consider preparing spiral binders for the arbitrators and the opposing team containing the four or five crucial documents, separated by tabs and accompanied by an index. In the documents, highlight the relevant passages. Then, argue along the lines of the following:

> *"It is the facts that are decisive for the outcome of this case. Thus, let us go through the facts. For that purpose, we have prepared a bundle with the most important documents which are, of course, already on the record. The first document is the Contract which you find at tab 1. We kindly ask you to turn to page 3 of the Contract where we have highlighted paragraph 5. In this very paragraph, the Parties have expressly agreed that ... (read out the paragraph loud). Let us now turn to Respondent's exhibit No. 3 at tab 2. ...."*

---

[17] According to *para.* 72 of the Vis Moot Rules, exhibits that are designed to clarify time sequences or other such matters may be used, but only if the arbitrators and the opposing team are in agreement. For technical reasons, the exhibits may not consist of overhead or Power Point projections or require the use of a stand.

Note, however, that opening bundles are not common in the Vis Moot unlike in many other moot courts. One possible reason is that the Moot Problem usually is relatively concise and does not include too many exhibits. Experience has shown that at least some of the arbitrators prefer making reference directly to the Problem over using an extra document that they are not yet familiar with. On a side note, when making reference to an exhibit, do not only state the exhibit number but also the page number of the file: "Let us turn to exhibit No. 3 at page 23 of the file."

Another reason why opening bundles are uncommon in the Vis Moot is that most arbitrators will bring their own bundles. In this case, it is sufficient to refer the arbitrators to the exhibits and the pages in the file. However, there will always be arbitrators who are not perfectly prepared. They will appreciate it if they are provided with an extra bundle. Against that background, it is advisable to bind three books containing the Moot Problem (possibly also with tabs) to be provided to the arbitrators, if required.

5.3 Entertain and Personalize

"Be entertaining" is a double-edged advice. After all, the Moot is not designed to be an entertaining event, and even less is a real arbitration. Yet, one reason for the arbitrators to take part in the Moot is the fun element. The arbitrators are happy if they do not hear the same stuff in all the pleadings they score. Of course, you risk that your approach is not liked. However, remember that "daring" involves an element of risk. If "risk" is one side of the coin, the other side is called "opportunity." Without accepting that risk element, you are unable to seize the opportunity. Finally, and maybe most importantly, you need to entertain the arbitrators in order to maintain their attention level. And that is also true in real arbitration.

The serious element of "entertainment" in arbitration is telling a story. Everybody loves stories (that is the reason why many people spend several hours per day in front of a TV set). Research shows that a non-fiction text or speech is much more likely to be read or listened to from start to finish if presented in a story-like format, which also makes them more memorable and convincing. That does not mean using a thriller-like style or being funny or polemic. But it surely does mean using figurative language and/or vivid comparisons. Here are some examples:

"What do you do when you buy a used car? You look at it. What do you do if you buy a used machine? You look at it. Claimant, however, …."

"Claimant wants to calculate the lost profit for nine years. That is a long period. Do you remember the year 2005? That was the year Pope John Paul II died. A lot can happen in nine years. However, Claimant believes that nothing will change …."

"Eight years ago I was thirteen years old and still waiting for my first kiss. Ages have passed since then. Ages? Well, in Claimant's eyes …."

"My client is Mark Spence. Mark Spence was a happy family father running a small business. That was before Mark made the one mistake he is guilty of in this case, i. e., contracting with Reason Enterprises, the Respondent in this case."

In particular, in the Moot, you must become memorable. So do or say something that is remembered – at least to the point when the arbitrators enter their scores into the grading sheets, *i. e.*, 60 minutes after you have started. Thus, try to be different. If your opponent is funny, you should not be funny at all. In addition, aim at surprising the tribunal. This will ensure you full attention. Here is some food for thought (however, try to assess in advance whether "your" tribunal will presumably like this kind of entertainment or consider it un-objective):

"I think that the argument we just heard from Claimant's counsel is correct, well, it is excellent, if not brilliant … (long pause). But the argument does not correspond with the facts of this case."

Or – quite aggressively: "Respondent has just told us many good and many new arguments. (pause) But the good arguments are not new and the new arguments are not good. In detail: …."

(three seconds of silence) "The oral statement we have just heard leaves one speechless. Speechless because …."

"You expect me to …. Sorry, I will disappoint you. …."

"We have just heard an entertaining, even funny opening statement. The problem is: This is not a funny case, it is not at all funny for my client, Mark Spence, who has lost …."

"Claimant is a cherry-picker. When the arbitration clause is in dispute, Claimant holds that the wording is to be neglected

and the sensible approach must be followed. When it comes to the Contract, Claimant holds that the wording is everything."

"Respondent wants to change history in this case. Since Roman times, the pacta-sunt-servanda-principle has been followed throughout the world. But not any longer, according to Respondent."

"Does the Arbitral Tribunal remember the last sentence that was spoken, just a few minutes ago? No? Well, that is usually the problem. Words are quickly spoken and vanish quickly. And that is why seasoned business parties agree on a written form clause to avoid those difficulties."

"Claimant is surprised. Surprised that Respondent belittles the very contract Respondent has entered into. Written contracts are there for a purpose, namely …."

"I have a question for Respondent: What were Respondent's expectations as to the arbitration clause which Respondent now considers invalid?"

"One of my favorite movies is Jurassic Park. There, everything is well-organized and it's a safe fun for the whole family. Until, well until Murphy's law applies: Whatever can go wrong goes wrong. What Respondent tells us today is that only theoretical something could go wrong with the fuses…."

Stories become more entertaining and more credible if real people are acting. Psychological research shows that a listener tends to sympathize with real persons. Hence, try to portray your party as a person. How do you achieve that? By referring to your client's name instead of using legalistic terms like "Claimant" or "Respondent." Talking about "*Mark Spence, my client*" evokes positive associations while an anonymous "Claimant" is less appealing to a listener. If your client is a company, as common in Moot Court cases, use the name of the company or personalize even further: "*Spence Inc. is a family owned business, run by the owner Mark Spence. Mark Spence is now confronted with wild accusations raised by Respondent…*". By the same token, you have no interest at all to personalize your opponent. Hence, stick to "Claimant" or to "Respondent," respectively.

5.4 About Jokes

As to jokes, our recommendation is straightforward: No jokes. That is too risky and may easily be perceived as non-professional. It is of course funny to start your presentation by saying "My opponents are from Harvard University but I have other arguments as well." However, most arbitrators will adopt the view that you are not taking the Moot seriously enough. In addition, almost all jokes are perceived as rehearsed, not made spontaneously, and as soon as a statement is considered as rhetoric figure employed on purpose, the arbitrators will react with a lot of skepticism. The sense of humor differs quite a bit and chances are high that you are not going to meet the taste of at least one arbitrator. And if that arbitrator punishes you with a low grade, your joke has truly backfired.

5.5 Customize Your Pleading for the Arbitrators

Psychological research show that people intuitively establish a link between the content-wise credibility of an argument and the perceived credibility of the person making that argument. That relation is clearly established if the listener dislikes the speaker. Whatever the disliked speaker states is automatically disqualified or "reactively devaluated," as a psychologist would put it. But the same credibility-transfer occurs also if the listener likes the speaker or perceives the speaker in general to be credible.

Now, it is rarely the case that you are personally acquainted with an arbitrator (and if counsel is, as in a real arbitration, that might indeed create other problems). So the question arises, what can a speaker do to be likable to the listener even if he or she might never have met the listener (arbitrator)? The answer to this question is twofold: People like people who are akin to themselves and people like people who act and speak as they do. In practical terms, those two findings overlap and result in the following remarks:

(i) An arbitrator with a lot of humor will favor a counsel who displays some humor while a stern arbitrator will be more pleased by a counsel's style concentrating on facts and not on funny rhetoric. As a rule of thumb, you should act more formally when dealing with eminent arbitrators than with young arbitrators.

(ii) Whenever you plead, consider how the arbitrators would plead if he or she stood in your shoes. If your arbitrator is a law professor, you can safely assume that he or she likes challenging legal theories more than discussing detailed technical facts. So you might want to concentrate on the former. If your arbitrator is from a non-English speaking country, you might choose to reserve your intricate Oxford English and huge vocabulary for other occasions.

(iii) Generally speaking, arbitrators with a common law background favor arguments based on the wording of a document or legal provision. That is because the "parol evidence rule" establishes stringent limits as to considering facts other than the wording of a document, *e.g.*, a contract. In addition, common law arbitrators might appreciate a reference to case law more than an arbitrator with a civil law background will usually do. Arbitrators with a civil law background are generally impressed by arguments based on the spirit and purpose of the law.

In Vienna, the names and the nationalities of the arbitrators are displayed at the doors. Thus, make use of that information where possible. We have already explained that it is important to use the arbitrators' names. The same is true when making reference to the opposing team's statement. So do not make reference to a "Learned Colleague" but to "Mr. Schmidt."

Moreover, there are some possibilities to further customize your pleading or argument, *e.g.*, by establishing a link to one of the arbitrator's home country. You may, for example, cite a leading case or commentary originating from that country:

> *"As your Federal Supreme court, Mr. Schmidt, has decided in June 2006 …."*
>
> *"As your fellow citizen, Dr. Schmidt, the famous Professor Schlechtriem …."*
>
> *"I believe there is a saying in your country, Monsieur Serge, which goes as follows: …. That is true, also for your case…".*

Finally, in the Moot, try to get into contact with the arbitrators before your hearing. If you arrive early, there may well be an opportunity to do some small talk with the members of the tribunal. This is easier than you probably think. Most arbitrators will be interested to know where you come from, *etc.*

5.6 Be Suggestive of Spontaneity and React to the Other Side

Many opening statements in the Moot are learned by heart and rehearsed again and again. This is not bad *per se*. What is, however, neither interesting nor convincing is a statement that clearly reflects the many rehearsals, namely a statement that does not sound like an oral argument, but like the repetition of a given text by an amateur actor. You will most probably not get a score for such a presentation that is different from the other teams' presentation.

Thus, try to make clear that your opening is spontaneous. Is it spontaneous? Of course, not! You are not a "pro" yet and – believe it or not – in many, even major arbitrations, opening statements are read, not given off the cuff. However, with a few tricks you can tailor-make your opening or make it look like tailor-made. We have already explained (above at V.5.5) how to customize your opening for the arbitrators. You can further customize it by reference to the opponent's opening. Very few are in a position to – under pressure – spontaneously react to the opposing team's arguments or questions of the arbitrators. Therefore, it is indispensable to be well prepared so that you know beforehand which arguments will probably be brought forward. If that is the case, you can plan your reaction in advance. And even if you have anticipated the argument, you can still say:

> *"We have just heard about interesting case law. Respondent alleges that …."*

Another key element to an excellent performance in the Moot – and also in a real arbitration – is flexibility.[18] Do not expect that you will necessarily be able to present your arguments without interruption. The more questions you get the more you will have to be prepared to change the order of your arguments or to omit a less important point in order to finish on time. So react to the situation. If a question by an arbitrator gives you the opportunity to make one of your arguments, seize the opportunity and adapt your statement accordingly. This is by far more professional and impressive than telling the tribunal that you would come to that point later on.[19]

At first sight, this may make you feel uncomfortable because it renders the whole exercise less predictable. However, it is much easier to demonstrate spontaneity and flexibility in rebuttals or in the question round than in a prepared statement. As a consequence, we, in principle, recommend that you keep your opening rather short, limiting yourself to the most important arguments. By doing so, you also show the arbitrators that you master your case because you have identified the crucial issues. We suggest that you concentrate on rebuttal or questions. Anticipating and rehearing those situations should play a significant role in your preparation for the oral arguments. Yet, you do not necessarily have to show that you are well-prepared but make it look as if you are reacting to the other side. Here is an example:

> *"Isn't that an astonishing argument that we have just heard? However …."*

---

[18] See also *Scalia/Garner*, p. 153 *et seq.*
[19] See also *Scalia/Garner*, p. 154 *et seq.*

5.7 Create Visual Images

The human mind memorizes information (*i. e.*, what you have just said) in pictures, not in language. In addition, the human mind understands information much easier and much quicker if it is conveyed by way of a picture than by way of language. Whoever gives a presentation is therefore well advised to make ample use of pictures in order to:

(i) create a memory effect (images are remembered, texts are not);
(ii) present information more understandably; and
(iii) entertain the arbitrators and thus make them more receptive to the conveyed information.

We have already talked about using figurative language (above at V.5.3). Over and above this, think of wordplays, such as:

> *"What Claimant tells us is that this printer is not a foil printing machine but a money printing machine."*

Or think of something that you can bring along (see also above at V.5.2). Showing a picture is even more powerful than simply describing/inventing a "verbal" picture. A picture is not necessarily a photo. A graph can well do the job. But the less complicated (*i. e.*, the less detailed), the better the effect produced. However, again, note that in the Moot, graphs are only admitted if the arbitral tribunal and the opposing team are in agreement.[20]

5.8 Show That You Are More Than a Lawyer

A professor at the University of California at Berkeley once said:

> *"The good law schools teach you to think like a lawyer. The great law schools, however, teach you to think, just to think."*

In other words: You increase your chances of succeeding in the Moot if you show that you are not just a good "lawyer" but an intelligent and educated person. How do you do that? A good way is to include, where appropriate, an apt quotation or aphorism. Here are some examples:

> *"'A man will fight harder for his interests than for his rights', said Napoleon Bonaparte, And that is exactly what Claimant does here."*

[20] See *para.* 72 Vis Moot Rules.

"Precaution is better than cure. That is why the Parties have agreed in their Contract that ...."

"When Claimant ..., he crossed the river Rubicon."

"Do not impose on others what you yourself do not desire." (Confucius)

"Napoleon held that 'The surest way to remain poor is to be honest.' That is probably why Respondent, when concluding the contract, omitted to say that ...."

"Aldous Huxley once said: 'Facts don't go away because we ignore them.' This holds true for the present case, Respondent is not going to change that."

"The German poet Erich Kästner once stated: 'The good – there is none. Until it's done.' How true that is. And when Claimant today tells us about its intentions, that doesn't change the one fact which matters, namely that Claimant did not do what was required, namely to send a notice to cure."

In some instances, references to Roman law will also be impressive. However, do not overdo this and be aware of needless Latin phrases. It is not wise to speak in a way that one or several of the arbitrators will not understand. Further, the arbitrators should not get the impression that you are simply showing off.

Rules for Winning

- *Be daring, be different, be first!*
- *Consider illustrative objects*
- *Entertain and personalize*
- *No jokes!*
- *Be suggestive of spontaneity*
- *React to the other side*
- *Create visual images*
- *Show that you are more than a lawyer*

6. About Questions

Why do we dedicate a whole chapter to questions? The reason for this is that questions are the most interesting part of the oral pleading. Some would even say they are the most important part of the oral pleading. Why is that? Well, let's be honest: It's one thing to prepare and hold a pleading, knowing you can always backdrop to the notes lying on your desk; it's another thing to give a sharp, spontaneous answer to a tricky question. By doing so, oralists can show their excellence. Questions thus give you the chance to really distinguish yourself. So do not be afraid of them but embrace a question as a chance kindly offered to you to increase your score. Some arbitrators interrupt you and ask questions during your pleading. Others let you hold your entire pleading and reserve their questions for a question round in the aftermath. Either way, you should consider the following:

6.1 Demonstrate That You Appreciate the Question

Remember that you aim at intellectual equality with the tribunal (see above at V.5.8). Thus, answering obsequiously "Thank you very much" when receiving a question is not a good option. On the other hand, it would be even worse to act like a teacher *vis-à-vis* the arbitrators ("This is an excellent question," meaning: "which indicates that you have understood the case."). Rather, try to find a way to show that you appreciate the question thereby displaying respect for the tribunal: "This question goes to the heart of the matter." In most cases, it suffices to seriously answer the question without any prelude.[21]

It is important not to convey the message that you dislike the question asked because it interrupts your speech. That is why, as stated above (at V.5.6), it is by far better to answer a question directly than to defer the answer to a later point in your pleading. Instead of feeling disturbed by a question try to perceive the question as an opportunity: The tribunal gives you an opportunity to say something on an issue that the arbitrator is really interested in. The question may give you valuable information regarding the arbitrator's perception of the case. Thus, there may be cases where a question does not "simply" require an answer but, at best, allows you to adapt your further argument to the tribunal's preferences.

If you have not understood a question, we recommend that you ask politely for a repetition of the question. This is by far more professional than answering a question that has not been asked or to say something meaningless.

6.2 Structure Your Answer

We have already explained the importance of a clear structure for your pleading (above at V.4.5). Nothing else applies for an answer to a question. It will help the audience follow your answer if you start by saying:

> "*There are three issues here. First, ...*"
>
> or
>
> "*Let me start with the second part of your question .... I now turn to the first part of your question, namely ....*".

[21] Compare also *Scalia/Garner*, p. 33 *et seq.*

6.3 KISS

Answering a question precisely and concisely is impressive. The arbitrators would like to get the answer to the question and then turn to the next issue. Thus, listen exactly to the question and do not annoy the arbitrators by lengthy elaborations which are not closely related to answering the question.

There may be occasions where a question by the tribunal gives you the chance to make a point that you wanted to make anyway. If that happens, you are lucky. However, even in those cases, resist the temptation to make too long a statement. Doing so would most likely weaken your answer.

6.4 What If You Don't Know the Answer

If you do not know the answer to a question in real arbitration, it is an option – sometimes the best option – to frankly admit that:

> *"I am not sure about the answer on the spur of the moment. In order to get it right, I will double-check after the hearing and provide a full answer in the next brief."*

In the Moot, you do not have that opportunity. So what else can you do? Simply admitting that you do not know the answer is certainly not the best strategy. The first thing you should double-check is whether your teammate knows the answer. You can do that if you have agreed beforehand on a sign indicating that your teammate is prepared to answer that question. For example, you can agree that your teammate quietly picks up his or her pencil if he or she feels comfortable to answer. Once you have received the message, you simply say:

> *"My colleague is the true specialist when it comes to this area of law. I refer to her…."*

What if you don't receive such coded message from your teammate? Well then you need to maneuver yourself out of that delicate situation. Politicians are trained to do that as you can observe in almost every talk show. A tested strategy is to generalize the question. If you are confronted with case law that you do not know you may, for example, answer:

> *"Yes, there may be case law arguing against my client. However, there is also case law which supports my client's position. This holds true for …."*

You can also avoid an answer by deflecting the Arbitral Tribunal's attention to a different issue:

> *"I am happy to answer that question but we must not ignore that this question is already based on the presumption that the contract is valid. However, the contract is not valid for three reasons ..."*

An intelligent response is to break down the question into sub-questions and then concentrate on the issue you can answer best. If, for example, the Tribunal confronts you with some unheard-of case law suggesting that the contract is void, you may answer:

> *"This question calls for a two-fold answer, namely whether the Scottish case law you referred to is at all applicable for the present case and secondly, if so, whether applying such case law would render the present contract invalid. As to the first question: The contract is governed by the CISG...."*

Gaining time often helps. If you don't have an immediate answer to the question, restate it for the arbitral tribunal and demonstrate to the tribunal that you have understood the relevance of the question:

> *"You are asking the question whether the general conditions typically used by Claimant have become part of the contract. That may be doubted because Respondent received a copy of those general conditions only after Respondent had signed the contract. That question is indeed relevant for the outcome of the case because ...."*

A final possibility is to bluff. If reference is made to some legal literature or argument that you do not know, you may state:

> *"I do not consider this view to be decisive because the underlying facts in the scenario discussed by those scholars were very different to the case in front of us today. Rather, Claimant's position is that ...."*

Besides all those strategies: If the argument is decisive in the arbitrator's eyes, he might well spot your strategy of evading an answer. Then you are fighting a losing battle. That is why you should try to avoid such situation by assiduously preparing for your pleading.

7. The Minutes After the Oral Pleading

After the pleading, the Tribunal will ask you to leave the room in order to allow for the arbitrators' deliberation. After that, you will be called back into the room for a short debriefing. The purpose of that is to assist you in improving your performance in future arguments. You will, however, not be informed about your score. You will only get to know your scores several weeks after the Moot (without the names of the arbitrators attached and without any details regarding the different criteria for the scoring).

8. Training

A good starting point for your training is watching a pleading from a previous Moot. It will give you an idea of the typical course of an oral pleading. At some point, the Vis Moot (East) began videotaping the final. Consider writing to the administrative team (info@cisgmoot.org) whether there is a DVD copy available for purchase (note, however, that there is no official DVD copy available from the Vis Moot in Vienna). Besides, you will find lots of material on YouTube.

Apart from that, here is some food for thought regarding your preparation for the Vis Moot.

8.1 Personality = Per Sound

The word "personality," when taken literally, is "through (per) sound". A significant part of your personality is indeed conveyed through your voice. Research has shown that the impression you make on others when giving a speech is to a great extent dependent on your voice and body language – and to a much lesser extent on the content of your speech.

Making yourself aware of how you sound is therefore important – not only with regard to the Moot. Try to get honest feedback from others and use video-taping where possible (for further details see below at V.8.5). Talking too quickly is a frequent mistake. Further, it will not help your argument if you are hard to understand acoustically, whether because your voice is too low or because of a poor enunciation. So adapt the volume of your voice to the room size. The aim is to be clearly understood without being unpleasantly loud. If speaking distinctly is not your talent, consider practicing with a cork in your mouth. This proven technique is used by many actors and will help you to enunciate each word clearly.

When you elect the team members for the oral pleading, it may be worth choosing colleagues with an agreeable voice. Another criterion for the election of speakers will probably be their knowledge of English. Yet, we recommend not overestimating this issue. Be aware of the fact that most arbitrators will not be native speakers of English either. Thus, somebody who is easily understood in English (with no strong accent, if possible) is a good choice. He or she does not necessarily have to be the best team member with regard to language skills.

8.2 Dealing with Nervousness (Thanks for Adrenaline!)

Many actors say that the day they are no longer nervous before going on stage is the day they should rather quit their job.

There is a lot of truth in this statement. Why? When you are nervous, your body releases adrenaline. This is a stress hormone which allows for a quick release of energy reserves in order to assure surviving in dangerous situations (fight or flight). The influence of adrenaline enables you to be at your best. You will be more attentive and think quicker because your body is prepared for immediate reaction. Thus, when getting nervous before your pleading, appreciate it!

However, too much nervousness or even performance anxiety will no longer enhance your pleading but can result in mental block. Probably the best strategy to avoid that situation is good preparation which includes training of the actual speaking situation (for further details, see below at V.8.3). The more you feel prepared, the easier it will be to rely on your strengths. Further, it is very helpful to have learned by heart the first three sentences of your presentation. All beginnings are difficult. But after you have started, you will very soon feel more comfortable with the situation.

In the minutes before your pleading, consider calming down by catching some fresh air and breathing deeply. Breathing deeply is also advisable immediately before you start and even during your presentation. It will help you make pauses – a fact that your audience will appreciate.

8.3 Write It Down And Rehearse

Writing down arguments or even parts of your pleading in direct speech is an important step in the preparation for the Oral Pleadings. However, as already explained above (at V.5.6), it is not the best choice to write down your opening statement word by word and to learn it by heart. Of course, it can be very effective to carefully think about the best presentation of an argument and to decide in advance upon the word choice, *etc.* This holds particularly true for the first two or three sentences and the closing remark. Further, it may apply for an individual argument but not for the whole pleading. The chances are too high that your whole prepared concept will be jeopardized by a question of the tribunal. Thus, we recommend a preparation and training that allows for flexibility, namely only outlining your individual arguments.

Justice Scalia and Garner even go one step further. They suggest not preparing a fixed outline of points in the order in which you wish to make them; rather, they recommend to make a list of five to seven points that you want to make, accompanied by a plan of how you intend to present each of them.[22] This can be done by way of speaking notes which each contain the three main arguments for a certain issue (see above at V.4.5).

When rehearsing, aim at making effective use of your notes and – at least partly – getting rid of them. Consider going through your pleading in the shower. Nobody can hear you and there is no possibility to use your notes. You will see that after months of dealing with the Problem, you know your case and are not anymore dependent on notes for each and every issue. Therefore, adapt your notes to your needs. It is easier to find a certain aspect quickly in your notes during the pleading if the notes are well-structured and not overloaded. What you know by heart does not need to be featured in your notes anymore. There is one exception: If you are worried about forgetting an issue under pressure, take your comprehensive notes with you to feel more comfortable. However, it would be a pity if you blocked yourself by adhering too closely to notes.

8.4 List of Questions

A good preparation does mean, in the words of Justice Scalia and Garner, to:

> *"ensure to the maximum extent possible that surprises don't occur."*[23]

Thus, look at the case from all perspectives. Identify the strengths and weaknesses of Claimant's as well as Respondent's position and prepare a defense for the weaknesses. Further, it is very helpful to

[22] *Scalia/Garner*, p. 154.
[23] *Scalia/Garner*, p. 150.

prepare a list of the – let us say 30 – most probable questions that you would expect from the arbitrators plus, of course, your reply to those questions.

Knowing the weaknesses of your position is paramount. It may be human nature to push those weaknesses to the back of your mind hoping that nobody will touch the issue. However, this is a very risky strategy. It is far better to anticipate a question pointing to a weak point and to carefully think in advance about an adequate reaction or defense. This can be openly conceding an issue because, as Justice Scalia and Garner put it:

> *"Don't try to defend the indefensible."*[24]

Of course, you would then move on to explain why the conceded point is not relevant for the outcome of your case. You may, for example, answer the question whether your client complied with a certain procedure prescribed under the Contract in the following way:

> *"We concede that Claimant did not comply with the procedure as foreseen in No. 6 of the Contract. However, in the present case, Claimant was not obliged to follow that procedure. This is because ...."*

8.5 Structured Feedback and Videotaping

A very important part of your training – if not the most important part – is receiving structured feedback. The persons giving feedback may be your team coach and/or other team members as well as an "opposing" team or the arbitrators in a pre-moot event (*cf.* below at V.8.6). It helps a lot if the feedback is supported by concrete examples and explanations. "Your performance was very good" does not help you improve. Try to ask back, if possible: "What exactly was good and why? What can be improved?" You will see that the whole team will learn a lot when analyzing why a certain argument was considered persuasive and why another argument was perceived as feeble.

It will help ensure valuable feedback if you structure the feedback by certain criteria. You may, for example, let yourself be inspired by the criteria relevant for the scoring in the Moot (see above at IV.1.5). It is a good idea to ask different team members to feel mainly responsible for one of the criteria. This facilitates the listener's task because he or she can really concentrate on body language, gesture and eye contact without having to pay attention to the legal quality of the argument at the same time.

---

[24] *Scalia/Garner*, p. 20.

Videotaping rehearsals is a very effective learning tool. This is because when you are concentrating on the content of your speech, you cannot be fully aware of how you look like when presenting. This could mean that you do not recognize that you have fiddled with papers for about 15 minutes or swayed back and forth during argument. Or you will only recognize when seeing the video that you have used too many "filler" sounds such as "ums" and "ers."

In addition, video analysis can assist you in improving your voice. Normally, you only hear your voice from the inside. It will probably sound different from the outside, *i. e.*, the listener's perspective. Usually, your voice actually is in a higher pitch than you perceive. However, a high and shrill pitch is often perceived as uncomfortable and – maybe even worse – interpreted as a sign of little confidence. Learning how to lower your pitch will help you not only in the Moot but in your career as a public speaker in general.

It can, of course, be uncomfortable to watch yourself on video. However, be assured that this exercise is not designed for blaming you. Rather, you are offered a chance for improvement by such kind of self-observation. Apart from that, you may also get positive insights from video analysis. For example you will recognize that if you are nervous during your presentation, the audience will detect much less of that then you would have thought.

8.6 Practice: Pre-Moot Events

Pre-Moot events are organized in various parts of the world and are somewhat part of the Moot experience. Pre-Moots are probably the best training opportunities because they closely resemble the Moot.

Getting Ready for the Race

A Pre-Moot is the mini version of the Vis Moot. It follows the same rules and uses the same problem as the actual Vis Moot. To this end, a Pre-Moot is a somewhat formalized competition with eight or more teams pleading against each other. Depending on the size of the Pre-Moot, there might even be first and final rounds and, most often, a winner and a second runner up will be chosen at the end. Accordingly, a Pre-Moot is to be distinguished from a mere training session organized by a law firm where two or four teams plead against each other and "only" receive feedback from seasoned attorneys afterwards.

When participating in a Pre-Moot, you can test your skills and arguments in front of a Tribunal. Depending on your success in the Pre-Moot, you can then slightly adapt your pleading or use different arguments altogether. At the same time, you will learn the ground rules and sequence of a Vis Moot pleading session. What is more, a Pre-Moot can help to overcome the panic that many of you will feel when having to present arguments in front of total strangers. You will get to see what it is like to plead your case – and will most likely find out that your worst nightmares will not come true but that you feel rather elated. To put it another way, a Pre-Moot functions as a training session for the actual race to test your muscles and physical shape.

The training session does not end as soon as the Pre-Moot is over. To make the most out of your Pre-Moot experience, it might be helpful to write down all the questions that were asked either to your team or to other teams during the Pre-Moots. You may then discuss those questions within your team and prepare an answer to them.

Finding a Way through the Pre-Moot Jungle

The "Pre-Moot-Industry" has been growing fast throughout the past few years. At least 55 (!) Pre-Moots were held in the 2016/2017 Moot. Moreover, there are small regional gatherings of universities that do not qualify as Pre-Moots but which also provide for test pleadings. And many teams are invited to Pre-Moot events held at law firms where the teams plead against each other and are well catered for afterwards.

Due to the sheer number and variety of Pre-Moots you may quickly lose track. To find your way through the jungle, we put together a "hit list" of Pre-Moots. In the following, you will find a compilation of the most prestigious Pre-Moot events around the globe (in alphabetical order) and all the information you need for a first impression. Of course, this list is not exhaustive and there might be other Pre-Moot events that would also deserve special mentioning – but that applies to any non-exhaustive list, doesn't it?

Willem C. Vis International Commercial Arbitration Moot
Selection of Pre-Moot Events

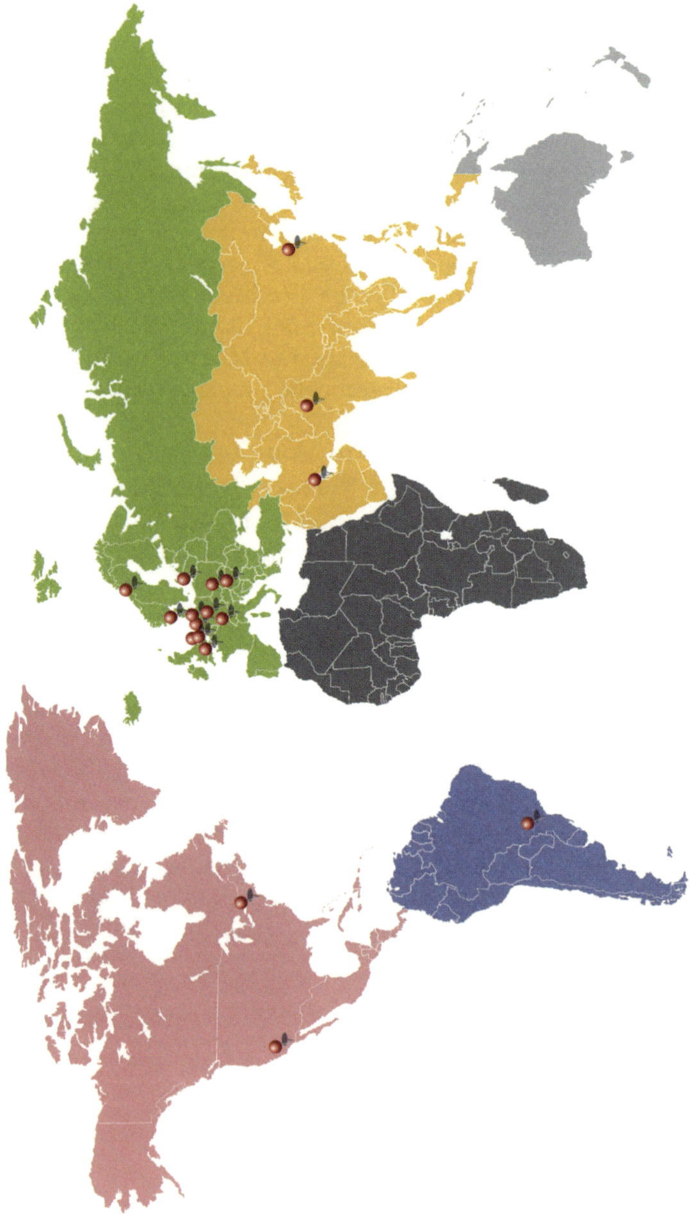

"ALL MUNICH ROUNDS"
(MUNICH, GERMANY)

- ✓ 20 teams from 12 countries (in 2017)
- ✓ established in 2010 / 3-day-event
- ✓ registration fee of 50 EUR per team
- ✓ http://www.mucdr.org/index.php?page=moot&sub=all_munich_rounds

"BELGRADE OPEN PRE-MOOT"
(BELGRADE, SERBIA)

- ✓ 79 teams from 39 countries (in 2017)
- ✓ established 2008 / 2-day-event
- ✓ no registration fee
- ✓ http://www.ius.bg.ac.rs/moot/premoot.htm
- ✓ special feature: At the *"Belgrade Arbitration Conference"* international professionals meet and discuss recent trends in international arbitration.

"BUDAPEST PRE-MOOT"
(BUDAPEST, HUNGARY)

- ✓ various teams from 24 countries (in 2017)
- ✓ established in 2011 / 3-day-event
- ✓ usually no registration fee (can vary)
- ✓ https://www.facebook.com/budapestpremoot
- ✓ special feature: Many social events (*e.g.* a "Sunset Cruise" on the river Duna) and academic events (*e.g.* a conference on topics related to the moot problem) take place on the occasion of the pre-moot; the Budapest pre-moot is one of the last pre-moots of the season - it traditionally takes place only a few days before the Vienna Vis Moot starts.

"CURITIBA PRE-MOOT"
(CURITIBA, BRAZIL)

- ✓ 24 teams from South American countries (in 2017)
- ✓ established in 2009 / 2-day-event
- ✓ no registration fee
- ✓ www.premootdecuritiba.com.br
- ✓ special feature: The Pre-Moot is usually accompanied by other academic events (*e.g.* in 2014, an UNCITRAL Seminar on "The CISG and Brazil" took place).

"CEPANI BRUSSELS PRE-MOOT"
(BRUSSELS, BELGIUM)

- ✓ 12 teams from 9 countries (in 2017)
- ✓ established in 2012 / 3-day-event
- ✓ registration fee of 100 USD per team
- ✓ http://brusselspremoot.be/

"DÜSSELDORF PRE-MOOT ROUNDS"
(DÜSSELDORF, GERMANY)

- ✓ 16 teams from 9 countries (in 2015)
- ✓ established in 2008 / 3-day-event
- ✓ no registration fee
- ✓ http://www.dus-moot.de/index.php/duesseldorf-pre-moot-rounds/registration-anmeldung
- ✓ special feature: social activities like "Brewery Night" and "Clubbing"

"Fordham Vis Practice Moot"

(New York, USA)

- ✓ 43 teams from 12 countries (in 2014)
- ✓ established in 2007 / 3-day-event
- ✓ registration fee of 25 USD per team member (2 coaches may participate for free)
- ✓ https://www.fordham.edu/info/23225/vis_practice_moot
- ✓ special feature: The Fordham Vis Practice Moot presents well-known keynote speakers every year and organizes social events in New York City as well as a "Showcase Round".

"Hannover Pre-Moot"

(Hannover, Germany)

- ✓ 28 teams from 11 countries (in 2017)
- ✓ established in 2007 / 3-day-event
- ✓ no registration fee
- ✓ http://www.jura.uni-hannover.de/premoot.html
- ✓ special feature: At the *"Hannover Pre-Moot Conference"* professionals give lectures about topics closely related to the current moot problem.

"Indian Vis Pre-Moot"

(Delhi, India)

- ✓ Various Indian teams (in 2017)
- ✓ established in 2011 / 3-day-event
- ✓ no registration fee
- ✓ http://www.jgu.edu.in/JGU/CMS/VisPreMoot

"ICC Pre-Moot"
(Paris, France)

- ✓ Various teams from different countries (in 2017)
- ✓ 2-day-event
- ✓ no registration fee
- ✓ https://iccwbo.org/event/2017-icc-vis-pre-moot/
- ✓ special feature: An *ICC YAF Conference* (ICC Young Arbitrators Forum) takes place on the eve of the Pre-Moot to give participants a chance to gather with other participants and exchange thoughts on international arbitration.

"Michael Thorsnes International Arbitration Competition"
(San Diego, USA)

- ✓ 22 teams from 3 countries (in 2017)
- ✓ established in 2008 / 3-day-event
- ✓ registration fee of 30 USD or 40 USD (depending on the date of application)
- ✓ http://www.usdvicam.com/usd-pre-moot.html
- ✓ special feature: A speaker panel will be held on the occasion of the Pre-Moot. The first and second place teams will receive an award of 200 or 300 USD (in 2017).

"Milan Pre-Moot"
(Milan, Italy)

- ✓ 18 teams from 10 countries (in 2017)
- ✓ established in 2008 / 2-day-event
- ✓ no registration fee
- ✓ http://www.camera-arbitrale.it/it/news/MILAN+PRE-MOOT+-+VII+edizione.php?id=471
- ✓ special feature: Each year, the Milan Chamber of Arbitration (CAM) organizes a conference on issues related to the moot-problem.

"MOOT CLINIC COPENHAGEN"

(COPENHAGEN, DENMARK)

- ✓ maximum of 6 teams
- ✓ 3-day-event to take place in September/ October
- ✓ fee of EUR 290 per team (incl. two coaches) for six clinic sessions ("introduction to the rules", "case analysis", "writing memorandum", "opening statements and submissions", "how to deal with questions" and "closing statements and rebuttal")
- ✓ http://www.moot-clinic.com/
- ✓ special feature: The Moot Clinic is different from any other Pre-Moot events. It takes place *before* the moot problem has been published in order to demonstrate what the oral pleadings will look like. This Pre-Moot event is for "early birds".

"MOOT SHANGHAI"

(SHANGHAI, CHINA)

- ✓ 24 teams from various countries (in 2017)
- ✓ established in 2011 / 4-day-event
- ✓ no registration fee for the first 5 team members (incl. one coach); 100 USD starting from the 6th participant
- ✓ http://mootshanghai.cn/
- ✓ special feature: several academic lectures held by arbitration practitioners.

"PCA PRE-MOOT THE HAGUE"

(THE HAGUE, NETHERLANDS)

- ✓ 10 teams from 7 countries (in 2017)
- ✓ established in 2008 / 2-day-event
- ✓ no registration fee
- ✓ https://pca-cpa.org/en/news/6301/
- ✓ special feature: The Pre-Moot takes place at the historic "Peace Palace" (*Vredespaleis*), which is the seat of the *International Court of Justice*.

"STOCKHOLM PRE-MOOT"
(STOCKHOLM, SWEDEN)

- ✓ 12 teams 12 countries (in 2017)
- ✓ established in 2009 / 3-day-event
- ✓ no registration fee
- ✓ http://sccinstitute.com/about-the-scc/news/2017/teams-from-all-over-the-world-gathers-for-the-stockholm-pre-moot-2017/
- ✓ special feature: A *"SCC Pre-Moot Conference"* takes place at the end of the Pre-Moot, usually exploring some of the issues addressed in the moot problem.

"VIS MIDDLE EAST PRE-MOOT"
(DOHA)

- ✓ 17 teams from 11 countries (in 2017)
- ✓ established in 2011 / 5-day-event
- ✓ no registration fee
- ✓ http://premoot.bcdr-aaa.org/en/pre-moot-events/
- ✓ special feature: 3 days of "Oral Advocacy Training" preceding the pre-moot. The location of this Pre-Moot changes every year (e.g. Vienna, Muscat, Abu Dhabi, Doha). In 2017, it was held in Kuwait.

"WARSAW PRE-MOOT"
(WARSAW, POLAND)

- ✓ 15 teams from 6 countries (in 2014)
- ✓ established in 2009 / 3-day-event
- ✓ no registration fee
- ✓ http://www.vis.wpia.uw.edu.pl/8th-warsaw-pre-moot
- ✓ special feature: A conference on changing topics is held on the occasion of the Pre-Moot, *e.g.* on "Money for Nothing? Security for Costs and other "Costly Matters" in International Arbitration".

Too Many Cooks Spoil the Broth

Pre-Moot events are an excellent way to prepare for the oral pleadings in Vienna and/or Hong Kong and it is great to see how many of them have sprouted up from the ground all around the globe. However, the fact that we listed no less than 18 recommendable Pre-Moot events shall not be misunderstood: This is not an invitation or recommendation to participate in as many Pre-Moots as possible.

Your decision on how many Pre-Moots to participate in is very individual and depends on various factors. Depending on the location of your team, the costs for participating might be disproportional to their benefit and you might not have the funds to travel around the world. And depending on your curriculum outside the Vis Moot there might simply not be enough time to travel around the world – even if you had the money to do so.

If there are no Pre-Moot events near your location and/or if you do not have the funds to travel to them, you should not feel disappointed. There are other possibilities for some "hands on" training: for example, you could have a practice session with another team via Skype. Or you can set up your own little Pre-Moot by inviting the team(s) "next door". Another option is to arrive earlier in Vienna and/or Hong Kong to meet up with other teams there. Try to think outside the box and you are sure to find a way!

If there are many Pre-Moot events in your region and if you have the funds to participate in as many Pre-Moots as you can fit into your schedule, try to be selective.

First, you should always calculate some (and enough!) time to reflect on your experiences and feedback subsequent to having attended a Pre-Moot. This is a necessary step in order to adapt and improve your pleading accordingly. However, when receiving feedback from the arbitrators be aware that this always comprises subjective elements. You may get contradictory advice from different people. Therefore, sometimes less is more. If you gather too much (contradictory) advice you might be left confused and dazed. Remember: too many cooks spoil the broth!

Second, and most importantly, you might actually end up losing a bit of your enthusiasm for the real highlights in Vienna and/or Hong Kong along the way if you "tour" from one Pre-Moot to another. Like a marathon runner, you will need to use your strength optimally to make it to the winner's podium.

VI. Seven Days in Vienna and/or Hong Kong

The Moot would be "moot" without its grand finale. More than half a year of research, arguing with team members, writing memoranda and pre-moot rounds finally pays off: the oral pleadings in Vienna and Hong Kong.

If you get to go to both of these spectacular and very different cities, you can call yourself lucky. If you participate in the oral pleadings only in Vienna or only in Hong Kong, there is no reason to feel less lucky. No matter where you participate in the oral pleadings, you will be infected by the Moot spirit.

1. Be Aware: The Moot is an Educational Tool With Competitive Elements – Not a Competition With Educational Side Effects

Once you have handed in your written memoranda, packed your bags and touched ground in Vienna or Hong Kong you might ask yourself: "What do I have to do to win the Moot?" Of course, the Moot is a competition and there will be winners, runners-up, and those who do not make it past the General Rounds. During the oral pleadings, the atmosphere is contagious. You will catch yourself thinking and praying: "If only we could make it past the General Rounds!" Once you made it to the final rounds, you will think: "If only we can perform better than our opponents!" It is only natural that a competitive environment generates competitors. It is nearly impossible not to become competitive.

At the end of the day though, the winner does not take it all. Of course, you want to give your best and that is great. But the real winners of the Moot – and it may sound trite – are those who do not forget to take a step back and enjoy the show. Also, a competitive mindset can prevent you from getting to know other teams. They are not "opponents" but fellow students who share the same enthusiasm for international law and arbitration. Most likely, there will not be other occasions in your life like the Moot where you get to meet so many law students from around the world. You can learn from each of them.

So if competition is not the actual purpose of the Moot, what exactly do we mean when we say "the Moot is an educational tool"? Before you decided to participate in the Moot, your legal studies were dominated by lectures, text books and case studies. It can happen quite easily that one forgets the purpose of those exercises: to apply and argue the law. The Moot gives you a first impression of what it is like to argue the law in "real life." It might not be enough to have read each and every case that deals with the relevant issues. Also, it might not help to know by heart the opinions of well-known professors on the relevant issues. If the other team argues complete nonsense, you will need to improvise. And if the arbitrators ask questions that you have not thought of before, you will need to come up with a clever and convincing answer on the spot. This is the real purpose of the Moot: you can test your skills and argue your case as a lawyer would in real life, but without the real life consequences attached to winning and losing for a real client.

2. Being Team-Spirited: The Oral Pleadings

In general, the Moot weeks in Vienna and Hong Kong follow the same pattern. It would be wrong, however, to declare that there are no differences between Vienna and Hong Kong. The Moot in Vienna is by far larger than its Asian counterpart. But whether "Vienna is calling" or if "Mooties go East," all roads lead to the final stage of each year's Moot; the Oral Pleadings.

2.1 Vienna Calling

Every year around Easter time, Vienna will become the international capital of arbitration. It might be true that "the arbitration world is a small one" (see further Chapter VIII) but it appears to be anything but small when seemingly every member of the arbitration community from around the world gathers in one place. For the local Viennese, this week must be quite a strange experience. A group of more than 2,000 (and annually growing) young people invade their hometown. They wear suits they are much too young for and speak languages that often cannot be pinpointed.

The Vienna Schedule

Over the years, the schedule for the oral hearings in Vienna has been fixed and is followed with clockwork precision. This works to your advantage because you can plan your stay in Vienna ahead of time (see Chapter II).

Thursday	MAA Welcoming Party
Friday	Official Opening Reception
Saturday – Tuesday	General Rounds of Argument
Tuesday – Thursday	Elimination Rounds of Argument
Thursday Evening	Finals and Awards Banquet

Welcome to Austria: Excuse Me, Where Do I Find the Moot?

Most Mooties will arrive in Vienna by plane and disembark at Vienna International Airport. Before the oral pleadings, you may have met a few teams from other universities at pre-moot rounds. Or maybe you have not met any other teams at all because pre-moot rounds were not an option for your team budget. In any event, you will recognize another Mootie when you see one. Just look out for young people that come in groups of four to eight and who might look just a little nervous but full of expectation and anticipation. This is your first chance to make new friends. Maybe you can even share a taxi or bus with another team in getting into Vienna (for transportation to and in Vienna as well as housing advice, see Chapter VI).

Vienna's Secret Tourist Attraction: the "Dachgeschoss"

The local Viennese must be baffled when they notice that the young suit-wearing foreigners who invade their hometown all have the same destination: the "Dachgeschoss." During the Moot in Vienna, the Dachgeschoss will be your most frequently visited stop.

The German word "Dachgeschoss" can be translated into "roof floor" and refers to the top floor of a building; *i. e.*, the floor right underneath the roof. In the language of the Vis Moot though, the "Dachgeschoss" is far more than just a part of a building. The top floor of the Juridicum, the building of the University of Vienna that houses the law school, is the command center of the Vis Moot. If Professor Eric E. Bergsten were the President of a nation called "Vis Moot," the Juridicum would be the White House and the Dachgeschoss would be his Oval Office.

Comparing the Dachgeschoss to the Oval Office, however, could raise unreasonably high expectations among first-time Mooties. The Dachgeschoss certainly has a charm of its own but you would not immediately think of a presidential office when you step out of one of the small Juridicum-elevators that have seen better days. The first eye-catcher of the Dachgeschoss is not the prettiest: blue linoleum flooring with a pattern of circles. The Dachgeschoss would be the perfect place to host a "back to the 80s"themed party. But the area is very spacious and the generous floor-to-ceiling windows offer a fine view of Vienna. On top of that, there is unlimited supply of water and coffee for everyone, free of charge.

The Moot administration is situated at one end of the Dachgeschoss. You will hardly miss it since the administration team is always busy organizing everything, from registering the Mooties to allocating the hearing rooms to distributing the tickets for special events. They are the brain of the Moot. Scattered around, you will find the MAA-desk as well as desks of publishers that sponsor the Moot who display their books on international arbitration and international commercial law. And then there are many tables and chairs as well as lounge seats for the teams to meet before the hearings, deliberate after the hearings, plan their next items on the agenda, or simply hang around and chat with new friends.

The Dachgeschoss also features a desk with a supply of Vis Moot T-shirts and coffee mugs, one each for every team member…

2.2 Mooties Go East

Created in 2003/2004, the Vis Moot (East) in Hong Kong is much younger and smaller than its Vienna counterpart. The Vis Moot (East) is based on the same principles, uses the same problem, and substantially identical rules. However, the two Moots are completely different, with different schedules, separate registration and separate winners. Also, the Vis Moot (East) takes place two weeks prior to the Vis Moot but does not serve as an elimination round for Vienna. Teams may register for both Moots but individual students who argue in Hong Kong may not argue in Vienna in the same year.

The Hong Kong Schedule

Like its European counterpart, the schedule for the oral hearings in Hong Kong is also prepared long before and is available at the website of the Vis Moot (East). This greatly helps you plan your stay in Hong Kong (see Chapter VI).

Saturday	MAA Welcoming Party
Sunday	Registration & Opening Ceremony
Monday – Thursday	General Rounds of Argument
Friday – Saturday	Elimination Rounds of Argument
Sunday	Final Round and Gala Awards Banquet

2.3 Whether in Vienna or Hong Kong: Let the Pleadings Begin

No matter if you touched ground in Vienna or in Hong Kong, the week will start off with the General Rounds in which each team will argue against four other teams. As the week proceeds, the teams who have received the highest scores in the General Rounds will move to the Elimination Rounds (*i. e.*, 64 teams in Vienna and 32 teams in Hong Kong). At the end of the week, the two teams that made it all the way through will have the honor to plead against each other in front of all other teams and arbitrators.

A Simple Equation: 2 x 4 = 8

One big advantage of the Vis Moot is that every participating team gets a chance to plead in the oral hearings. Unlike other moot courts, there is no elimination round prior to the oral hearings based on the evaluation of the written memoranda. But having said that, each and every team member does not necessarily get a chance to practice pleading skills. Some law schools put together large teams with more team members than pleading slots in the General Rounds. The number of team members is discretionary but experience has shown that between four and eight people make a good team (for more details on team composition, see Chapter III).

If your team has more than eight members, a simple arithmetic exercise reveals that not everyone can participate during the General Rounds (*i. e.*, four pleadings with two team members each). But even in smaller teams, speaking in front of the arbitral tribunal is not a given. Some teams decide to send only their "best horses" to the front. This might be a good approach if you wanted to win a competition. The Moot is, however, not a competition but an educational exercise (see above at VI.1). Preferably, every team member should get the chance to argue in front of the arbitral tribunal. If you participate both in Vienna and in Hong Kong, you have more pleading slots available.

The Cheerleader Syndrome

Some teams – especially those from universities nearby – might be accompanied by an entourage of affiliated teams, former Mooties and members of their university. If you have to plead against a team that fills the entire hearing room, do not be intimated. It is only important to impress the arbitrators, not the spectators in the peanut gallery. Focus on your arguments and let your adrenaline do the work: You will be wide awake and ready for any question from the arbitrators.

If you are from a team with a strong fan base, please keep the following in mind: Don't intimidate! It is great that you can rely on a group of people that believe in your abilities but be aware that other students are lone fighters who cannot rely on such on-site support. Some teams even travel to Vienna or Hong Kong without a coach because this would exceed their budget. You would act within the Moot spirit if you showed a small team that you acknowledge their position. Why not invite them to join your group for drinks at the official moot court bar (see Chapter II) after the pleading?

Not All Arbitrators Are the Same!

Arbitrators come in a wide range of shapes and sizes. This is not a reference to their age, gender or other superficialities, but to the amount of preparation they have undertaken before coming to

Vienna or Hong Kong. Traditionally, the most prestigious scholars and arbitrators travel to Vienna to act as arbitrators in the oral hearings. The Vis Moot would be less impressive if only a bunch of students and coaches came together to judge each other. But the arbitration elite also gather in Vienna to meet long-time-no-see friends and to mingle with their kind.

Once you find yourself in Vienna or Hong Kong, you will know the Moot Problem by heart. You will be able to cite cases without referring to your notes and you will know from the top of your head that Procedural Order No. 1 can be found on page 47 of the file. And of course, you will have prepared specific and witty answers to the most common questions an arbitrator could possibly ask....or so you think!

But the range of questions by arbitrators is endless. Some arbitrators also act as coaches of other teams (of course, they are not allowed to judge a team they are affiliated with). Those arbitrators can be tricky because they know the Problem inside out and will surely find your weak spot. They will notice immediately if you are unfamiliar with some of the details, or they may spontaneously deviate from your rehearsed arguments. Other arbitrators, however, have not even touched the file before coming to Vienna or Hong Kong. Those arbitrators can be tricky, too, because their questions are unpredictable. For example, an arbitrator could ask you how such a machine – that is defective and now part of the Moot Problem – works in general, and why Claimant was unable to fix the machine himself. An arbitrator could also inquire if Respondent concedes that the arbitral tribunal has jurisdiction to hear the case so the parties can concentrate on the substantial issues rather than arguing procedural issues. There is no correct or incorrect reaction to such situation – just be prepared that the arbitrators are not prepared.

Arbitrators are encouraged to behave in the exact same way they would do in real arbitral hearings. Consequently, they might bombard you with questions the second you have introduced yourself and your co-counsel and before making your first arguments. Arbitrators might also sit in silence until you have finished your pleading and ask only one single question. This is part of the Moot experience and it should not bother or concern you. It only shows that different backgrounds lead to different approaches – just like in the world of real arbitration.

Getting to Know the Other Side

Once you have registered onsite in Vienna or Hong Kong you will be provided with your team's schedule. Now, you are getting down to serious business: Who will be the four teams that you will plead against in the General Rounds?

The Moot organizers will try everything to avoid pleadings between universities from the same country. What is more, they also try to mingle the teams as much as possible. One of the unique features of the Vis Moot is that it provides for a very international environment. In an ideal Moot world, you would be pleading against four universities from four different continents. You would be introduced to four completely different legal systems and pleading styles.

There are, however, more universities participating in the Moot from Europe and the US than from countries like New Zealand, Ethiopia or Bahrain (for an overview, see our world chart in Chapter II). It is therefore more likely for you to compete against a European or an American university than pleading against teams from more exotic countries. There are pros and cons to this aspect. On the one hand, if you are from a European country with a civil law background, the pleading style and line of arguments of the African competitors will take some getting used to. Likewise, the African team will wonder why you do not show any enthusiasm when pleading your case. In such a pairing, it might be difficult for you to stay on track with your own line of arguments. On the other hand, it will be those pleadings that will stay in your mind forever and that make up the Moot spirit. Additionally, those are the pleadings where you can show your advocacy skills the most.

No matter where your pleading partners for the General Rounds are from, you should get to know them before the actual pleading starts. In fact, this is a two-fold-task: First, you could prepare for the pleading by finding out how the other team "ticks." Do they have a common law background or a civil law background? Is the university new to the Moot or part of the Moot's "ivy league" (*i. e.*, those who have participated in the Moot since 1993)? Second, it is always nice to get to know the other teams personally. Why not have drinks with your "future opponents" at one of the numerous receptions that take place at the beginning of the week? In case you do not make it before the actual pleading, show up a little early and have a quick chat with the other side. Maybe you can already agree on an order in which you would like to present the issues. If the tribunal later asks whether the parties have reached an agreement in this regard, you have something to offer.

In any event, getting to know the team on the other side can help you to feel prepared and ready for your pleading and show the arbitrators why your team deserves the full 200 points.

3. Being Social: Receptions and Parties

The oral pleadings will be a great experience. But what you will probably remember for a lifetime are the receptions and parties that accompany the weeks in Vienna and Hong Kong. Those events come in handy because you will not have to arrange for meetings with newly found friends – you will meet them anyway at one of the receptions or parties that are scheduled for the day.

3.1 Receptions and Parties in Vienna

MAA Welcome Party at Palais Eschenbach

Traditionally, the first stop of every Vienna stay is the MAA Welcome Party at Palais Eschenbach on Thursday. Technically speaking, the MAA Welcome Party takes place before the actual start of the Moot on Friday. But especially for the fact that the General Rounds will not start before Saturday contributes to the relaxed atmosphere at Palais Eschenbach.

As a classical Austrian palace, Palais Eschenbach serves as an ideal location to welcome the Mooties from all around the world to Vienna. Its stunning chandeliers and the tasteful interior decoration create a unique atmosphere. The first big get-together of the week is a great opportunity to meet teams and coaches before the Official Opening Reception takes place the day after. This is probably also the reason why the Welcome Party at Palais Eschenbach happens to be a success year in and year out.

Official Opening Reception

On Friday, the Official Opening Reception at the Wiener Konzerthaus signals the festive start of the Vis Moot competition in Vienna. If you already thought Palais Eschenbach is a fancy venue, then wait until you see the Wiener Konzerthaus. As one of Vienna's most beautiful venues, it provides enough space for the increasing number of participants every year. The Mooties will be welcomed by the organizers and several other speakers. In addition, Professor Harry Flechtner will perform his legendary CISG song and an exclusive tune in honor of the latest Moot Problem. Afterwards, everyone is invited to have a glass of wine and to chat with other participants. On this occasion, you will also witness the huge number of people that are actually attending the Moot in one way or another.

Although not mandatory, most teams will wear festive evening dresses. The Official Opening Reception serves also as a great start of the first evening program, which will eventually move on to the official Moot bar, the Schwarzberg.

The Moot Bar: Schwarzberg (until 2014: Ost Klub)

In fact, there are two hot spots where Mooties, alumni, coaches and arbitrators meet over drinks in Vienna. The most traditional one is the Schwarzberg. It is located in the centre of Vienna and its doors are open almost every night during the Moot. The Schwarzberg does not charge entrance fees and offers drinks at very reasonable prices.

After long Moot days, the Schwarzberg offers you the chance to get out of your suit and spend time in a more casual atmosphere. The guests may compete against each other in exciting table soccer matches, have a couple of drinks at the bar, or dance on the dance floor. Apart from the Schwarzberg, the Aux Gazelles has evolved to a very popular location for anyone involved in the Moot. The Aux Gazelles is the ideal location to enjoy the social side of the Moot, providing for a bar, lounge and dancing area in a picturesque European-African setting. It is located right next to the subway exit at "Museumsquartier".

The MAA Walking Tour and Goulash Dinner

The MAA Walking Tour usually takes place on Saturday or Sunday. A professional tour guide leads you to well-known tourist attractions as well as to some of the secret attractions that you would probably not find if you were exploring the city by yourself. At the same time, you will learn about the history of Vienna, especially about the golden age when Vienna was the capital of the Austrian-Hungarian Empire. Even those of you who have been to Vienna before are encouraged to join the walking tour because there are tours for beginners and "advanced" Mooties.

After the walking tour, everyone is invited to enjoy a traditional Austrian-Hungarian goulash dinner. Tickets are available at the MAA's website.[1]

Visit the United Nations

Another interesting possibility to spend one of your afternoons is a visit to the United Nations. It usually takes place on Monday. Those who register get an exclusive insight about the UNCITRAL headquarters in Vienna and the history and work of the United

---

[1] www.maa.net.

Nations. The participants will be introduced to the work of the United Nations by experienced guides. Subsequently, there is the chance to attend a lecture about the business of the United Nations particularly with regard to its work in international trade law. Again, tickets are available on the MAA's website.[2]

Farewell Party at the Bollwerk

By Wednesday, when the majority of the teams have dropped out of the pleading rounds, it will be time for the farewell party at the Bollwerk. Those "unlucky" teams that may not plead in the Final Rounds the next day get the chance to say goodbye to Vienna in a proper manner. Sometimes, even teams that are still in the competition will show up at the Bollwerk to dance the night away. Those teams deserve your praise and appreciation for demonstrating the real spirit of the Moot.

The Bollwerk offers more space than the Schwarzberg. From experience, the additional space is urgently needed since everyone wants to take the last opportunity to party with all old and new friends. The Farewell Party therefore guarantees an appropriate ending for the probably best experience of your life.

The Awards Banquet

Thursday, the last day of the Vienna Moot, starts off with the semi-finals. Once the arbitrators have rendered their decision on which two teams will proceed to the grand finale, the Moot crowd will move to the Vienna Congress Centre for the Final Hearing and the Awards Banquet. This will bring the Vis Moot to its formal end.

If you have not noticed the number of people involved in the Moot until then, you will certainly be impressed by the spectacle that unfolds in front of the Congress Centre. Hundreds and hundreds of Moot participants, arbitrators, coaches and professors will make their way to the big showdown. Again, most attendees will wear formal attire although this is not mandatory.

The pleading of the two teams that made it all the way to the finals will take place in front of all other teams and arbitrators. After the Final Hearing, everyone will be asked to leave the auditorium so that it can be prepared for the banquet lunch at 3:00 p.m. In order to attend the Awards Banquet, tickets are required and have to be presented when re-entering the auditorium. Upon registration on the first day of the Moot, five tickets are reserved for every team. Any additional tickets have to be purchased from the Moot organi-

---

[2] www.maa.net.

zation team located at the Dachgeschoss. Those tickets usually sell out quickly, so make sure to buy enough tickets early.

The Banquet lunch will be served while the teams and arbitrators listen to the announcement of the various awards. The last announcement will be the one of the prevailing team of the Final Hearing. And then, the moment arrives: Your Vis Moot is officially over.

3.2 Receptions and Parties in Hong Kong

The Vis Moot (East) might be smaller than its Viennese counterpart, but the receptions and parties in Hong Kong are certainly no less exciting.

The MAA Welcome Party

On Sunday, the MAA Welcome Party will be the first social event students and arbitrators can attend during their stay in Hong Kong.

Since the MAA Welcome Party is scheduled before the actual start of the moot, many teams will still be on their way to Hong Kong and may not be able to attend the Welcome Party. In the 14th Vis East Moot, the Welcome Party took place at FoFo's rooftop bar, which is located in the middle of Lan Kwai Fong. This is the first chance to get in touch with Hong Kong's vibrant nightlife.

The Official Opening Reception

The Vis Moot (East) in Hong Kong officially starts on Sunday and is inaugurated by Louise Barrington at the Official Opening Reception. Various welcome speeches are delivered and the Mooties will be able to get a first impression of the number of students that are participating in the Vis Moot (East).

Just like in Vienna, the ceremonial part of the Opening Reception is followed by an invitation to stay for a glass of wine and to mingle with other attendees of the Vis Moot (East). Once the Opening Reception has finished, everyone will move on to the Moot Bar.

The Moot Bar

Every Vis Moot needs a bar. If you are looking for a place where teams, arbitrators and coaches come together after mooting all day long, the MAA will not disappoint you in Hong Kong.

However, there is not *the* Hong Kong Moot bar. Instead the venue changes from year to year. In the 14th Vis East Moot in 2016/17, the place to meet mooties, alumni, arbitrators and coaches in Hong Kong was the China Bar in Lan Kwai Fong. One special feature for Vis East participants who showed their Vis East badges was the happy hour until 12 midnight.

The MAA Antique Open-Deck Party Tram Tour

In a buzzing city like Hong Kong, you wouldn't necessarily expect the (relatively slow) tram to be the most popular and famous public transportation. Not until you get to know Hong Kong! You should therefore take the chance and join the MAA Antique Open-Deck Party Tram Tour. The MAA has booked two historic double-decker open-top trams on which you can enjoy the ride through the illuminated streets of Hong Kong at night. It is advisable to register early, as spaces fill up quickly.[3]

Although the name of this tram tour features the word "party," please note that this is not the Moot bar on wheels. Drinks won't be served. The MAA encourages you to bring them yourself.

Admittedly, this is not the usual way Hong Kong citizens use the tram to get from point A to point B. If you have the feeling that you have partied enough, you can exit the tram halfway through and enjoy the horse races at the Happy Valley Racecourse.

The MAA Visit to Happy Valley Horseracing

Horseracing is one of the British traditions that left its mark in Hong Kong: Hong Kong citizens love horseracing. To get a taste of this part of Hong Kong culture, you should join the MAA Visit to the Happy Valley Racecourse. If you already went on the MAA Open-Deck Party Tram Tour, then you only have to leave the tram halfway through. If you want to get to Happy Valley straight away, just take the MTR Island Line to Causeway Bay, leave the station through Exit A and follow the signs to the race course. Bets start at HKD 10. Good luck!

Sunset Boat Trip and Seafood Dinner

If the receptions and parties in Hong Kong top their equivalents in Vienna, then it is because of the Seafood Dinner on Lamma Island. This is one of the most fascinating social events in Hong Kong. Just a beautiful boat trip away from Hong Kong Island, Lamma Island or "Pok Liu" welcomes visitors with its numerous fish restaurants. In contrast to the vibrating atmosphere throughout the rest of Hong Kong, Lamma Island offers you a piece of untouched nature and a break from the metropolitan vibe that makes

[3] Visit the events page on www.maa.net.

Hong Kong so special. Registration takes place at the Vis Centre (seats are limited).

At the Seafood Dinner, the Mooties will be served several courses of familiar and unfamiliar dishes. Everyone is encouraged to try out the exotic seafood and to wine and dine in a relaxed atmosphere. In the course of the evening, a Karaoke contest will be staged. Louise Barrington will "invite" every team to perform a traditional song from their region, so make sure to be prepared!

Farewell Party

The downside: Every Vis Moot competition has to come to an end. The upside: This calls for an appropriate farewell party! The location for this event is determined annually since reservations in Hong Kong depend significantly on other events that are taking place in the city at the same time. The MAA, however, confirms that one thing is guaranteed: this event "is traditionally a blast."

The teams that are lucky enough to be exempted from pleadings in the Final Rounds get the chance to shake off the stress of the past months and to bring this chapter to an end in proper fashion.

The Gala Awards Banquet

On Sunday, the last day of the Vis Moot (East) will start with the final hearing of the oral rounds in front of a large audience. The winner will be announced at the Gala Awards Banquet which takes place immediately afterwards. The participants will be served lunch while they cross fingers for the announcement of the awards for the best speakers and best memoranda in the competition. Just like in Vienna, five tickets are reserved for every team but additional tickets may be purchased separately. Lastly, the teams and the coaches get the chance to congratulate each other and to plan to meet again next year!

4. Being in Vienna: How to Make to Most of Your Stay

The week in Vienna is packed with oral pleadings, receptions and parties but it is also nice to step out of the Moot crowd every once in a while and simply enjoy the city. Especially if you are not from a European country with castles, cobble stoned streets and old city neighborhoods you will be stunned by the city of Vienna.

4.1 How Do I Get Around in Vienna?

Vienna's public transportation network is extensive and covers all 23 districts ("*Bezirke*"). The districts are arranged in a circle with the city center being in the 1st district and then moving outwards like a snail shell. Vienna's transportation network includes buses, trams and underground metro lines.

Tickets generally cover all modes of public transport and are available for different periods of time, such as for 24 hours or calendar weeks. For purposes of the Moot though, the weekly tickets are tricky. If you arrive in Vienna on Thursday, a weekly ticket will only be valid until Sunday. Because the weekly tickets run per calendar week (and not for seven days in a row), you will need a new ticket at the beginning of the week on Monday. It is therefore advisable to buy a "*8-Tage-Klimakarte*" instead. This ticket consists of eight strips ("*Streifen*") and can be used for eight days. As soon as you punch one strip, it is valid until 1 a.m. of the following day. You can also share the "*8-Tage-Klimakarte* " by punching one strip per passenger and day. As of 2017, the "*8-Tage-Klimakarte* " costs EUR 38,40 and can be purchased at booths of the Vienna Transportation Service ("*Wiener Verkehrsbetriebe*") which are located in bigger stations or at tobacco stores.

There are no turnstiles or other ticket barriers when entering a tram or bus. You are obligated to punch your ticket aboard. There will be random ticket inspections to ensure that passengers do not dodge the fare.

4.2 Where Do I Stay in Vienna?

Vienna offers many housing alternatives. You can stay in a regular hotel, a bed and breakfast (called "*Pension*") or even at the YMCA. Since there are numerous possibilities to find nice hotels online (*e. g.*, via "tripadvisor") there is no need to recommend specific hotels in this guide. If you plan to stay in a hotel in Vienna, you should, however, keep in mind that there are many Mooties and arbitrators from around the world who will need a roof over their heads. The hotels close to the Juridicum and close to the reception venues will be fully booked quickly.

Another housing alternative – and probably the best one – is renting an apartment for the week. In recent years, this form of housing became quite popular amongst Mooties. Renting an apartment has many advantages: (1) an apartment is generally less expensive than hotel rooms for everyone; (2) you will be able to prepare breakfast and dinner at home rather than having to spend your money in restaurants; (3) those of you who plead will have a place to study and prepare for the hearings ahead of you; and (4) you have an excellent place to hang out together with your team members before going out at night (which might however collide with advantage No. 3).

So how do you find the perfect apartment in Vienna? You can start your search by looking at one of the following websites: "www.ferienwohnungenwien.com" or "www.apartment.at". You can also ask among former Mooties of your university if they have any suggestions. In most cases, an apartment is passed down from one Mootie generation to the next.

When choosing your apartment, there is only one thing that matters: location! However, your dream apartment does not have to be in the city center. In fact, apartments in the 1st district of Vienna will be very expensive. You should make sure though that the apartment is not too far in the outskirts because then it will be difficult to get to the city center. You are fine as long as the apartment is located anywhere in districts No. 1 to No. 9. Your apartment should preferably be close to the Vienna tram line. In this case, you are flexible enough to get to the pleadings during the day and to the receptions and parties at night. But do not expect to hop on a tram when you stumble out of the Schwarzberg at 2 a.m. in the morning. Most public transportation only run until around midnight. Afterwards, you will need to get a taxi to get home but there are always a few taxis waiting in front of the Schwarzberg.

4.3 What To Do in Vienna?

Vienna can be a cultural overdose; there are so many museums, galleries, theatres and old palaces to visit that you could spend several weeks doing just that. If you cannot afford to see all of Vienna, you will have to concentrate on the highlights.

Stephansdom

The "Stephansdom" (St. Stephen's Cathedral) is Vienna's most famous church. It is the seat of the Archbishop of Vienna and situated in the city center. The Stephansdom is not far from the Juridicum so you can easily walk there after your pleading. You will recognize the Stephansdom by its richly colored roof. The roof consists of a mosaic of 230,000 (!) yellow, green, white and brown glazed tiles.

Once you have reached the Stephansdom you should definitely have a look inside. Afterwards, you can reward yourself for your cultural interest with something from the "Manner" shop situated right next to the Stephansdom. Manner produces all kinds of wafer products and other confectionary and is genuinely Viennese (Arnold Schwarzenegger is a big fan of Manner). In fact, the company logo is a picture of the Stephansdom because the shop next to the Stephansdom was the first one to be opened in the 1890s.

Schloss Schönbrunn

The "Schloss Schönbrunn" (Schönbrunn Castle) is one of Vienna's major tourist attractions. It was built in the 17th century as a hunting and recreation residence. The Schönbrunn complex includes more than just the castle, though. First and foremost, there is the "Tiergarten Schönbrunn" (Schönbrunn Zoo), the oldest zoo in the world that dates back to 1752. There is also an orangery, an English garden and a palm house. You can easily spend the whole day in Schönbrunn, have coffee and some "Sachertorte" (see below at VI.4.4), and enjoy springtime.

Hofburg and Belvedere

You need not travel all the way to Schloss Schönbrunn to visit a Viennese castle. There are two famous castles located right in the city center, the "Hofburg" and the "Belvedere." The Hofburg is the former imperial residence and was the home of the Habsburg dynasty. It also comprises the "Hofreitschule" (Spanish Riding

School), a center for classical dressage. There are public performances and sometimes public viewing of training courses is possible.

Should you want to see the famous "Kiss" painting by Gustav Klimt, just go to "Schloss Belvedere" located near the Schwarzenbergplatz.

Prater

The "Prater" is Vienna's version of Disneyland. However, it has been around a little bit longer than Walt Disney's amusement parks. In 1766, the Emperor Joseph II declared that the area in Vienna's 2nd district shall be free for public enjoyment. Soon afterwards, cafés and Viennese coffee houses were established. The main attraction of the Prater is the "Wiener Riesenrad" (Viennese giant wheel) which dates back to 1897. Despite its age, it is still up and running and if you dare a ride, you will have perfect views of Vienna from 64 meters above the ground.

4.4 Food Culture: What Do I Eat in Vienna?

Food is very important for getting to know the culture of the place you are visiting. In Vienna, there are at least three things you should try: (1) Wiener Schnitzel; (2), Viennese coffee; and (3) Sachertorte.

The "Wiener Schnitzel" is a flatly pounded piece of veal that is first coated in egg and breadcrumbs and then pan-fried which gives it a golden crust. In the cheaper version, you will be served pork instead of veal, which is called a "Schnitzel Wiener Art." The Wiener Schnitzel is usually served with potato salad and cranberry jelly (yes, the combination does taste delicious). The best place to eat Wiener Schnitzel is the restaurant "Schnitzelwirt" at Neubaugasse No. 52. The most famous place for Schnitzel is the restaurant "Figlmüller" at Wollzeile 5 in the 1st district. On their website, they actually call themselves "the home of the Schnitzel".

If you go in large groups, call restaurants beforehand to make a reservation. It might be difficult to accommodate larger groups on short notice.

Viennese coffee is different from coffee elsewhere in the world. Strangely, most people first associate coffee with Italy but coffee from Vienna is just as good – no, it's better. There is not simply one type of Viennese coffee but many alternatives. The best alternative would probably be a "Wiener Melange"; a mild coffee comparable to a cappuccino with equal parts of steamed milk and foam.

The "Sachertorte" is Vienna's famous cake and would taste great with your Viennese coffee. Unlike many other cakes, the Sachertorte goes without cream inside and rich sugar decoration on the outside. It comes along like a plain and innocent chocolate cake covered in dark chocolate icing…but the taste!

The "Original Sacher Torte" was created in 1832 and is only available at one of the Sacher Shops. The Sachertorte "flagship store" is the Café Sacher adjacent to the Hotel Sacher at Philharmonikerstraße 4 in the 1st district. But other cafés and shops also sell Sachertorte. For a real Viennese experience, try "Café Central" in Herrengasse 14. This Viennese coffeehouse dates back to 1876. The atmosphere at "Café Central" – Gustav Klimt's favorite place – is unparalleled, especially when you come in while the piano player provides some background music.

4.5 Views From Inside: Vienna in a Nutshell

Finally, if you want to get to know the real Vienna, you need to ask a Viennese. That is exactly what we did! Here is first hand insight information on Vienna from our colleague Stefan Riegler from Baker McKenzie Vienna:

Which is the best tourist attraction everyone has to visit when being in Vienna for the first time?

The most enchanting tourist attraction undoubtedly is Schönbrunn Palace, the magnificent Baroque residence of the Habsburg emperors.

Which is the best non-tourist attraction everyone has to visit after having seen all the tourist attractions in Vienna?

An absolute insider tip is the "Third Man Tour" – immerse yourself into the city under the city![4]

Where would you spend your day off if it's raining cats and dogs?

A rainy day is just perfect for the Albertina Museum, followed by an extended stay in one of the Vienna coffeehouses.

Which place or street describes the vibe of Vienna the best? Why is that so?

The Graben (Vienna's most famous street in the city center) and the Prater on a Sunday – whether it's shopping, doing business or relaxing, eventually every Viennese goes there.

Talking about food and drinks: What is THE Viennese specialty everyone should try while being in Vienna?

Wiener Schnitzel!!

Which souvenir would you buy and take home to remember your trip to Vienna?

There's no need for a souvenir – just go there again, and again …

Which behavior or activity is an absolute "no-go" in Vienna?

You can get some to-go coffee at any place in the world, but when you are in Vienna, take your time and have a real coffee in a proper café.

What is your best-kept secret about Vienna that only Viennese know about?

We are not as grumpy as we appear to be.

5. Being in Hong Kong: How to Make the Most of Your Stay

Hong Kong is a great place to explore! Especially if Asia is far from your home country, the people and culture will be captivating. You should try to step out of the Moot crowd every once in a while and experience the vibe of the city yourself.

5.1 How Do I Get Around in Hong Kong?

Hong Kong tourists are traditionally overwhelmed by the huge crowds that seem to be traveling 24 hours a day. Basically, in Hong Kong almost every spot can be reached via subway, bus or taxi.

The most convenient way to use the MTR (mass transit railway) and the KCR (Kowloon-Canton Railway) is by purchasing the so

[4] http://www.drittemanntour.at/en/index.html.

called "Octopus Card." The Octopus Card is a rechargeable stored value card and is a widely utilized payment system for basically all public transport in Hong Kong. Additionally, the Octopus Card can also be used for payments in virtually all kinds of stores.

You can purchase the Octopus Card at every bigger rail station for HKD 150 where HKD 50 are held as a deposit and the remaining HKD 100 can be used as regular card value. When you return the card, you receive the deposit and the value left on the card.

If you use a cab, make sure that you also bring the description of your destination in Chinese with you because not every taxi driver will be able to talk English.

5.2 Where Do I Stay in Hong Kong?

To put it plainly, it can be a challenge to find affordable accommodation in Hong Kong. Sure, Hong Kong offers an incredible number of hotels but they are not cheap. Luckily, the organizers of the Vis Moot (East) help out by making special arrangements with hotels in various prize categories. You will find a list of those accommodation possibilities including their special rates for Moot Court participants via the official website of the Vis Moot (East)[5]. Like in Vienna, however, the best hostels and bed and breakfast options will be passed down from one Mootie generation to the next.

5.3 What To Do in Hong Kong

Hong Kong has many great tourist attractions to offer. Some of the interesting places are farther out and you might need at least half a day to explore (*e.g.*, the Big Buddah on Lantau Island). Other spectacular places are just around the corner and maybe you would not even call them a tourist attraction (*e.g.*, the ferry ride from Kowloon to Hong Kong Island).

The Victoria Peak

One spot that every Mootie should visit during the stay in Hong Kong is the Victoria Peak. With 552 meters above see level, the top of the highest mountain on Hong Kong Island offers the perfect opportunity to take impressive pictures during the day as well as at night.

---

[5] http://www.cisgmoot.org.

The peak can be reached easily by bus as well as by the Peak Tram. At a maximum steepness of over 48 %, the Peak Tram itself is an amazing experience and probably the most spectacular way to reach the Peak. If you are lucky and catch a clear day, the Victoria Peak offers breath-taking views of the island and the mainland.

Big Buddah

Another famous landmark of Hong Kong worth seeing is the Tian Tan Buddah or simply the "Big Buddah" on Lantau Island. With a height of 34 meters, the Big Buddah is one of the biggest Buddhist monuments in China and the biggest one in Hong Kong. This impressive statue is located on the top of a mountain on Lantau Island and symbolizes the harmonic relationship between men and nature, people and religion.

If you consider visiting Big Buddah you should at least expect a half-day trip. You can reach Lantau Island either by ferry or by MTR. You may then use one of the bus routes or take the gondola lift which guarantees to make for a unique view of the island.

Star Ferry Ride from Kowloon to Hong Kong Island

If you think a ferry ride is not a tourist attraction, think again. The Star Ferry Company carries passengers across Victoria harbor, between Hong Kong Island and Kowloon on the mainland.

Aboard the ferry, you will have spectacular views of the city. You can just sit, relax and enjoy the view that unfolds in front of you. Coming from Hong Kong Island, you can either board at "Central" or at "Wan Chai." From both piers, the ferry will take you across to "Tsim Sha Tsui" on the Kowloon peninsula. Once you have arrived at Tsim Sha Tsui do not head straight back to Hong Kong Island but proceed to our next tourist suggestion: the Avenue of Stars.

The Avenue of Stars

At first glance, the Avenue of Stars seems like an imitation of Hollywood's Sunset Boulevard. At second glance, it might still be an imitation but one with a view! Kowloon's Avenue of Stars pays tribute to Hong Kong's film industry, with names such as Bruce Lee and Jacky Chan.

But from the Avenue you can also enjoy breathtaking views of the city, especially of all the skyscrapers that are lined up on the other side of Victoria Harbor. It seems like Hong Kong knows quite well that its skyline is one of the prettiest in the world. And in case the many twinkling lights are not enough for you – there is a light and sound show called Symphony of Lights every night!

Stanley Market

If you have seen enough of Hong Kong's skyline and buzzing city center, take a bus tour to Stanley Market for some serious Hong Kong souvenir shopping. Be aware though that the bus will ride along a windy road and getting car sick might be a problem.

Stanley has once been a fishing village and its market has ever since attracted people. Nowadays you do not go there to buy fish but t-shirts, electronics, small wood crafts and jewelry. Even if you are not interested in buying anything specific, Stanley market is worth a visit for strolling through the tiny streets and taking in the atmosphere of the place.

5.4 Food Culture: What Do I Eat in Hong Kong?

Food culture plays an important role in Hong Kong. You will find everything from small street carts to big fancy restaurants overlooking the city. Of course, McDonald's and Starbucks have taken over the city but do you really want to go home telling everyone that your Hong Kong food experience was a Big Mac?

If you want to get to know some Chinese food, there is one great place to go: the Temple Street Night Market. Ok, there are some funny things on the menu but would you not agree that the same applies to your country's dishes? Temple Street Night Market has at least three advantages: The food is inexpensive; the food is always fresh because of the many customers; and you will be entertained while dining. You can simply sit at one of the many plastic tables on one of the colored plastic chairs and watch the crowd that passes by. It is a great place.

5.5 Views From Inside: Hong Kong in a Nutshell

Finally, only Hong Kong people can show you the real Hong Kong! We asked our (former) colleague James Kwan from Baker McKenzie Hong Kong to reveal some of Hong Kong's best kept tourist secrets:

Which is the best tourist attraction everyone has to visit when being in Hong Kong for the first time?

Take the tram from Garden Rd to "The Peak" – the short trip will be rewarded with a great view of Hong Kong's skyline and the harbor.

Which is the best non-tourist attraction everyone has to visit after having seen all the tourist attractions in Hong Kong?

In this highly unlikely event, take the ferry to Macau, the former Portuguese colony so rich with cultural monuments dating back to colonial times, and enjoy some Portuguese food.

Imagine a one-day-holiday in Hong Kong: How would you spend your day? Where would you stop for lunch and dinner?

A rich dim sum breakfast should prepare you best for the following tour: first walk it all off on a short hike from Parkview to Quarry Bay, go to Stanley for the open market and lunch in the area, head to Mongkok ladies' market and Yau Ma Tei Temple Street for some local flavors, go shopping for sports gear, DVDs, and electronics in Mongkok (if you're into brand items Canton Rd., Tsim Sha Tsui is the place), have a drink at Aqua (1 Peking Rd., Tsim Sha Tsui) providing spectacular views of Hong Kong harbor, and dinner in Tsim Sha Tsui, then take the ferry back across the harbor to Central – with late night drinks in Lan Kwai Fong to round off the day.

Where would you spend your day off if it's raining cats and dogs?

The perfect place for a rainy day is IFC mall in Central, Times Square in Causeway Bay, or iSquare/K11 in Tsim Sha Tsui (all attached to a MTR station), both offering excellent shopping opportunities and typical restaurants (and a cinema!).

The Captain's Bar at the Mandarin Oriental and the Dicken's Bar (Excelsior Hotel, Causeway Bay) showing football and Aussie sports are also recommended.

Which place or street describes the vibe of Hong Kong the best? Why is that so?

Central – the place is buzzing with energy and never sleeps! It is a major business district with shops, restaurants, and bars – both high end and local.

Talking about food and drinks: What is THE specialty of Hong Kong everyone should try while visiting?

Well, I'm not sure where to start: Shrimp dumpling at a dim sum restaurant – Tim Ho Wan (the world's cheapest Michelin Star restaurant), is highly recommended. Better go early to line up! Maxim's Palace at City Hall Central do dim sum the traditional way – with the trolleys. Or Peking duck … and Won Ton noodles … with Tsingtao beer, of course …

It's a Saturday night and you want to go out with friends. Where and at what time would you go?

We would certainly go to the Soho area for dinner, and then check out the bars at Volar, Dragon-i, and Beijing Club, each of them at Lan Kwai Fong.

Which souvenir would you buy and take home to remember your trip to Hong Kong?

Much more than a souvenir, namely a little work of art is a postcard with one's personal name translated and hand printed in Chinese calligraphy (at Stanley Market).

Which behavior or activity is an absolute "no-go" in Hong Kong?

Surfing during a typhoon #3 signal and above.

What is your best-kept secret about Hong Kong that only citizens know about?

If you need to go by taxi across the harbor (Hong Kong to Kowloon and vice versa), hail one with the 'For Hire' sign covered up – and look what happens …

VII. Where to Go From Here: Life Goes on After the Moot

Maybe you will feel a certain kind of emptiness once you have said your farewells to new friends, packed your bags and boarded your plane back home. Is this really it? Why has it gone by so fast? No more pleadings tomorrow? These emotions are the first signs of a disease which is nearly incurable and possibly lasts for a lifetime: the Vis Moot disease.

But your pain can be soothed. The end of your life as a Mootie does not have to be the last time you met the Vis Moot crowd. There are various ways to stay in contact: you can join the Moot Alumni Association (MAA), participate in future Moots by judging the written and oral arguments of a new generation of Mooties, and consider working in the "real" arbitration world. But be warned that those activities will rather intensify than cure your Vis Moot disease.

1. Stay Involved: Moot Alumni Association

The Moot Alumni Association (MAA) is the perfect platform to stay in touch with all new friends and colleagues who have crossed your path during the Vis Moot. It is open to Mooties, coaches, arbitrators and everyone else who has been involved with the Vis Moot.

The MAA was founded in 1996 by a group of Mooties who wanted to stay in touch beyond their time together in Vienna. Time has passed and the MAA has grown from a bunch of Moot alumni to an international network of attorneys, professors, managers, research scholars and students who all share one thing: their participation and involvement in the Vis Moot.

Your first step to get involved is a membership subscription via MAA's website.[1] The MAA runs several projects for you to get involved in, both directly related and unrelated to the Moot. For example, each year the MAA organizes the welcome parties for Mooties and arbitrators in Vienna and Hong Kong. Of course, there is also the MAA Walking Tour and Goulash Dinner in Vienna, and

[1] http://www.maa.net.

the MAA Antique Open-Deck Party Tram Tour in Hong Kong (for more details, see Chapter VI). Additionally, the MAA hosts the Generations in Arbitration conference (GIA) which is a combination of a student seminar and practitioners' workshop that takes place a few days prior to the start of the oral hearings in Vienna and Hong Kong. But there are even more activities of the MAA than could be mentioned here.

Have a look at the MAA's website and see for yourself how you can get involved and stay involved with the Moot crowd.

2. Come Back in a Different Role: Become a Moot Coach and/or Arbitrator

You have seen what it is like to be a Mootie, now you can see what it is like to be on the other side.

At many universities, former Mooties coach or at least co-coach the next generation of Mooties. This is a clever move since former Mooties will have the experience needed to give the right advice. Also, former Mooties will be as enthusiastic (or even more enthusiastic) to hand in well-written memoranda and to draft convincing pleadings. Once they graduate from law school, Moot Court coaches are also permitted to judge the memoranda of other teams and act as arbitrators in Vienna and/or Hong Kong (as long as they are not affiliated with those teams). This is wise, too. No one else is better suited for the job of a Vis Moot arbitrator than a former Mootie. Former Mooties know the stress the participants went through before handing in their memoranda. And they also know the tension and anxiety that fills the room before the beginning of a pleading.

You will benefit tremendously from coaching and judging others because it will enhance your skills in international commercial law and international arbitration. On top of the educational exercise though, coming back to Vienna and Hong Kong as an arbitrator has the advantage of giving you a chance to meet other, more experienced members of the arbitration world. During your time as a Mootie, you will most likely have focused on meeting other Mooties. You will have gathered at parties and receptions to share your interest in international commercial law and to simply have a good time together. In your role as arbitrator, you will also gather at parties and receptions to do the exact same thing. But this time it might be Martin Hunter you are having a glass of wine with, or an associate of a law firm that focuses on international commercial arbitration who can tell you about his daily routine in the arbitration world. Sometimes, "networking" can be exhausting but during the Vis Moot, it just comes naturally and you will go home with many new ideas and inspiration for your future.

3. Looking Ahead: Job Opportunities in the Arbitration World

The world of arbitration is a small one. To participate in the Vis Moot is your first step to become a member of this world. To become a coach and/or arbitrator is your second step. To work in the field of international commercial law and arbitration could be your third step.

3.1 There Is More Than One Career Path in International Arbitration

It would be wrong to state here that there is a certain career path you would have to follow to land a job in arbitration in a law firm, arbitral institution, university or government. There is always more than one alternative to start a career in international arbitration. It is a fact though, that deepening your skills in international law and maybe even studying the law of a foreign country are helpful tools to start a career in international arbitration. For example, you can take a post-graduate course such as an LL.M. in international arbitration or participate in a summer course on international law (*e. g.*, the summer program of the Hague Academy of International Law). If your university offers exchange program with universities abroad, you could even spend one semester studying at a foreign university and thereby learning more about a foreign legal system and foreign language at once.

3.2 Arbitration Needs Input

When thinking of a career in international arbitration, you should be aware that arbitration is not an end in itself. Parties engage in arbitral proceedings because of material issues of the law. There are numerous topics that are frequently resolved by arbitration such as construction agreements, telecommunications agreements, M&A deals or intellectual property agreements. The parties might have concluded a contract for the construction of wind turbines and now find themselves in a dispute over the timely conclusion of the project. It is therefore crucial to not only be an expert in arbitration but have in-depth knowledge of the industry or area involved. To develop and deepen this knowledge is a further tool to start a career in international arbitration.

3.3 Take Your Chances

Keep your eyes and ears open for career opportunities. Especially during the weeks in Vienna and Hong Kong, you will have the chance to meet many interesting people, some of whom have already established a successful career in international arbitration. Use your chance to ask for their advice and recommendations. Some successful careers in arbitration have started over a beer and a game of table football at the Schwarzberg.

4. An Exclusive Club: Women in Arbitration

There is one "club" that is open exclusively to some of the Vis Moot participants. And there is only one criteria ... you have to be female!

Topics like "diversity" and "female representation" are widely talked about in the business world – arbitration being no exception. Various programs and workshops have been launched to help young women being seen and heard in a world that has been male-dominated for a very long time. At the Vis Moot, the ratio of male and female participants is almost equal. There seems to be no "glass ceiling" for women striving to work in international arbitration. But when it comes to real life, the ratio of male and female representation looks somewhat different. Here, men still outnumber women by far.

This guide is not the appropriate place to investigate why women are under-represented in international arbitration. Rather, this subchapter is meant to encourage women to continue on their way into the international arbitration community.The Vis Moot predicts a successful future for prospective female arbitrators. To that end, at the 24th Vis Moot 2017 for example, the award for the best oralist was a triple tie for first place between three women.

4.1 The Present: Women in Arbitration Are Outnumbered

In 2016, the ICC published its first statistics on gender balance. At that time, women arbitrators represented just over 10 % of all appointments and confirmations of arbitrators in 2015.[2] While there has been a slight increase compared to previous years,[3] women are still under-represented in international arbitration.[4] This is particularly true for arbitrator nominations, although the numbers are not much better when it comes to lead counsel statistics.[5] According to GAR, only 11 % of partners at the top ten international arbitration teams are women.[6]

But rather than focusing on the glass being half empty, let's focus on the glass being half full: There are already women who are active and successful in the field of international arbitration. Some of them are also active in the Vis Moot and you might well plead in front of an all-women panel. If time allows, this is the perfect chance for you to obtain some valuable tips and hints on how to succeed as a female arbitrator and thus on how to slowly change the ratio of male and female representation in international arbitration.

4.2 A Change in Progress: Perception of Women in the Business World

In recent years in particular, a momentum of change seems to shake up the business world. A famous case study of Harvard Business School indicates that the perception of women in the field of business slowly changes.

In 2003, two professors from Columbia Business School and New York University conducted the study for the first time. Two groups of students were given a case study describing the success story of an entrepreneur named Roizen. In the first group, the entrepreneur's first name was "Heidi", in the second group, the first name was

---

[2] *See* ICC press-release on "ICC Arbitration posts strong growth in 2015" dated 11 May 2016: http://www.iccwbo.org/News/Articles/2016/ICC-Arbitration-posts-strong-growth-in-2015/.

[3] *Philippe*, Speeding Up the Path for Gender Equality, in: TDM vol. 14, issue 1, January 2017, p. 1–5; cp. also *Nelson*, The representation of women in arbitration – one problem, two issues: http://kluwerarbitrationblog.com/2012/11/02/the-representation-of-women-in-arbitration-one-problem-two-issues/ (last visited 23 January 2017).

[4] *Oger-Gross*, Gravitas: persuasion and legitimacy (or why calling on parties and their counsel to appoint more diverse arbitrators may be wishful thinking), in: TDM vol. 12, issue 4, July 2015, p. 1.

[5] *Philippe*, When Did the Doors to Dispute Resolution Open for Women?, in: TDM vol. 12, issue 4, July 2015, p. 11–12.

[6] *See Nelson*, http://kluwerarbitrationblog.com/2012/11/02/the-representation-of-women-in-arbitration-one-problem-two-issues/ (last visited 23 January 2017).

changed to "Howard". This was the only difference. When the students were asked for their impression of Heidi and Howard, the students favored Howard as a boss arguing he seemed to be more appealing whereas Heidi came across as "selfish" and "not the person you would like to work for".[7] Facebook's COO Sheryl Sandberg explained it as follows: "*[T]his experiment supports what research has already clearly shown: success and likability are positively correlated for men and negatively correlated for women. When a man is successful, he is liked by both men and women. When a woman is successful, people of both genders like her less*".[8]

So far, so bad. However, ten years later in 2013, the case study was repeated at New York University's Business School. This time around, students rated the female entrepreneur as more likable and desirable as a boss than the male.[9] A possible explanation for the different outcome is the fact that more women have taken over leadership roles in the 10 years since the study was conducted for the first time. As a result, students nowadays may be more receptive to the idea of a successful woman, and, as "The Atlantic" put it:

> "*In their minds, female leaders are transforming from a scary concept to an appealing reality.*"[10]

Nevertheless, a lot of work and effort still lies ahead of us. In international arbitration, one notable initiative to increase the number of women appointed as arbitrators is the "Equal Representation in Arbitration Pledge" launched in 2016.[11] As of 27 February 2017, more than 1600 individuals and organizations (including major arbitration organizations) have signed the pledge.[12]

---

[7] *See*, e.g., http://www.pwnparis.net/newsletter/2013-09/post/6_lean_in_septembre.html (last visited 23 January 2017).

[8] Sheryl Sandberg, *Lean In – Women, Work, and the Will to Lead*, 2013, p. 40.

[9] *See* http://www.theatlantic.com/sexes/archive/2013/03/are-successful-women-really-less-likable-than-successful-men/273926/ (last visited 23 January 2017).

[10] http://www.theatlantic.com/sexes/archive/2013/03/are-successful-women-really-less-likable-than-successful-men/273926/ (last visited 23 January 2017).

[11] http://globalarbitrationreview.com/article/1036332/the-pledge (last visited 23 January 2017).

[12] http://www.arbitrationpledge.com (last visited 12 April 2017).

4.3 The Future: More Women in Arbitration around the World

The momentum of change for gender diversity is likely to enhance career opportunities for women. And being a female can suddenly become a unique selling point with a high recognition factor. But it goes without saying that being a female is not by itself enough for getting into the arbitration scene. Like your male colleagues, you have to enhance your legal knowledge, develop your soft skills and stand out from the crowd. But hey, you participate in the Vis Moot – so you can already tick those boxes.

Another factor that cannot be underestimated and that can be perfectly trained at the Vis Moot is networking. The Vis Moot is a perfect networking platform because you all have something in common. But also after the Vis Moot, networking works best if you have something in common. Thus, once the weeks in Hong Kong and/or Vienna lie behind you, you may consider participating in other arbitration events. It comes as no surprise that the topic of female representation has created quite a few all-women organizations within the arbitration community. In particular, there is the well established network "ArbitralWomen".[13] ArbitralWomen is an international non-governmental organisation with the primary objective of advancing the interests of women and promoting female practitioners in international dispute resolution. It encourages diversity in the Vis Moot and arbitration through a scholarship program which is sponsored by various law firms to teams consisting of equal or more women than men. ArbitralWomen also organizes seminars all over the world to combat unconscious bias against women in arbitration. And its founding co-president is no stranger to Vis Moot participants. It is Louise Barrington, the founder and director of the Vis Moot East.

But ArbitralWomen is not the only chance to meet other women interested in arbitration. There are also more informal gatherings, such as luncheons or seminar series exclusively open to women. Those of us who authored this Vis Guide, regularly participate in the "Frankfurt Women in Arbitration Lunch" – much to the envy of our male colleagues who would love to join in. But what do you do if there is no such networking event in your city? The answer is easy: you could start one of your own.

---

[13] As regards the foundation of ArbitralWomen, cp. *Philippe*, in: TDM vol. 12, issue 4, July 2015, p. 19–20.

VIII. Views from the Dachgeschoss

On the occasion of 22nd and the 24th Vis Moot in Vienna in March 2015 and April 2017, respectively, Lisa Reiser, Fabian Roemer and Max Oehm had the chance to interview teams from around the world. The teams were particularly chosen from different continents and cultural regions. They shared their entire Moot experience with us – from how it all started to where they go from here.

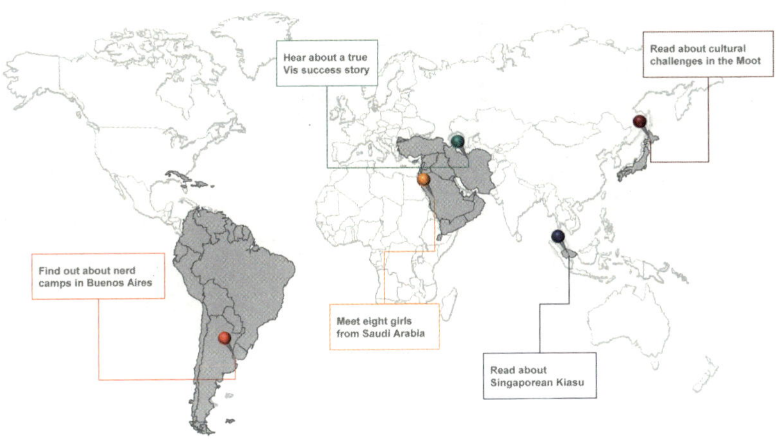

One might expect that being a Mootie in a Japanese team is a completely different experience than being a Mootie in a team from the Middle East, not to speak of what it must be like being in a team with eight girls. But this is not what the teams told us. A Mootie from South East Asia can share stories remarkably similar to a Mootie from Latin America. Find out what the stories of the five teams are.

Here are the best tips from your peers:

1. University of Buenos Aires/Argentina: One Team to Win the Moot!

The 2017 Vis Moot team of the University of Buenos Aires, Argentina, bore a heavy burden: their predecessors won the Vis Moot 2016! We wanted to learn about their secrets and understand how it is like to be a Mootie in a Latin American team. We had the pleasure of talking to them about their experience during this year's Vis Moot.

BM Thank you so much for taking time for the interview today. We have four topics we want to talk to you about today. The first one is about becoming a Mootie: What were your reasons to apply for the Moot team at UBA?

UBA I felt that I had to do something different within the University experience. The University of Buenos Aires is a public University, with lots of students and courses. Thus, students are not always aware of all the opportunities available. The Vis Moot is certainly one of those opportunities, among other international programs. Actually, I saw a post on Facebook and decided to apply. Fortunately, there are scholarships by the University of

Buenos Aires for the participants. So, the doors were opened, you simply had to enter them and I felt that the moment had come to try something new.

I actually saw a post on Facebook and I decided to go. It was a good trip to Vienna. A free trip, of course it depends on what you call free.

BM What was the application process at your University?

UBA You have to take part in the Commercial Arbitration and CISG class, which lasts two months. On top of that, there is a respective seminar once a week. At the end of the seminar you have to write a ten page memorandum as claimant or as respondent, and then you plead for five minutes against the assigned opponent.

BM That sounds like a mini Moot…

UBA Exactly. And there are sometimes up to 30 applicants for the four places available. However, our team does not only consist of four participants. We have a big group of coaches. Most of them were part of previous Moot teams.

BM How do the coaches get involved during the selection process?

UBA One of the main characteristics of how we structure the selection and the entire Moot at the University of Buenos Aires is that we are very self-managed. So, there are older professors that we have as references and we go to for guidance. But we self-manage most of the things we do.

We are looking for a team. We are not choosing the best individuals, we are choosing a team. We talk for hours and hours during the decision process. We always tell the new students that this is not just a one year commitment. If students sign up they know that there is an implicit-explicit commitment to possibly become a coach later on. There comes a time to return some of today‘s coaches investment back to the next generation of Mooties.

BM By the way: Congratulations to winning the Vis Moot last year! There are not that many teams that win the Moot. It is a very big thing. How is it for this year's team to follow in these footsteps?

UBA On the one hand, it is a lot of pressure on us. It is not put on us by the coaches, but the title itself. On the other hand, the title opens a lot of doors. For example, we have been to three Pre-Moots. We do this every year with the team, but this year it was special because we are the successors of the last year's winning team. And, in addition to this, I personally took it as very high standard to reach. During the whole process, I tried to take up the challenge. We want for the success not to be singular but for the University of Buenos Aires to stay as one of the top teams of the Moot.

Not as a Mootie, but as a coach: It is really interesting and nice to see the reactions on other peoples' faces being different. When you say: "I am from the University of Buenos Aires". Instead of saying "oh, Messi" or "oh, I think that is in Brazil, right?" they say "oh, you won last year".

BM What is the Vis Moot history at your University?

UBA I have tracked the history. It dates back to 1996. So, our University has participated for a long time. That means, there is a big family behind the Vis Moot. We try to stay very close and to help each other. We have at least one alumni meeting per year. Because of the opportunities that the Moot gives to the people, many of the alumni come from far away. I would say about half of the former participants live abroad and often this is related to the fact that people have participated in the Moot. So, it is nice to get together.

BM That is so great. Coming back to the topic we are currently talking about: Do you get any university credits for participating in the Moot or is it basically taking up your free time?

UBA We are lucky to receive credits, but it is never enough to compensate for work the Vis Moot entails. We should get like two years off for this. Anyway, we get four credits which equals one subject.

BM What were your expectations when you applied for the Moot?

UBA When you are entering into the selection process you know that the coaches tell you that you are going to have to work hard if you get on the team. You say "okay, I am going to work hard". And, once you are on the team, you realize what working really hard means. I did not imagine that it was going to be like this. However, all the hard work is worth it because you see how you improve, how the team improves and this gives you strength to keep on doing it. You know that your final destination is Vienna. You are nervous and you are excited at the same time.

BM Thank you, this brings us to the second topic we want to talk to you about: Being a Mootie. Did you have any team building exercises during the Moot?

UBA I am going to start by the funniest thing that I found out about the Vis Moot at our University. We have a "nerd camp". I mean, we get together for two days when we are preparing for the pleadings in January. It is like a slumber party or something like that but without the party. Luckily with the slumbers. We discuss about the Moot all day long and do several team building exercises. It is a lot of fun how we do this. Especially since we do it at a pool when it is summer in Argentina.

BM Did you have any events before the written memorandum phase?

UBA Well, we had the selection process until October when the case was released. We then started drafting the memorandum. And well, the team building exercise was to see each other's faces 30 hours a week. That is the most successful team building exercise I can think of.

With a little shame and a lot of pride, I can share that the team has a song, a dress, and a team shirt.

BM That sounds great. What turned out to be completely different from what you expected?

UBA When you apply for the Moot, you do not know what it is about. You just want to do something different. I think that the size of all of this is too big to imagine. It changes your life completely. It opens a lot of doors. It has a strong impact on your career and also you make a lot of friends. I think that one cannot imagine it before.

You get to know yourself a lot better. You have to work so hard and you have to work with other people all the time. So, you start to understand how you work alone and how you work in a team. That is something precious.

BM Coming to the third topic: Being here in Vienna. Do you see yourself as ambassadors for Argentina when you are here in Vienna/Europe?

UBA Last year we were the only Argentinian team here and, in a way, we were representing our country. This year we have another university from Argentina, so we are not the only ones. But still, we think that people have seen Argentina through us. So, this is kind of cool. It is a big opportunity to place Argentina somewhere on the maps of people. We take it with pride.

BM Is there any cliché about Argentina you think is totally true?

UBA They are all true. We got the best meat and the best football players. We are loud and we are dramatic.

BM Was it difficult for you to come here to Vienna?

UBA Luckily not, we do not need a visa. Also, the university has been really helpful. It provides for all of our expenses. We are especially thankful for this because the University of Buenos Aires is a public, that means free university. So, the fact that our education is free and on top of that we get a scholarship to travel to Vienna is a privilege for us.

BM Let us get a bit personal here: Any romantic relationships for you during the Moot?

UBA No, we do not have time for romance. And also, never within the family. We are like brothers and sisters to each other.

BM I think you are not telling us everything but that is absolutely okay. Let us come to the next question: How do you like Vienna?

UBA We love it. There are no words to describe this beautiful city. But honestly, we know we are not here for sightseeing. We are trying to be competitive. Last year, I was only able to see Vienna after the competition. I was not a good tourist. And as a team we even have a hashtag for this: #wedidntcomefortourism.

BM That is amazing, I really like your hashtag. Now, let us come to the last topic: Looking ahead. What do you think comes after the Vis Moot?

UBA Coaching next year's team, that is the default rule for us.

BM And besides that?

UBA When I come back, I have to re-socialize, undergo a process of making friends again.

I think in the short term, I am going to be depressed for a while because we have been sticking together for nine months. My teammates are like my new family. Also, I am going to miss the case, because I spent so much time thinking about the case and the arguments.

BM What is your most valuable advice that you would like to share with future Mooties?

UBA Try to enjoy the whole process. Even when you are working under a lot of pressure and relatively parting with your friends, you should focus on your greater goal – which is going to Vienna. I think it is all worth it. So for me, it would be to enjoy every opportunity and every second of everything and never give up. You reap much more than you sow.

And, it is definitely worth it. It is a lifetime worth of experience. You can make a lot of new friends and build a very strong network within your team as well as between the former and future teams. This brings many new opportunities.

BM One last question: If you had to decide right now, would you pursue a career in international arbitration?

UBA Yes, absolutely!

BM Thank you very much. This was very interesting and a lot of fun talking to you.

2. University of Jeddah/Saudi Arabia: Meeting the Saudi Girls

We were particularly excited to meet the 2015 Vis Moot Team of Dar Al-Hekma University (DAH) in Jeddah, Saudi Arabia, because, until a couple of years ago, women in Saudi Arabia were not allowed to practice law.

Nevertheless, the all-girls university Dar Al-Hekma has been part of the Willem C. Vis Moot for four years now – and the girls have participated very successfully. In 2015, the team of Dar Al-Hekma University won the Middle East Pre-Moot in Jordan. And they took home not only one award but awards for best oralists, best memorandum for claimant and best memorandum for respondent.

More than enough reasons for us to meet the girls in Vienna!

BM First of all, thank you very much for coming. It's a pleasure to have you here. Our first question would be: What were the reasons you applied for the Moot? Why did you want to take part in it?

DAH The first time that our university participated in a pre-moot and then in the Vis Moot as well was four years ago. After that, the Moot became something that our university strives to do because only here we get to experience the legal field, how to be a lawyer and how to advocate before graduating. We all wanted to take the opportunity to participate in the Vis Moot in order to get the real international feel of the field. Also, the Vis Moot is one of the few extracurricular activities at our university that are actually awesome.

As Saudi ladies, it is important for us to stand out in our community. It is important to be independent, to thrive and to show the community that women are capable of participating in such great events. It is important to be noticed. A lot of this came with the help of many people at our university and even in the Saudi community in general. For instance, our late king was a big advocate for women to thrive and to have a place in the society. Plus, our generation is the next generation that will form the international legal system in Saudi Arabia.

We are Pioneers.

BM That sounds great and like something every student at your university would like to experience. When you applied for the Vis Moot at your university, was it a hard competition?

DAH Our coach Prof. Olga Nartova introduced the Vis Moot to the university. First, the Moot was not something very known to the girls at the university. But this year, we had a larger group applying because year after year, the Vis

Moot has been getting its popularity at the university. At the end, this year's team boiled down to eight girls out of 17 applicants.

BM Okay but one cliché: eight girls in one team – that sounds like trouble.

DAH It was – but more on a professional level. Everyone wanted to prove to herself that she can do this and that she is better than the others. It was a competition on a professional level, for example: who can write better, who can research better and who can speak better. Due to the competition, we exceeded our own expectations.

BM And now since the hard preparations are over and that you have arrived in Vienna, did the Vis Moot meet your expectations? Is it what you expected?

DAH It is far better than what we expected! Especially that for six months when you research, read and write memos not knowing when you come to Vienna, you will meet a lot of amazing people. For example, Professor Schwenzer stays in the same hotel as us; we had breakfast with her. Where else would that happen? The Vis Moot star-struck us.
The Moot definitely opened our eyes to a new world. It is something that we never expected. Even when we were drafting the memos, we could not have foreseen how great it would be in Vienna. You meet people from all around the world. You get to know professionals and other students, who are all kind of in the same place as you. This gives you hope that you can do it, you can match others. We saw ourselves maybe as the underdogs and then we came to Vienna and we felt that we were doing and performing well. Now, we know that we can do it.
Opportunities like the Vis Moot are not present in our country. If you just sit there and do your work and study, you are not going to be able to have the opportunity to meet with people from all around the world. We could never get the network back home that we got through the Vis Moot. So participating in the Vis Moot really enhanced our lives.

BM If you had both options, would you prefer to work in your country or would you prefer to work outside your country, and why?

DAH I would like to help my country and I would work as an international lawyer. Working outside Saudi Arabia gives you experience that you need. But there comes a time that you have to go back home and give back to your community by working and educating others at home. That is how our country progresses. We are all part of the evolution.

BM I think, it is very interesting that you see yourself as pioneers and representatives of your country. That's very special.

DAH The difference with us is that everyone looks at us with a different eye. We are like aliens to many.

BM You do not look like aliens.

DAH If we tell someone that we are from Saudi Arabia, the reaction is always the same: "*Oh my God, you are a Saudi Arabian woman? How can you travel?*" Because of such reactions you feel the obligation to prove everyone wrong. It is a burden that we have to carry, but we choose to take it on. Saudi Arabia is progressing. All of us want to help our country to progress. We do not only want to be known as the very uptight religious country. We are open to new. And this reflects on us as well, not just for the country but also for us citizens.
If someone asks us: "Where are you from?" And I say "Saudi Arabia" the reaction I would like to get in the future is "Oh, I would love to visit that place." Rather than: "Really? How come you go out dressed like this? How come you can travel?" It is a stigma that is attached to us and it is really hard to let go of it.

BM Well, I have to admit that I also expected you to wear capes.

DAH We're normal people. Yes, we wear capes at home, but it is not restricted to the extent that you have to wear it in a certain way or color. Wearing the cape is a custom that has developed rather than being a rigid law.

BM You already mentioned that there are so many clichés and things that people expect of Saudi women. If you had the chance to prove everyone wrong, which cliché would you like to clarify?

DAH Expect us to speak proper English. We are well educated. Hold us to the same standards as other universities, do not be surprised when we meet a certain standard.

BM So when the Vis Moot concludes next week, sadly, what's the most valuable piece of advice you would give to the next generation of Vis Mooties?

DAH Seize the opportunity. Take it and do your best! Work hard and then let it be. Be patient.

BM What do you mean by "be patient"?

DAH For some reason, we could not believe what our coach was telling us. When we were drafting the memos, we got frustrated by the end of January. We did not want to do the Vis Moot anymore. We did not want to go to Jordan for a Middle East Pre-Moot, let alone to Vienna. We were done with the entire competition. However, our coach was pushing us. She said: "*No! You have to work. You will see when you get there, you will see that it is worth the pain.*" She did not tell us about what would happen in Jordan or Vienna. She never told us any stories but she would only say: "*You will see. No matter how many times I tell you, you will not get it until you get to Vienna. Until you see it for yourself.*" And once we landed in Vienna, once we came here, all the sweats and tears were worth it. It is worth it! Our coach is the only reason why we got this far. Even though we are talented and smart, this does not matter. She got us here. And now, we want to freeze time. We do not want the Vis Moot to end. We want to be participants of the Vis Moot for the rest of our lives.

Thank you very much for sharing your experience with us!

3. Singapore Management University/Singapore: Talking about Singaporean Food-religion and *Kiasu*

Over the last couple of years, the Vis Moot teams from Singapore have been extremely successful. Especially the team from the Singapore Management University is always a strong contender in the competition. We wanted to meet this year's team consisting of Andre Soh, Melissa Ng, Sim Yi Jie and Giam Zhen Kai with their coach Deya Shankar Dubey to talk about their Vis Moot experience.

BM First of all, thank you very much for doing this interview. We have a few questions regarding your experiences participating in the Vis moot. My first question would be: How did you become a participant at your university?

SMU At our university we have a quite long selection process. It begins with a module called "International Moots 1" where we are given a public international law problem. We have about two weeks to prepare a written memorandum and thereafter we go through five practice rounds which are video-taped. In the selection round we were judged by the different coaches for the different Moot teams of our university. Thereafter, they would look at presumably all the videos of our rounds. And then they will decide who fits in best with which team.

BM So you do not apply specifically for the Vis Moot but you apply for Moots in general and then the coaches decide who is best placed in which Moot?

SMU Yes, but when we apply, we get the chance to indicate which Moot we prefer. But ultimately the coaches decide.

BM Was the Vis Moot your preference or did you have other preferences?

SMU It was my preference. I thought arbitration is a very good practical thing to get into. And I really like contract law, so arbitration was right up my alley.

BM I assume you did not know each other before participating in the Moot. Did you do any teambuilding exercises?

SMU We had dinners. Singaporean food is a separate religion. Food is something that brings happiness to everyone. No matter how much you hate each other during the memo writing phase, food brings people back together.

BM How did you experience working in a team? Any obstacles that needed to be solved with food?

SMU I remember our first written submission was made in a rush because it was due a few days after our final exams. So there was one day after we finished our finals that we all just locked ourselves into one room, and were shouting at each other for like a couple of hours, debating intensely about the arguments for the memorandum. It was painful but it was a very good learning experience. We all had different styles of writing and thinking, so it was quite amazing to see how all your different teammates will come up with something different and a different take on the same issue.

BM Was there something in the Moot that turned out to be completely different from how you expected it?

SMU We have been briefed by our seniors that came from the Vis Moot before on what to expect. Nevertheless, I guess there are some things you can never really be prepared for until you are in the middle of it, e.g. the intensity of the training and the actual work itself. We taught ourselves a lot on the training process and the months before we actually went for the Moot were pretty intense, especially because we were having school in the same time.

And also pleading was something completely new to us. When we started pleading we thought that having a lot of knowledge would be enough to win the case. But communication skills are actually far more involved. I think that is something essential that I learned: communicating to the tribunal instead of just schooling them.

BM And how did you train your communication skills, how did you prepare for the oral hearings in Vienna?

SMU In SMU, the law school actually just recently moved into a new building and one of the, well, I would say proudest features of the school is that we have a Moot court now. Every international Moot team of our university had to have audience rounds. So every Friday we went to our Moot court and spectated our friends from the other teams and they spectated us as well. It was a good preparation and possibility to prepare for later rounds when there is an audience. I think that was something new that really helped in the whole preparation phase.

BM What did you like better, the written phase or the oral phase?

SMU Definitely the oral phase. It is more intense and goal oriented.

BM Do you see yourself as ambassadors for Singapore when you come here to Europe, to Vienna?

SMU Definitely for SMU but I guess for Singapore as well in a sense because there are only two Singaporean law schools, NUS and ourselves. So in the sense we are unavoidably ambassadors of Singapore, I hope we are living up to it. And our government is actually very supportive. One of the senior minister of state has judged some of our new teams. She has been extremely supportive in all of our endeavors, she always encourages the students, speaks to them, judges them. So I think in that sense if NUS or SMU wins a Moot, it is ultimately Singapore. You just feel a sense of pride that it is Singapore.

BM Is there any cliché or anything that is absolute true about Singapore?

SMU We are what we call Kiasu. It is a Hokkien term which actually means "scared to lose". So, I think it means that we are very competitive. If everyone is doing something, we actually rather follow them than not follow them. To give an example: In university, if someone starts studying a specific book for some exam because he heard the professor saying it were important, everyone else will go and borrow that book even if it is not important at all.

BM Oh, I remember that when I was in Singapore everyone always rushed to be first in the Underground, even if the car was completely empty. I guess that is somewhat different here in Vienna. So, how do you like Vienna so far? Have you done any sightseeing yet?

SMU Unfortunately not yet, but we would like to. We heard Vienna is like time travelling and we were told of all the places to visit. Hopefully, we do not get to go there because if we do get to go there it means that we have been kicked out. But I really like Vienna because I was researching on historical figures I am interested in. So one figure was Empress Elisabeth of Austria, and I realized that her picture is everywhere. Like on chocolates in supermarkets. Mozart is everywhere also.

BM Unfortunately, the Vis Moot is soon going to end. Looking ahead, what comes after the Moot? Do you plan to have a career in international arbitration?

SMU Recently there was an interview with a renowned Singaporean Arbitrator in the papers. He suggested for young lawyers before going into international arbitration to try and cut your teeth in litigation first. He thinks that once you get there, at a more mature stage in your career, international arbitration is the next step forward. So I think if we have the chance we will definitely consider it.

BM Coming to my last question, what is the most valuable advice that you would give future Mooties?

SMU Do not be afraid of the hard work. It pays off. Eventually you will come to a point that you will look at your team and you will feel a sense of gratitude for having made an amazing experience. And be open-minded about things. Accept criticism with a pinch of salt and just take everything as a learning experience because you will really see yourself grow very much in this whole period of preparation. I think all of us are not like how we were when we first started.

BM Well then, thank you very much. This was very interesting.

4. Hokkaido University/Japan: A Clash of Cultures?

Only a week before this interview, the team of Hokkaido University in Sapporo had achieved the biggest success in their University's Moot history: An honorable mention for the memorandum for Respondent in Hong Kong. We had the chance to sit down with Kazuha Tsuchihashi and Fumina Tominaga of the Japanese university and their German Coach Tobias Strecker to talk about the Moot, language barriers and cultural adaptation.

BM Thank you for agreeing to have this interview with us. Starting with the probably first aspect of the Moot: At your university, how does one become a Mootie?

HOK In my university there usually is a course for arbitration, our university has a class for the Vis Moot. So, I just applied and wrote an essay for the professor to read. Basically everyone can participate. We were ten students. Two students decided to leave in the past semester. And now we have eight students.

Coach There was a preparation seminar in the summer semester that started with ten members. Of these ten members then nine decided to join the Moot Court Team that started in the winter semester. One of them left the team at some point because he found that the pressure is too high and that it takes too much time to be part of the Moot Court. Unfortunately, one member could only go the Pre-Moots because her new job started during the Moot Court in Hong Kong, and she could not join us there. So, we ended up with seven team members in Hong Kong and two of them are now here in Vienna. The other five did all speak in Hong Kong.

BM What were your expectations of the Moot when you entered?

HOK For me, because I had already participated last year, I already knew some aspects of the Moot. For this year, I expected to know the oral hearing. I wanted to be able to improve my presentation and look like having more self-confidence. That was my expectation for the oral hearing. And for writing the memorandum, I wanted to learn how to use the cases, commentaries or decisions of the court. Learning, how to include those things into my argument or memorandum, that was my expectation.

Coach Do you feel that it is a very different experience participating for Western teams and for Japanese teams?

HOK Of course we are not good at English. So, English is always the obstacle. We are not native speakers, so there are some language barriers. But in my opinion, in the Moot Court, most people do not think I have no legal knowledge when I cannot explain something in all detail. They understand my arguments, so it is quite exciting as well.

BM It is definitely a challenge for non-native speakers to participate. Did you feel that in the Moot Court you were requested to do things that you would normally not do in Japan?

HOK In the Moot Court, I think, we had to be more outgoing persons and …

Coach Present arguments with confidence.

HOK Yes. But in Japan, we are recommended not to talk so much. Just express important things. We do not say too much, but we are thinking something. We mostly understand what you are saying. Sometimes, we are very quiet and very shy just because we cannot express our thoughts.

BM Because of the language?

HOK Yes, because of the language. But also because of the culture. Maybe people from some part of Japan tend to be more outgoing and not shy. We have such kind of members in our team.

BM Before we go back to cultural differences, you said what your expectations of the Moot were – did the Moot so far, in the written phase, meet your expectations? What was expected and what was different?

HOK The Moot Court is beyond my expectation. It is more excellent. It takes a lot of work, but I was motivated by other Mooties from all over the world. It is really exciting.

BM When you started in the very beginning, did you do any team building exercises, anything to make the team grow together?

Coach You could tell him how we went to Izsakaya and the German Christmas market. Maybe you have to explain what Izsakaya is because I guess nobody outside Japan knows.

HOK Should we really explain about the Izsakaya?

BM Of course, yes.

HOK I do not know how to explain because for Japanese it is very ordinary. But …

Coach What do you do at an Izsakaya?

HOK Drinking.

Coach So would it be fair to say that Izakaya is a Japanese drinking restaurant where you could go with your friends or with your colleagues after work and there you have something to eat but you also drink while you are there together and you are usually in your own area, in your own space, so doors will be closed, so you are only there with your own table?

HOK Sometimes, free drinks and there is a time limit of two hours.

Coach You can drink as much as you want. And sometimes, afterwards you go to karaoke.

BM And did you?

HOK Yes. Until 5 AM.

BM	And what was that about the Christmas market?
HOK	We are from Sapporo. It is a city and the sister city is Munich.
Coach	Because both cities had Olympic Games in 1972, when Munich hosted the summer games and Sapporo hosted the winter games. That is when they decided to be partner cities. Now there is a Munich style Christmas market in Sapporo with "Glühwein" or mulled wine.
BM	Okay, very German indeed. Speaking of culture and culture transfer between Munich and Sapporo – What is important about Japanese culture? What is maybe different from what people think?
HOK	There are not a lot of Samurai in Japan and there are no Ninja.
BM	I was about to ask where your swords are! Do you want to share something about Japanese culture that you have found surprising when you first spent time there?
Coach	What was really interesting for me in coaching a Japanese team was understanding what a western event the Moot Court actually is. And that for Japanese students it is not just an experience to learn about the law that is applicable and to improve English, but it is also a very cultural experience. I felt that for a lot of students, they first had to understand that western people have a very different style of dealing with disputes and conflicts. And I think that can be an interesting process to really leave the ways you have learned to behave in certain situations and where the Moot Court can require a total different way.
BM	What were the biggest challenges?
Coach	When I first came to Japan and I told the team how to present arguments in this competition, I had the impression that some of the students thought I was a little bit crazy for what I asked them to do. They did not really believe that this was really something they should do because it just seemed very impolite to some of the students to behave like that. And only after the Pre-Moot in Munich, I felt that the team realized that it is actually something that other teams do too.
BM	Can you maybe give an example of the things, what would you have been uncomfortable with doing that he told you to do?

HOK — For me it was uncomfortable to behave like an actor in a drama. I did not expect this. I did not think in the real world a lawyer behaves like an actor. First, I thought, okay, he says so but I do not need to be like this. For me it is too much.

Coach — What is too much?

HOK — I think the Japanese teams thought that when we speak about something legal, we should be serious. We do not know how to present. In Japanese courts, the lawyer just reads something. Not like an actor, so we cannot imagine the style. The most difficult thing for me was his advice to speak in English all the time. But when we discussed something it was too hard to speak in English. But after the Munich Pre-Moot, we realized that it is the most important thing.

Coach — It also was an interesting experience for me to see, how difficult it is to learn a language that is so far away from your own. Having learned European languages before, I really underestimated how difficult it would be for me to learn Japanese.

HOK — Many people say the English does not matter. That bad English is ok. But I do not think so. A good English speaker has a great advantage. English is important.

Coach — How did you cope with other aspects? I heard from some Japanese teams that they believe you should not use your hands to gesture while talking, or that some find it very uncomfortable to look directly into somebody's eyes. Did you feel uncomfortable with these aspects of the presentation? Was it unusual for you?

HOK — As I remember these aspects were very difficult for me at first, but now using the hands while talking, now it is ok to me. Looking into eyes directly is still difficult for me. But I understand that it is good to look into someone's eyes, because I can see if the person understands my argument. But it is still difficult.

BM — If you go back into a purely Japanese context, is this something you would try to get rid of again because you think your Japanese conversation partner would find it impolite if you use your hands too much or look him/her straight in the eye? Would you have to reduce it again now?

HOK — Maybe you have to reduce it.

BM Let me ask about your experience in Hong Kong and in Vienna. When you came to Hong Kong – what did you think?

HOK Hong Kong is a nice place because they have 7/eleven. It is a Japanese company. Besides that: at first, we did not like to go to parties and we did not like that our coach forced us …

Coach Your coach *recommended* you to go!

HOK … now I think it is great to go to the social events because you can meet people from all over the world. It is a very rare experience, so now I think we should go to the social event of this Moot.

BM From an academic perspective, you said the memorandum was successful?

Coach Yes, for the first time, Hokkaido University won an honorable mention this year for the Respondent memorandum in Hong Kong. Now we are the third Japanese team that has ever received a price in the Vis Moot.

BM That is impressive. Tell us about that moment.

HOK This is the first time to receive an honorable mention. At the moment Hokkaido University was called as honorable mention, I could not believe this was true. Two of the team members started to cry. So, okay, I understood this was a great thing.

Coach Didn't you cry too?

HOK Yes, (laughs). Yes.

BM That must have been wonderful, congratulations. So, now you are in Vienna and you have had three pleadings. Are you happy so far with how the pleadings went and are you enjoying it?

HOK Yes, I think. In particular, today's pleading. It was my best pleading in these two years. So, I am very happy.

Coach I am actually very impressed with the two. They worked really hard during the last year and I think they learned a lot. They improved their presentation styles very much and it's a great pleasure to see how students develop so much throughout this experience.

BM Apart from the Moot, have you been looking around in Vienna? Have you eaten a Schnitzel, as you should? And eaten Sacher Torte, the typical things?

HOK We have done it last year. It is funny, we have kind of Schnitzel in Japan. It is called Katsu, fried pork.

BM After the Moot is over, what do you think you will miss most?

HOK Of course I will miss the coach because he leaves our University. And the team, because we worked together on the memo six months. So, I will miss the team and my coach.

BM What will you miss about coaching?

Coach Of course, I will miss my team. It is a mutual relationship. Of course the coach is there to teach the team but at the same time the coach learns a lot from a team. And especially when you coach a team in a country with such a different culture than your own, it is a very learningful experience. I had a really great team of very dedicated students that was there for each other and very committed to team work, which was terrific.

BM Thank you all so much for this interview.

5. Allameh Tabatabai University Tehran/Iran: Living the Spirit of the Vis Moot

5. Allameh Tabatabai University Tehran/Iran

The 2015 Vis Moot Team of Allameh Tabatabai University (ATU) of Tehran was the first Iranian team to participate in the Vis Moot. Phil Ray coached the team from the outset with "*a little help from friends*" in the international arbitral community. We had the chance to speak to Phil in Vienna where he shared his view of the team's "*long and winding road*" from Tehran to Vienna.

BM Phil, thank you so much for agreeing to the interview. You are one of the coaches of the Iranian team.

P. Ray Right. I became the remote coach of the Iranian team and the journey started on the 21st Vis Moot at the MAA Generations Workshop. During a coffee break I chatted with n Iranian attorney and Vis Moot arbitrator, Encyeh Sadr.

BM Wait, it all started in a coffee line?

P. Ray That's correct: in the coffee line Encyeh said: "*Next year Iran will have its first Vis Moot team*". And I said: "*That will be a challenge*". That was in March 2014.
Only a few months earlier, the Iranian team was inspired to do the Vis Moot after reading Erik Bergsten's preface to "*The Principles and Practices of International Commercial Arbitration*" by Margaret Moses. They asked themselves: "*Why don't we just do it?*"
After obtaining support from their ATU law school Dean, they began the initial team selection with about ten students and ended up with these five team members. Before the Vis Problem was issued, the team had few resources. In September 2014, Iran team student coach, Ali Dehdashti, was trained in a 3-day DIAC workshop in Dubai by Uni-Cologne Professor Klaus-Peter Berger, who later introduced Ali to you, Lisa Reiser.
But the actual written and oral advocacy training was voluntarily supported by online tutorials from US, Canadian, and UK experts. After this online training, the team submitted high quality memoranda and learned effective oral advocacy skills, before they began the Pace IICL online pre-moot and online practice rounds with US, Italian, Bosnian, German and Australian teams.

BM Sounds like very intense training.

P. Ray Very intense! But the team soaked it up! For their next level of oral advocacy training, the team went to Amman, Jordan for the 5th Middle East Pre-Moot with ten other teams from eight countries. The great thing about this

Middle East Pre-Moot was the students' getting to know each other – regardless of their differing religious and political cultures – and learning how to support each other's development of oral advocacy skills. One of my most memorable impressions is how great the Iranian all-guy team got along with the Saudi all-gal team, becoming best buddies and overcoming any Shia or Sunni differences.

After the Middle East Pre-Moot, the team took off for the PCA Pre-Moot in The Hague, and then to the Belgrade Open Pre-Moot. I joined them again in Belgrade. From Belgrade, we went to Zagreb for friendly practice rounds at Uni-Zagreb, where all six of us stayed in one hostel room – a challenge but good for team-building. From Zagreb, we travelled to Vienna to continue preparations for the team's Vis preliminary rounds.

BM I see that you and the team have come a long way. And by that I do not only refer to your trips through the Middle East and Europe, but also to your support of the Iranian team's Vis education to create a framework for future Iranian teams' educational opportunities – a Vis Moot success story, definitely. Thank you for this Interview, Phil.

After interviewing their coach Phil Ray, it was time to meet the team of Allameh Tabatabai University in Tehran in person. It consisted of Nima Nasrollahi Shahri, Masood Mahboob, Amir Hossein Tanhaei, Ali Naimi Zaker and their student coach Ali Dehdashti. We were more than curious to hear about their experience and adventures of the last six months since the Vis Moot had started.

BM Thank you so much for agreeing to the interview. I am very, very curious to hear about your experience with the Vis Moot so far. So first of all, Phil already told me his view and his story. But what were the reasons? Why did you apply for the Vis Moot in the first place?

ATU The whole education system in our country is based on memorizing the text books. After eight years of experience in practicing law in Iran, I came back to university for a LL.M. and when I found out about the Vis Moot concept and competition, I realized that this is a really good opportunity to learn the law by practicing. It was like a completely different education opportunity for all the students. So I proposed participating in the Vis Moot to the university and they happened to like the idea and I was fortunate to find these guys who are so determined and industrious.

BM And once the team got together, what were the biggest obstacles you had to face?

ATU We faced a lot of difficulties and to overcome these difficulties we had to be disciplined. It wasn't just financial problems, even for very short sentences from a book, we needed help from outside Iran because we did not have access to the sources. Because of the sanctions and the devaluation of the Iranian Rial, a lot of universities could not afford to pay their annual subscription fees for data bases so the services were cut in most universities. So, we had absolutely no access to any books, no access to online publications and no access to data bases like Westlaw, LexisNexis or Kluwer Arbitration. And due to the sanctions, we even could not buy books online because we were not able to pay for them through our credit cards.

BM So, that was the biggest challenge you had when you were drafting the memorandum.

ATU Yes. Especially when we got to the point that we had to add resources to our memos. We had problems because the area of arbitration is something that is growing fast and is in progress and we did not have the access to the books that are updated. So, the thing that we had to do was asking other lawyers out of the country and we specified some pages, for example, we need page 28/29 of book XYZ and ask them to scan and send us a copy of it.

BM So, apart from the resources, is there anything else in the political system in Iran that prevented you from competing or that made it a little bit complicated?

ATU No, absolutely not.

BM Now, that you are here in Vienna, do you see yourselves as ambassadors of your country?

ATU We see ourselves as ambassadors of a rich ancient Persian culture and we try to represent that, try to show others the beautiful country we come from and how misunderstood people are about our nation and our country. Because, you know, when we talk to Westerners they have a very distorted image of what things are like in Iran. They think, it is a primitive society with camels on the streets which is really not the case because Tehran is quite a modern capital, very much resembling some European capitals such as Madrid. So that is what we are trying to make people understand.

BM Do you think that also in the future, there will be a team from Allameh Tabatabai University?

ATU Yeah, for sure. In fact, there are already six students at home now who are practicing and studying together. Five of them are girls.

What is more, for the next year, we are trying to bring more teams from more Iranian universities to the Vis Moot. Maybe next year, we have like three or four teams from different Iranian universities. Because this is a great learning opportunity for every Iranian law student and if we have more than one team in Iran, we can practice internally.

BM If next year's team of Allameh Tabatabai University is already in place, what would be your most valuable advice for the team? What should they keep in mind when participating?

ATU For all of us, the Vis Moot was the first time that we really enjoyed education and the most important advice can be: enjoy education and in a way that you feel, this is real life. The biggest successful story of our team is that, last year, our team member Masood did not speak a word of English. He has definitely gone the farthest, he's gone a very long road. Now he speaks good English and pleaded in the practice rounds.

BM So, I have actually come to my last question: If you could decide now, would you pursue a career in international arbitration?

ATU Sure. Yes. We have really developed that interest in advocacy. We have developed a real passion for arbitration.

The team of Allameh Tabatabai University won the "Spirit of the Vis Moot Award" due to their enthusiasm and hard-working endurance during the preparations for the Vis Moot. Congratulations!

IX. Views from Around the World

Baker McKenzie is a truly global law firm with arbitration practitioners all over the world. We asked a few of our colleagues to share their war stories with you and to give some advice on good mooting.

1. Behind Closed Doors: Arbitral Proceedings in the Real World

What is the biggest difference between the Moot and real arbitral proceedings? Which details are similar?

Jon Ebner, a partner in Baker McKenzie's Chicago office, shares his experience.

Of course, there are many differences and similarities between the simulated arbitration experience provided in the Moot and an arbitration experience in the real world. It may be helpful to focus on just a couple of these aspects, which include the arbitrator's motivation, and the chance to practice the art of oral persuasion.

Difference: The Arbitrator's Motivation and Bias

You should take full advantage of the opportunity offered by the Moot, which is, as mentioned above, intended to be an education tool. It is truly rare that you will be able to participate in an experience where the main purpose of the exercise is to simply help the participants learn. Later, in private practice, you cannot expect that the arbitrators who agree to serve on a tribunal do so because they want to help the lawyers become better lawyers. You should be aware of this dynamic and take full advantage of the opportunity presented by the Moot: realize that most of the arbitrators are there because they want to help the students learn, and agree to serve as arbitrators motivated mainly by altruism.

In real life, you should be aware that the arbitrators are compensated financially for their time. They are not there to help you learn, but only to apply themselves and to fairly decide the case. So first and foremost, a professional appointment is a "job" for the arbitrators, and one which they approach professionally and with a certain amount of distance from the lawyers and the parties. But at least two of the three arbitrators are appointed by the parties. That means that the parties select arbitrators whom they hope be "sympathetic" to their side of the case. This does not mean that an arbitrator feels some obligation to rule in favor of the party who appointed them; quite the opposite. However, as a lawyer in the real world it is wise to select an arbitrator whom you believe will truly understand your side of the case. For example, if the claimant's case is founded on a misunderstanding of a scientific principle, the respondent may want to choose an arbitrator who has a scientific background and who will understand the respondent's defense on a deeper level. This means, in practice, that a lawyer may believe that one of the arbitrators may be "sympathetic" to their case, that the arbitrator appointed by the other side may be "hostile" to their case. This dynamic should not exist in the Moot.

Similarity: Practicing the Art of Oral Persuasion

Apart from the altruistic motivation of the arbitrators in the Moot, the overall Moot experience is designed to replicate, as nearly as possible, the experience of arguing a case in arbitration proceedings. In the Moot as in real life, this requires (1) a thorough understanding of the facts, (2) a thorough understanding of the law, and (3) the ability to convert a lawyer's mastery of the facts and law into a compelling oral presentation that is likely to persuade the listener. Of course, it is this last point that is most important in the Moot, and which is also simultaneously the most important skill required by any oral advocate. In short, the principles which apply to oral persuasion in the Moot and in real life are exactly the same.

Part of being an effective oral advocate is by watching the listener and getting feedback about whether you are persuading them. This generally requires a good amount of flexibility on your part and a willingness to adapt your presentation to the arbitrator's response. Sometimes the arbitrators will tell you that they do not understand your position, and will ask tough questions. As noted earlier, you cannot plan out a script of your presentation for this very reason. If the arbitrators' interests do not match up neatly with your planned presentation, you will need to quickly adapt and focus on the questions raised. It may not be enough to simply answer the question asked and returning to your outline, it could be that the question asked – and the way it was asked – necessitates revising your focus for the remainder of the presentation, even after you have answered the question.

But even apart from direct questions asked by the arbitrators, they will give you indirect, perhaps even subliminal, feedback that they are not even aware of, in many different ways. You should carefully watch the arbitrators to see how they are responding to your presentation. When you paused after making an important point, did any of them nod in agreement? Or did they cross their arms and seem to disapprove? If so, you may want to make the point in a different way. In the real world, practitioners learn from each oral argument they make, and part of this learning comes from watching and responding appropriately to the arbitrator. The Moot is your chance to try out different techniques and find out which style works for you.

2. Addicted to the Moot: Why So Many Arbitrators Come Back Year After Year

Grant Hanessian is a partner in the New York office of Baker McKenzie and chair of the firm's International Arbitration practice group in North America. He travels to Vienna year after year to participate in the Vis Moot.

Some ten years ago, I entered the hearing room for my first assignment as a Vis Moot arbitrator a bit late, and more than a little disheveled, having come to the Juridicum directly from the Vienna airport after landing that morning on a flight from New York. I had reviewed the memorials but knew nothing about the teams other than the fact that they represented universities in China and India. I was not familiar with either university – in fact I had not even heard of the city in which one of the universities was located.

I expected to find the oralists, a couple of coaches and my co-arbitrators. Instead I found a room packed with Indian and Chinese students, coaches and supporters. As chairman of the panel, I welcomed everyone, apologized for my lateness and tried hide my bewilderment. At that time I had been practicing international arbitration for nearly twenty years – admittedly almost exclusively in the United States and Europe. Although I had met and worked with many international arbitration lawyers of Indian or Chinese nationality or origin, most of them practiced with western firms and virtually all had been educated at western law faculties. My understanding at that time was that there was virtually no English language arbitration in China and no international arbitration of any consequence sited in India. Yet here was a room full of arbitration students and teachers from China and India.

I asked the parties if they had agreed on the time allocations – which of course they had. I nodded to the claimant to begin. I watched with growing admiration as both teams presented very capably. My initial surprise that students from universities in China and India were so knowledgeable about international commercial arbitration gave way to a sort of astonishment that they were performing at such a high level in English.

As I sat there that day I thought to myself: "This is the future of international arbitration."

Ten years earlier, at the first Vis competition in 1993, it probably would have been more appropriate to speak of "CRIB" countries rather than "BRIC" countries in the context of international commercial arbitration. At that time none of the four BRIC countries (Brazil, Russia, India, China) had an effective international commercial arbitration national law, a national arbitration institution with a significant number of international cases or an international arbitration bar. Things are very much different now, of course: BRIC countries and other "emerging" markets provide many parties, counsel and arbitrators in international commercial arbitrations.

Certainly the availability on the Internet of international arbitration rules, awards, treatises and other materials has significantly eroded previous barriers to entry into the field, but the Vis competition has played no small role in these rapid and profound changes. From its origin in Vienna in 1993 with eleven teams (all from Europe, the U.S., Canada and Australia), the Vienna moot in 2012 attracted 280 teams from 67 countries – 49 teams from the four BRIC countries alone. India sent the third highest number of teams, 17 – following only the U.S. and Germany. Brazil sent 13 teams, the same number as the U.K. and France. And of course there is now also a Vis Moot (East) competition in Hong Kong, at which 83 teams from 26 countries competed in 2012.

On the second night of my first Moot experience in Vienna, I attended a party at the Baker McKenzie offices in Vienna. This event (my first Vis party) was attended by hundreds of Vis participants. The energy in the room was palpable and infectious – I had never seen such a large gathering of young people interested in what had always seemed to me a relatively small and somewhat academic practice. Also in attendance were a number of senior arbitration figures, some of whom stayed quite late, freely sharing with students their insights into the arbitral process and their careers.

The four days I spent in Vienna on that first trip were among the most professionally invigorating and inspiring of my life. I have been coming back ever since. There are many aspects of the Vienna Vis experience I look forward to each year – continuing old friendships and beginning new ones, the Würstelstands, the Heurigens, the Musikverein and the Naschmarkt. However, what mostly brings me back is the opportunity to experience the commitment and enthusiasm of so many hundreds of students from all over the world – and to participate ever so slightly not only in the development of a new generation of arbitration lawyers but in the continuing expansion of a truly global system of commercial dispute resolution.

3. Arbitration in Brazil: Professional Sailing through Tropical Waters

Isabell Weaver Gernand and Luis Peretti are Of-Counsel and Senior Associate at the Brazilian law firm Trench, Rossi e Watanabe Advogados in association with Baker McKenzie. They explain why arbitration is on a rise in one of the BRICS States.

Looking back – Some history

Brazil is a traditional promoter of arbitration. The first reference to arbitration appears in the Constitution of the Brazilian Empire of 1824 which allowed individuals to appoint private judges (or arbitrators) to adjudicate their disputes. The Commercial Code of 1850 also allowed for the arbitration of disputes[1]. In the same century, Brazil resolved its border disputes with France and Argentina through arbitration. The peaceful determination of its borders through negotiations and mediation was one of the greatest achievements of Brazilian diplomacy.

The trend shifted in the 20th century. Arbitration remained a valid choice, being regulated in the 1939 and in the 1973 Civil Procedure Code. However, arbitration agreements that were concluded before

[1] José Augusto Delgado, *A Arbitragem no Brasil: evolução histórica e conceitual*, Digital Library of the Brazilian Superior Court of Justice, available at: http://bdjur.stj.gov.br/jspui/handle/2011/8302. (last visited 8 March 2017).

the dispute arose were not considered binding. The parties would need to state their consent to arbitration again in order to start arbitration. Besides that, arbitral awards had to undergo proceedings for recognition at state courts before they became enforceable. This required lengthy proceedings which defeated the purpose of arbitration. That changed with the new Brazilian Arbitration Act in 1996[2], which provided for arbitration agreements to be binding and abolished the requirement of recognition of arbitral awards before state courts as a condition for enforceability.

In the years following the enactment of the Brazilian Arbitration Act, the binding character of arbitration agreement stirred much debate, as the Brazilian Constitution guarantees "free access to courts". Scholars argued that to recognize arbitration agreements as binding would prevent parties from access to Brazilian state courts, which would result in a conflict with the constitutional principle of "free access to courts". The Brazilian Supreme Court ended the dispute in 2001 by declaring that the binding character of arbitration agreements does not violate the Constitution.[3]

In 2002, Brazil ratified the Convention on the Recognition and Enforcement of Foreign Arbitral Awards (New York Convention)[4], putting into place the necessary toolkit to allow the development of arbitration. Courts and Congress adopted and maintained a favorable stance and supported and passed rules that allowed arbitration to develop. As a consequence, arbitration centers mushroomed in major cities in Brazil, namely in São Paulo and Rio de Janeiro. Arbitration in Brazil has significantly evolved in the last ten years. Nowadays, Brazilian parties are keen users of arbitration in both international and domestic disputes. Arbitration is perceived as more expeditious and specialized than state courts. In 2015, 96 Brazilian parties were involved in proceedings administered by the International Court of Arbitration of the International Chamber of Commerce ("ICC"), making Brazil the sixth largest ICC client in terms of nationality.[5] The increasing global significance of arbitration in Brazil will be fostered by the ICC opening offices in São Paulo in 2017 to handle Brazilian-related arbitration.

---

[2] The text in English is available at the Brazilian Arbitration Committee's website: http://cbar.org.br/site/legislacao-nacional/lei-9-30796-em-ingles.

[3] Brazilian Supreme Court, Appeal in the procedure for the recognition of foreign judgments No. 5.206–7, MBV Commercial and Export Management Establisment c. Resil Industria e Comércio Ltda. 8 maio 1997.

[4] Decree 4,311 of 2002.

[5] International Chamber of Commerce, ICC Bulletin: 2015 ICC dispute resolution statistics, Paris: ICC, 2016, p. 4.

Some surprises in the tropical waters

Brazilian parties and counsel are savvy operators of international arbitration, and international arbitrations with situs in Brazil or involving Brazilian parties normally follow globally recognized standards. However, when it comes to domestic arbitration, Brazilian idiosyncrasies may surprise those who for the first time sail through these tropical waters. Differently from international arbitration, domestic arbitrations in Brazil may have certain peculiarities. The Brazilian Civil Procedure Code may have some impact on domestic arbitral procedures and the common arbitral rules. For instance, in Brazilian domestic arbitration, the parties can call a "legal representative" to appear and testify, not quite as a witness, but rather as an informed representative that makes statements regarding the party's business operations and the case in dispute, notably from the perspective of that party. Though such legal representatives are not "real" witnesses, most domestic tribunals consider their statements like witness statements. The tricky part is further, that each party cannot request its own legal representative to be heard, but can only request the examination of the other party's legal representative. So parties have to consider carefully whether they call the opponent's legal representative to testify because this does not automatically lead to a testimony of their own legal representative.

Domestic arbitral hearings are further influenced by Brazilian Civil Procedure Law when it comes to challenging witnesses. Witness testimony may be barred if a witness is considered to have a conflict of interest related to the parties, e.g. in case the witness is a party in another lawsuit against one of the parties. It is often the case that challenges regarding witnesses are made, argued and decided during the hearing and not through briefs in advance. If the arbitral tribunal does not provide for other rules beforehand, it may happen that witnesses fly in from overseas to attend a hearing just to be challenged and finally disqualified as a witness.

Looking forward – What is beyond the horizon

Arbitration in Brazil will grow. Brazil is the fifth largest country in the world with significant import and export of goods from all over the world.

The Brazilian government, legislations and courts have been providing consistent support for arbitration. This trend is consistent with a broader movement towards an increase in the importance of party autonomy in Brazil. This trend translated into new provisions included during the reform process of the Brazilian Arbitration Act in 2015[6]. The new statutes clearly provide that also public entities can agree to arbitration proceedings. Before, it was often argued that public entities could not enter into arbitration agreements at all.[7] This will lead to a massive increase of public law contracts with arbitration clauses and hence, to more arbitration in Brazil.[8] Notably, state entities are involved in almost every industry sector in Brazil, in particular construction, energy and transport.

Arbitration is now in harmony with the Brazilian state courts, not an enemy to them anymore. A telling example of this is the fact that arbitrators today are authorized to render interim measures and to review, uphold, amend or even repeal decisions on interim measures rendered by the state courts[9]. And though the power to compel enforcement of awards lies with the state courts, arbitrators are allowed to request court assistance in order to ensure compliance with their decisions.[10] Enforcement of a foreign award has also become easier as it has become more difficult to successfully raise the public policy defense that would allow refusing enforcement of foreign decisions.[11]

---

[6] Law No. 13,129 of 26 May 2015 altered some of the provisions of the original Brazilian Arbitration Act, Law No. 9,307 of 23 September 1996.

[7] Brazilian Arbitration Act, Article 1, first paragraph: "*The public administration may resort to arbitration to resolve disputes relating to waivable patrimonial rights.*"

[8] Provisional Measure 752/2016, commented by *Muniz/Peretti*, New rule on the Brazilian privatization program provides for arbitration. Global Arbitration News, available at: https://globalarbitrationnews.com/20161125-new-rule-brazilian-privatization-program-provides-arbitration/.

[9] Brazilian Arbitration Act, Article 22-A and 22-B: "*Before the institution of the arbitration, parties may resort to the courts in order to request precautionary or urgent measures […].*""*Once the arbitration is instituted, the arbitrators will have the power to uphold, amend or repeal the interim our urgent measure handed by the courts […].*"

[10] Brazilian Arbitration Act, Article 22-C: "*The arbitrator or arbitration panel may address an arbitral letter to the competent organ of the national Judiciary so that the latter may compel the enforcement of the act requested by the arbitrator within the boundaries of its territorial jurisdiction.*"

[11] For instance, the Federal Supreme Court has granted exequatur to a foreign judicial decision aiming at collecting gambling debts from a resident of Brazil, although gambling is illegal in this country (STF, Decision on the rogatory letter No. 9970/United States, United States District Court for the District of the New Jersey v. Osmar Zambardino, 18 March 2002). In another case, the Superior Court of Justice granted exequatur to a foreign judicial decision that failed to apply the civil law principle of the exception of non-performance (*exceptio non adimpleti contractus*), which is part of the Brazilian Civil Code, and stated that such rule is not a public policy matter (STJ, SEC 802-EX, reporting Justice José Delgado, judged on 17 August 2005).

The trend towards increased party autonomy in arbitration has even affected the regulation of the civil procedure in state courts and in alternative dispute resolution proceedings. With the adoption of the New Civil Procedure Code in 2015,[12] parties are allowed to agree on certain procedural aspects and to regulate many aspects of civil litigation,[13] such as the number of submissions of briefs, the organization of the evidence taking, etc. A Mediation Act entered into force in 2015,[14] which further fosters to resolve disputes through consensual means.[15] A recent decision from the Superior Court of Justice also recognized dispute boards as a binding conflict management tool.[16]

Brazil is already an arbitration powerhouse. The possibilities regarding party autonomy provided in recent statutes (encompassing mediation, arbitration and litigation) and the desire for more efficient and flexible means in dispute resolution will boost Brazil's arbitration practice.

4. The Positive Paradox: How the VIS Moot can Change the Future of Arbitration

Filip Boras is a partner of Baker McKenzie Vienna. He explains why the VIS Moot confronts Viennese people with a paradox and how the VIS Moot can be a game changer in promoting arbitration in difficult times.

For a Viennese the Vis Moot leads to a paradox when thinking of arbitration:

Doesn't matter which of the large German language newspapers a Viennese reads, he or she must meanwhile be convinced that arbitra-

[12] Law 13,105 of 16 March 2015.

[13] Brazilian Civil Procedure Code, Articles 190 and 191: "*If the lawsuit relates to rights that can be amicably settled by the parties, the parties with legal capacity may stipulate changes to the lawsuit proceedings in order to adapt them to the case particulars, and they may also agree on their burdens, powers, faculties and procedural duties during or before the commencement of the lawsuit.*"

[14] Law 13,140 of 26 June 2015.

[15] *Muniz/Peretti*, The dawn of the age of mediation, Global Arbitration News, available at https://globalarbitrationnews.com/20150722-brazil-the-dawn-of-the-age-of-mediation/.

[16] Superior Court of Justice. Special Appeal No. 1,569,422-RJ. Repporting Justice Marco Aurélio Bellizze. Judged on 26 April 2016.

tion is bad. This is true no matter what he or she thought about arbitration before, or whether he or she knew what arbitration is at all. Headline stories on arbitration speaking of "*parallel justice*" taking place "*behind curtains*" and in "*expensive hotels*" are not rare in daily newspapers. The newspapers make sure that you believe you know what arbitration is and that you know it is bad. They all imply in one way or the other that arbitration takes place "*in the shadow of the legal system.*"

But once the media successfully convinced you that arbitration does not serve the interests of justice and after even you as an arbitration practitioner started to cast doubts on the current system (Can it be true that the broad public and political majority is wrong? Can it be true that the political party I always voted for is against my job?), suddenly something inexplicable happens: Students from over 300 universities come to Vienna to compete in one of the most prestigious moot competitions in the world – the VIS Moot. Can it be true that so many talented young students all over the world want to compete in a legal field that is almost "*beyond the rule of law*"? This contradiction does not make sense.

The first question is: How do we resolve this paradox? You might think this is biased, but I truly believe that it is to be resolved in favor of the VIS Moot participants. We all became lawyers, because already at an early age we were the ones who raised our voices first to say: This is unfair or that is not ok. It is the young, who still have a great portion of instinct freshly available. I am convinced that the young talents from 300 universities coming every year to Vienna are not dedicated to a process which is somehow unjust, but that their instinct tells them that this is the right thing to do.

Once we have settled who is "right", the second question is: Do we have to care about the other side of the paradox – about those who still think that arbitration is bad? After all, one could argue that all this criticism is directed towards investment arbitration involving states ("ISDS") and not commercial arbitration. And since the VIS Moot deals with commercial arbitration and CISG problems, there actually is no paradox. This is correct only on first sight, but fails to take into account the reality of the debate: the difference between commercial and investment arbitration may be well understood by arbitration practitioners and VIS Moot students, but it is lost once the debate reaches the public. There the debate does not make halt at criticizing ISDS, because the broader public does not distinguish between commercial and investment arbitration. Neither does the media when it speaks of "arbitral tribunals" ("*Schiedsgerichte*"), but usually drops the "investment" prefix. The damage inevitably spills over to commercial arbitration. Damage to arbitration is done.

The distinction between investment and commercial arbitration serves only as an ill turn here, because many practitioners feel in a trappy safe heaven by thinking of the debate as an isolated investment arbitration issue. In result, they prefer to abstain from the debate (under the motto: at least the commercial arbitration work is safe). After all, many of us do both, commercial and investment cases during our career. In sum, we should definitely care for those who are on the other side of the paradox, because this majority can seriously impact the future of our practice.

The third and key question is: How do we convince the other side of the paradox? More specifically, how do we convince the public that arbitration is a valuable and established dispute resolution mechanism in international trade and commerce – of course, with space for improvement?

So far, the arbitration community has chosen to employ a low-key tactic in defense: Speak about the issue at conferences (where the critics are not present) or write an article here and there in a daily newspaper that most likely gets lost in the shuffle of negative ones. In the past years, the arbitration community has failed to find a meaningful response to the PR armada of political parties and NGOs. All that is left is the hope that this entire debate will somehow go away. Don't even the best stories become boring at some point? At least one can hope that the debate could shift to the right spot, from the procedural to the real substantive question: the fundamental question whether to grant foreign investors protection or not.

But hope is not a plan, I learned at my first business plan session. And this public debate on arbitration seems to be highly tenacious and recurrent. It is much more likely that the entire free trade and investment protection debate is likely to last long and issues will get even more cloaked into a question over arbitration.

Here, the Vis Moot can play a game changing role. But not because of the record number of teams participating and the increasing number of practitioner events accompanying the VIS. No. It is because of the energy that you can feel during the VIS Moot. If each one of you devotes this incredible energy and instincts; if each of you educates your friends and family, your colleagues, your fellows members in organizations; if you tell them about arbitration and its role in international trade and commerce; if we all do this, arbitration will turn to a winner in this public debate. The public attention arbitration currently enjoys is unique and can serve as a chance, but only if each one of us does a part of the job. Enter the debate; don't avoid it, because there is nothing to hide. We can be proud of our international arbitration community – the VIS Moot being its best part. Start today and spread the word!

5. Reality Check: If You Think the Moot Cases Are Unrealistic Wait until You Hear About My Case

We asked our colleague Edward Poulton, partner of Baker McKenzie in London, to tell us about the strangest, funniest, most interesting facts that he came across during his career in international arbitration. He had a lot to tell us about!

Have you ever heard about…

a machine that freezes turkey so fast it doesn't need to be described as "frozen"?

a lady who thinks having 10 brothers and sisters is a formal HR qualification?

a case where everyone involved was named after a different type of bird?

an opponent who looks like a pirate (but, unfortunately, without a parrot)?

a witness who starts to clean the tribunal's desk with a hand-held vacuum cleaner?

The reality of working in the world of dispute resolution involves confronting strange facts and interesting characters almost at every turn. The five situations above are only some of the odd and wonderful matters I have come across in my career as an international arbitrator. The variety of the situations and people (not to mention legal arguments) we meet is one of the reasons why our job is so interesting and, often, why we decided to focus on this area of work in the first place. Long may it continue!

Different fact patterns

An arbitration can arise in almost any industry, which requires arbitration practitioners to be prepared to throw themselves into anything, from complicated formulae for Korean-manufactured polymers to the inner workings (and market in) Thai ceiling fans. I had to become an expert on car registration processes (including IT and logistics) for 2 investment treaty claims against Mexico, not to mention the need to be able to function after lunch washed down with tequila. I have delved into the weird and wonderful world of laying fibre-optic cables across Swiss mountains, the public international law aspects of off-shore gas exploration, the Greek market for domestic appliances, the freezing of Brazilian poultry and the intricacies of swaps and derivatives (probably the most terrifying of all).

The legal cases have occasionally been pursued against a backdrop of political interference or unexplained death (accident/suicide/murder?). Often, they involve an intense level of personal animosity between the parties, which one of counsel's roles is to rise above.

Interesting people

Arbitrators and opponents (both parties and their lawyers) come in all shapes and sizes, as well as nationalities and legal traditions. It is a vital part of being successful in an arbitration to understand your tribunal (including its inner workings) and your opponent, so that you can anticipate, and adapt to, the dynamic which develops as the case progresses. In few other fields can things become so lost in, or improved by, translation.

You will also encounter characters and moments which make particular matters unforgettable. For example, I will always remember the opponent who confused himself so much in an attempt to come up with an analogy helpful to his submission that he ended up making my submissions for me. Or the arbitrator who, because he was reading the submissions (obviously for the first time) rather than listening to the cross-examination, would repeatedly ask the witness a question about something he had addressed minutes previously.

It is also a privileged world, in which one can engage in intellectual and procedural jousting with some great legal minds, and also interact with (and cross-examine) ministers, CEOs and experts in the most exotic fields of engineering or economics. Each of these encounters is challenging, but also enriching.

Strange hearings

Always be prepared for the unexpected. Most witnesses these days will be sufficiently well-prepared that they will come up to proof, and defend the facts set out in their witness statements. However, every now and then, a witness is so spectacularly bad (or the lawyers' tactics so flawed) that a "eureka" moment can occur. I once cross-examined a witness who had made a very short statement 2 days before the final hearing. The statement dealt only with his interpretation of a single one-page letter, which he exhibited to his statement. You can therefore imagine my surprise (not to say glee) when, upon presenting him with said letter, he was unable to confirm or deny whether he had seen it previously. I will never forget my opposing counsel's face, particularly when the Chairman of the Tribunal raised his eyebrow at him enquiringly.

Having said that, it is equally important to develop an inscrutable poker face for those moments where your own witness, who seemed so able and confident in meetings with you, suddenly turns into an incoherent and contradictory ball of nerves in the face of aggressive (and sometimes not even that probing) cross-examination. I recently observed a very senior executive fall down so spectacularly in the face of cross-examination that he, subconsciously I suspect, decided that the best way to end his ordeal quickly was to agree to everything opposing counsel asked him, even where it was in direct contradiction to his written statement. Luckily for our case, this witness-equivalent of the 'Stockholm syndrome' made him seem so incompetent and clueless that the tribunal generally ignored his evidence altogether.

Summary

In summary, the Vis Moot fact patterns are not far-fetched. They capture quite accurately the type of case which an arbitration practitioner can expect to land on his or her desk at any time. You'll never know what you'll have to learn about next and if that doesn't excite you then it's not the profession for you.

6. International Arbitration in Japan: The Glass Half Full

Joel Greer, a partner of Baker McKenzie Tokyo, gives insights from a country in which arbitration is not yet a widely embraced means of dispute resolution.

Seven years ago, I co-authored a report on international arbitration in Japan in which we reviewed the progress arbitration had made here since the enactment of a new, modern arbitration law (the first such revision in over a century) and the introduction of new rules for the Japan Commercial Arbitration Association (JCAA) in 2004. Both developments were significant legal reforms, but they alone could not boost the historically very modest level of arbitration activity in Japan. Nonetheless, we concluded our assessment by noting:

6. *International Arbitration in Japan: The Glass Half Full*

> *"If it may be an exaggeration to consider the past six years a new dawn for international arbitration in Japan, equally it would be a mistake to assume that this period has been a false dawn .... With more time, and more accumulated positive experiences, Japanese and non-Japanese parties alike may begin increasingly to arbitrate in Japan and thereby to dispel doubts that the new dawn has finally arrived."*

Since writing those words, there have been "*more accumulated positive experiences*" with arbitration in Japan. Progress, while still modest, is discernible in various ways.

For example, between 2005 and 2009 the average number of arbitrations filed annually in the JCAA was around 13. Between 2010 and 2015, that number rose to 21. This figure, of course, is low when judged against comparable averages at the Singapore International Arbitration Centre (SIAC), the Hong Kong International Arbitration Centre (HKIAC), or other major arbitral institutions. Nevertheless, it represents an increase of over 60 % from the 2005–2009 period.

It is fair, therefore, to ask whether one might view this growth more optimistically (the glass half full) or pessimistically (the glass half empty). I prefer the former, for reasons that go beyond the statistical data.

For example, the JCAA has made important strides to update its rules, both in 2014 and 2015. The 2014 update in particular involved substantial amendments, including the addition of provisions for emergency arbitrators and joinder of third parties, useful revisions regarding interim measures, expedited procedures, and consolidation, and modifications to help make JCAA proceedings more efficient. A number of these changes followed amendments to the rules of the SIAC, HKIAC, and ICC. As such, while the JCAA rules currently may be underused, there is little question that they are on a par with the rules of major arbitral institutions.

Japan also has a mature judiciary with a reputation for impartiality, and although Japanese courts have less experience in addressing arbitration-related issues than courts in certain other jurisdictions, the publicly available decisions rendered so far have generally been pro-arbitration. Among these decisions are cases addressing the validity of arbitration clauses, including flawed clauses, the law applicable to arbitration agreements, the separability of arbitration agreements, and the enforcement of arbitral awards.

Indeed, the case law in Japan has advanced fairly rapidly in recent years, and it can be expected to keep growing in the future. This development, combined with the sweeping reforms of Japan's arbitral legislation, means that Japan is making important headway in establishing itself as a dependable seat of arbitration.

From my own experience working with Japanese companies over the past decade, I can say that awareness of and curiosity about international commercial arbitration has certainly risen. The inquiries I receive from business executives have become better informed and more sophisticated, and, increasingly, these executives have had at least some first-hand experience with arbitration.

Japanese corporations also are beginning to take advantage of their rights under investment treaties to which Japan is a party. In 2015, a Japanese firm filed an arbitration under the International Centre for Settlement of Investment Disputes rules against the Spanish government pursuant to the Energy Charter Treaty. Japan is a party to over 40 investment and other economic treaties, and it will be interesting to see whether more Japanese companies seek to exercise their rights under these agreements.

Finally, efforts in Japan to foster greater understanding and appreciation of arbitration among practitioners are proceeding apace. Most of Japan's leading law schools today include classes on international commercial arbitration, and organizations such as the Japan Association of Arbitrators, Japan Bar Association, and the JCAA are involved in various training and outreach activities to promote arbitration. The Chartered Institute of Arbitrators has established a local presence and coordinates training and speaker events. And at the 2014 International Bar Association annual conference in Tokyo, numerous arbitration-related events were held and attended by participants from Japan and around the world.

All this is not to say that more cannot be done to encourage the use of international arbitration in Japan, or to deny that Japan and Japanese corporations have not embraced arbitration as quickly as have other jurisdictions and companies in Asia. It is, however, to recognize that there have been and are tangible signs of progress and to anticipate that this progress will continue.

As it is with countries, so it is with individuals: they develop at different rates. You have already learned much in preparing for this exciting event, and you will learn more by participating in it. Don't be discouraged if you think some of your competitors may be better prepared, or others possess a talent you lack. Take the opportunity to learn about your own strengths, weaknesses, and – perhaps most important – what you enjoy from the experience.

7. International Arbitration in Asia: Significance of Culture in International Arbitration

It is often said that one must be alive to cultural nuances when arbitrating in a different land. Are arbitrations in the East all that different from those in the West? Leng Sun Chan SC, an arbitrator as well as a partner of Baker McKenzie.Wong & Leow in Singapore and the firm's Global Head of International Arbitration, weighs in on the debate.

Cultural sensitivity is like emotional intelligence. In the context of arbitration, it is a useful trait for counsel to have. After all, psychology is an integral aspect of the art of persuasion. One cannot apply psychology without knowing the subject and the audience. On the other hand, the importance of culture in international arbitration can be overstated.

The former Chief Justice of Singapore, Chan Sek Keong, described culture as "the way of life of any ethnic community, as determined by or influenced by its language, religious beliefs and practices, customs or even its food." When you speak of culture, whose culture are you referring to? The culture of the country where the arbitration is taking place? Or that of the parties? Or the tribunal?

How different culturally is an arbitration under the Rules of the American Arbitration Association in New York from an arbitration administered by the Singapore International Arbitration Centre in Singapore? Familiarity with the rules, laws and conventions of each seat is, in my view, more important than understanding the cultural differences between America and Singapore.

Race, language and religion may always be the great divides in societies and nations. But in international arbitration, where the seat of arbitration might have nothing to do with the origin of the transaction or the residence of the parties, the national culture of the seat has little effect on the outcome of the arbitration. What is more important, where the seat is concerned, is the legislative framework, the infrastructure supporting arbitration and the attitude of its judiciary towards arbitration. It does not matter whether the country celebrates Christmas, Deepavali or Hari Raya Aidilfitri or whether as, in the case of Singapore, it celebrates all three plus the Buddhist Wesak Day thrown in.

Should you then consider the culture of the disputants? Of course. Whether you are counsel or arbitrator, you must understand the background of the parties in order to understand where they are coming from or what they are getting at. Then again, this is true of all human interaction, be it in the corporate space, in a courtroom or in arbitration.

It has been said, for example, that traditional Asians are non-confrontational. They are not comfortable with direct confrontation and prefer more subtle forms of disagreement. So subtle, in fact, that one might walk away thinking that one has an agreement sealed with a nod and a smile when all that one has are, well, just a nod and a smile.

It has also been written, even judicially acknowledged, that Asians place stock in the concept of good faith in contracts.

Very recently, the Singapore Court of Appeal broke ranks with the English courts in upholding the enforceability of an agreement to negotiate in good faith. In *HSBC Institutional Trust v Toshin Development* [2012] SGCA 48, the Court of Appeal observed that "*it is fairly common practice for Asian businesses to include similar clauses in their commercial contracts.*" It finds that the "confer in good faith" clause is consistent with Singapore's cultural value of promoting consensus whenever possible. It endorses the following arguments of Associate Professor Philip J McConnaughay in "Rethinking the Role of Law":

> *A core term of many Asian commercial contracts – the "friendly negotiations" or "confer in good faith" clause – captures the essence of contractual obligation in the Asian tradition. Such clauses typically recite that, if differences or disputes arise during the course of the contractual relationship, the parties will discuss and resolve the matter amicably. The Western view of such clauses is that they impose no real obligation at all; at most, they represent a mechanism for making unenforceable requests for novation, or perhaps an initial formality in a multiple-step dispute resolution process culminating eventually in compulsory adjudication intended to enforce precise contractual terms. But these views presuppose a Western understanding of the contract itself, which is not shared in Asia.*

On the other hand, there is danger in romanticizing the Asian way of doing business. The East can be as hard-nosed as the West when it comes to doing business. One is better served by understanding the laws of a particular Asian country than assuming that good faith will always carry the day in Asia. After all, Asian countries can have significantly different legal systems. Some are common law, some are civil law and some are a hybrid of the two. Indeed, "good faith" is not a defining component of the contract law of all Asian countries. Some, even Singapore despite the HSBC Institutional Trust Services case, places primacy on the language of the contract. Indeed, it is probably more accurate to say that good faith is a feature of civil law systems, be they East or West.

What about the culture of the tribunal? It is of extreme importance to know who your arbitrators are, to at least be familiar with their background even if you do not know them personal. This is where international arbitration differs from a national court when it comes to culture. When you have a dispute in a national court, you know that the judges, the counsel and perhaps one or both of the parties carry the pysche and values of the country. In international arbitration, the tribunal members are not necessary from the seat and are more likely than not to come from a mix of nationalities, even legal traditions. You should therefore be sensitive to the beliefs and inclinations of each member of the Tribunal. But this is no more and no less than other things that you must take into account. That will include the educational and professional background of your arbitrators.

It has been said that an arbitrator from the civil law tradition does not favor the lengthy and aggressive cross-examination that is the hallmark of a common law counsel. Likewise, many Asians may take a dim view of rude behavior from counsel. But there is danger in stereotyping. There are many lawyers from England and the United States whose manners are impeccable just as there are civil law or Asian practitioners with excessive testosterone.

The fluid exchange of experience and education between different parts of the world mean that we have more in common than we do differences. This is especially so in the sphere of international arbitration. It is a bit like the Olympics. The contestants come from contrasting backgrounds but they play by the same rules once they step into the arena. The game is familiar and its rules are the universal language for all contestants.

You who are participating in the Vis Moot will see for yourselves how different and yet similar the world is when you congregate in this fascinating and hugely successful event in Vienna and Hong Kong. Enjoy the experience.

8. International Arbitration in Australia: Chances and Challenges

Mini vandePol is a partner in Baker McKenzie's Hong Kong office (previously the Melbourne office). After five years as the chair of the Asia Pacific Regional Dispute Resolution Group, she was appointed as the chair of Baker McKenzie's global Compliance & Investigations group in 2014.

Arbitral Proceedings in Australia

Arbitration in Australia is slowly growing in importance as a practical solution to transnational disputes. In August 2010, Australia opened its first arbitration center in Sydney: the Australian International Disputes Centre. In 2012, Chief Justice Warren of the Victorian Supreme Court stated that she expected that an announcement relating to the construction of a similar center in Victoria would be made "very soon."

The impetus for the construction of the Sydney center, and the potential construction of the Melbourne center, came from the growing preference among corporations to use arbitration as a means of determining their disputes and a desire to conduct those arbitrations in Australia. In 2008, a PricewaterhouseCoopers survey found that 73 % of corporations prefer to use arbitration to resolve their cross-border disputes rather than transnational litigation. In 2009 a survey conducted by the Australian Centre for International Commercial Arbitration (ACICA) revealed that the number of cases handled by major international arbitration centers increased by between 50–150 % from 1999 to 2009.

Challenges for Arbitrators and Attorneys Working in Arbitration

The prospects for international arbitration in Australia are bright. Nonetheless, arbitrators and attorneys in Australia face some practical challenges:

Constitutional Challenge

In 2010, the Federal Government amended the International Arbitration Act 1974 (Cth) (IAA) to make the Model Law the default law governing the conduct of arbitral proceedings in Australia. Under section 34 of the Model Law, parties may only challenge an award of an arbitrator in limited circumstances, most significantly where the Court finds that the award conflicts with public policy. This has led to concerns that a Court enforcing an arbitral award might be seen as a "rubber stamp" for the decisions of an arbitrator.

Divergent Judicial Interpretations of the Relevant Statutes

Although Australian Courts are broadly supportive of arbitration and, in particular, of international jurisprudence, there have been some diverging interpretations of the Australian arbitration statutes. For example, while Justice Foster of the New South Wales Supreme Court took an expansive approach to the question of who is an award debtor for the purposes of an arbitration agreement, the Victorian Court of Appeal recently found that an award creditor bears an evidentiary onus of establishing the existence of an arbitration agreement. The Court of Appeal decision has been criticized as inconsistent with the intent of the intent of the New York Convention on Recognition and Enforcement of Arbitral Awards (1958).

Chances for Young Practitioners and Law Students

The Australian Centre for International Commercial Arbitration (ACICA), the Australian Commercial Disputes Centre and the Australian Maritime and Transport Arbitration Commission (AMTAC) and the Chartered Institute of Arbitrators (Australia) all provide opportunities for young lawyers to get involved and influence the growth of arbitration in Australia. The Australasian Forum for Arbitration has been established for the benefit of young practitioners working in Asia. These associations have taken an active role in promoting Australia as an arbitration seat. For example, on behalf of Australia, ACICA has recently entered into a formal agreement with the Abu Dhabi Chamber of Commerce and Industry to promote the use of international arbitration to resolve disputes.

Young lawyers can also pursue qualifications through undergraduate and postgraduate degrees, as well as accreditation courses to qualify as arbitrators in Australia and internationally. Several Australian university competitions offer young lawyers the opportunity to practice and hone their skills in arbitrations on both the domestic and global stages.

With Australia's established and independent legal system, as well as a stable economic and political environment, Australia is well placed within the rapidly growing Asia Pacific region to provide a forum for international arbitration.

Young practitioners should seize the opportunity Australia offers to grow into one of the most highly skilled and dominant arbitration centers in the Asia Pacific.

9. International Arbitration in Eastern Europe: Chances and Challenges

Vladimir Khvalei is a partner in Baker McKenzie's Moscow office, heading the firm's Dispute Resolution Practice Group of the Russian Commonwealth of Independent States (CIS). He shares his views on arbitration in Eastern European countries.

On the face of it, international arbitration in the CIS should not differ from that in other jurisdictions in any way, considering that almost all CIS countries are members of the New York and European Convention and their national laws are either identical (as in the case of Russia and Ukraine) or based on the UNCITRAL Model Law.

Yet international arbitration in the CIS has a number of distinctive features – some de jure, others de facto. Those distinctions are due to the existing procedural traditions in CIS countries, most of them surviving from the legal system of the former Soviet Union.

The number of arbitration courts and arbitration rules differs within the CIS

Russian legislation of the early 1990 s introduced very liberal requirements for establishing permanent arbitration courts, which required no special permission or registration. For those institutions to become validly constituted, it was sufficient to approve relevant rules and procedural regulations. As a result, arbitration courts were created at regional chambers of commerce and industry, trade associations, and major (and smaller) Russian companies. According to some estimates, Russia today has more than 500 permanent arbitration courts, although the exact figure is unknown, since these institutions, as it was mentioned above, are not subject to registration.

However, a lack of arbitration traditions had a serious impact on the rules of the newly-established arbitration courts. Some merely borrowed the Rules of the ICAC at the Russian Federation Chamber of Commerce and Industry (the "ICAC at the RF Chamber of Commerce and Industry" or the "Russian ICAC") with only minor changes, others drafted their own rules by using Russian procedural codes as examples. It is thus not surprising that some rules often contain provisions that clash with the very nature of arbitration by authorizing, for example, arbitral tribunals to involve third parties to the proceedings on their own initiative or revising final awards because of newly-discovered circumstances.

However, the situation is different in other CIS countries. Due to legislative restrictions there is only one international arbitration institution in Ukraine, two or three in Belarus, and four in Kazakhstan.

Companies in CIS countries still prefer litigation over arbitration

For a number of reasons, companies in CIS prefer to submit their disputes to state courts rather than to arbitration primarily because the former are quicker and cheaper than the latter, while overlooking such advantages of arbitration as the opportunity to elect arbitrators, the absence of procedural formalism, the arbitrators' ability to understand the commercial nature of the dispute, confidentiality of proceedings, and the finality of the award.

It is difficult to compete with state courts with respect to the amount of time that it takes to resolve a dispute, as the trial courts in Russia are as a rule to issue a judgment within three months after initiation of action. If appealed, the challenged act will only take effect after the appellate court rules on the case, with the appeal proceedings usually to take no longer than 2 months. Thus, as a general rule, the aggregate time of proceedings before the decision takes effect should not exceed six months.

Arbitral proceedings in CIS countries are no different from any other arbitral proceedings?

Although it may be hard to believe for a foreign practitioners not familiar with arbitration in CIS countries, CIS arbitration courts resolve disputes in terms comparable to other arbitration systems.

For example, cases submitted to the IAC at the Belarus Chamber of Commerce and Industry, as a rule, are completed within six months. The ICAC at the Ukrainian Chamber of Commerce and Industry is also well known for its speed: in 2011 74 % of cases were resolved within two and six months, 18 % within seven and nine months, and only 8 % took more than nine months.

As filing fees for state courts in CIS countries, more often than not, are insignificant, local arbitration courts have to take them into account when establishing their own schedule of fees

This competition of arbitration courts in the CIS with state courts allows these arbitration institutions to look particularly attractive compared to Western European arbitration courts in terms of costs.

Low costs of CIS arbitration for the party have another consequence: the fees paid to the arbitrators are very modest.

Thus, serving as arbitrator under the Rules of the CIS arbitration courts do not generate income considered to be significant by practicing lawyers, because the fees paid are not really comparable to the amount of time spent. This is one of the reasons why practicing lawyers are not often appointed as arbitrators.

This problem is partly resolved by involving law professors. As they do not have the same pressure for generating revenue as lawyers from a law firm, they are able to devote some time to acting as arbitrators, and usually consider it as a very useful exercise which allows them to get some experience in practical application of the law. However, the problem remains that a party might not succeed in appointing its arbitrator of choice because the chosen candidate, i. e. an experienced M&A lawyer for a post M&A dispute might not be willing to work for the arbitrator fee stipulated in the fee schedule.

If you want to become involved in arbitration in CIS countries

Because of the advantages described above, arbitration in CIS countries is gaining popularity. This is a great opportunity for students and young practitioners coming from one of the CIS countries.

If you want to become involved in arbitration in CIS countries, you already took the first step by participating in the Vis Moot. After the Moot, you could further develop your arbitration skills by participating in seminars, online trainings and arbitration-related workshops organized by ICC International Court of Arbitration, LCIA and other arbitration institutions.

Another good option is getting to know other lawyers from CIS countries. For example, you could join an association of arbitration practitioners such as Moscow Arbitration Forum (MAF 40) or the Russian and CIS Arbitration Network ("RCAN"). Both organizations have been created to foster informal discussions and facilitate networking among young arbitration practitioners with an interest in Russian and CIS arbitration. Amongst other activities, these organizations set up events attracting major arbitration experts and promote arbitration-related initiatives. While RCAN has introduced corporate membership fees, participation of individuals doesn't require any contribution. You can join RCAN via Linked-In network. MAF-40 does not have any participation fees at the moment.

There is also Young Arbitrators Forum of the International Chamber of Commerce (ICC YAF) that has similar goals as the above arbitration networks but functions on a global scale. Membership in the ICC YAF as well as participation in its events organized for young arbitration practitioners is free of charge. For the past several years there have been a number of ICC YAF events held in CIS countries, thus providing a forum for discussion of CIS-related arbitration issues.

There are also conferences on arbitration held in CIS, mainly supported by major international and arbitration institutions. Russian National Committee of the International Chamber of Commerce – the World Business Organization (ICC Russia) in cooperation with the ICC International Court of Arbitration holds annual arbitration conferences in Moscow dealing with issues related to Russia as a Place for Dispute Resolution. The last one was held in Moscow on December 7, 2012. The American Bar Association Section of International Law organized its 4th Annual Conference on the Resolution of CIS-Related Business Disputes in Moscow on 21 September 2012. International Bar Association will stage a conference in June 2013 entitled "International Arbitration and related matters" in St. Petersburg.

Speaking about the latest developments in international arbitration related to CIS countries one should mention the agreement of major law firms in the CIS territory to establish the Russian Arbitration Association that would serve the goals of promoting both international and domestic arbitration in Russia and CIS countries. With law firms being actively involved in arbitration as parties' counsel and therefore interested in more transparency, predictability and higher quality of arbitration proceedings, the creation of the Russian Arbitration Association is regarded as a major step toward the formation in CIS countries of an arbitration mechanism corresponding to international standards.

However, if you strive to become part of the arbitration community in the CIS, you should mind the following: It is not easy to become an expert in arbitration. It is even more difficult to become a recognized authority by your colleagues. If one chooses to be a corporate lawyer, it would take less time to get recognition and would require less effort. International arbitration is an area where people below 45 are considered as young practitioners. Therefore, the one who wants to move to this area should be prepared for a long trip.

10. Farewell Mootie: How to Come Back in a Different Role

The Moot is not the end; it's the beginning! Urs Zenhäusern, a partner of Baker McKenzie Zurich, identifies ten points which may help you to reach your goal to become a successful arbitration practitioner:

One: Become an excellent lawyer

Becoming, being and staying an excellent lawyer is a prime requirement for a successful career in every field of law. It is of particular importance if you want to become an arbitration lawyer: firstly, a dispute submitted to arbitration is always about a subject that requires a profound knowledge of a certain area of law, *e.g.* contract law, with all its "subdivisions" (sales, distribution/agency, licensing, *etc.*), M&A, construction/engineering, intellectual property, e-commerce, *etc.* To know the applicable arbitration rules is just the "skeleton" that one needs to have; but it is not sufficient for successfully representing a party in a dispute or for acting as arbitrator. Secondly, parties in international arbitration cases are often represented by major law firms. This means that you, at one stage in your career, will have to join a major law firm. These law firms tend, however, to accept only the best. If you are not an excellent lawyer, your application will be rejected.

Two: Go to a state court

Arbitration was "invented" as an alternative method of dispute resolution for cases for which it was found that the traditional state courts do not offer adequate solutions. In order to understand why arbitration is, or can be, different from dispute resolution by state courts, it helps if you know how a state court works. Before being admitted to the bar exam, you may have to practice in a law firm, or as a clerk at a state court. If you go to a state court, you will have at a very early stage of your career the opportunity to actually participate in adversarial proceedings where two parties and their lawyers present their arguments. You will also see first-hand how the judges deal with these arguments and how they take their decision. One year at a state court may well give you more insight into the "art" of dispute resolution than five years in a law firm during which you may be involved in perhaps 10 arbitration cases, as compared to the 50 or litigations you might see during your stay at a state court.

Three: Become part of the arbitration community

Participating in a Moot Court is a first step in becoming part of the arbitration community. But there is more. Nowadays, there exists a great number of arbitration associations offering all kind of arbitration services, including conferences, seminars and other events where arbitration practitioners of your local jurisdiction, and sometimes also those of other jurisdictions, convene. Join these associations and events and try to become an active member, so that your professional colleagues know that you exist and that you want to become a player in the field of arbitration. Many national arbitration associations have sub-sections open to young practitioners, such as the "ASA below 40", which regularly organize meetings and conferences for young arbitration practitioners who are less than 40 years old. This is an excellent forum for meeting all those lawyers who just as yourself are trying to make their first experiences as arbitration practitioners.

Four: Try working with an experienced arbitration practitioner

"Learning by doing" is still a good way for becoming an expert in a particular area of law. However, the chances that somebody has waited for you and will let you try an arbitration case are rather slim. Therefore, try to learn by watching an experienced arbitration practitioner how he or she does it. But remember: to work with such a person will often make it necessary that you join their law firm, and as you will recall, this may require you to become, and to be, an excellent lawyer.

Five: Be curious, be interested, go into the details

Each dispute brought to arbitration is different in that there is always a particular story behind it. You should be curious in getting to know this story and to explore what really happened. More than in any other field of law the principle of *audiatur et altera pars* is of essence: what your client is telling you about the background and the origin of the dispute will often be completely different from what your opponent will tell the arbitral tribunal. To avoid (negative) surprises, in particular during witness examinations, you must always challenge what you are being told and what you read. Never take things for granted. Be critical, try to understand what motivated a person to do what he or she did, but do not accept an easy explanation. Go into the details, find the unexpected and do not just stop when things are getting difficult.

Six: Learn how to write and how to speak

As an arbitration lawyer you will prepare comprehensive written briefs in which you will have to set out the factual and legal arguments in a way that an arbitrator is convinced that the position of your client is the right one and should be protected. Profound legal writing skills are, therefore, of importance and this is something you will not learn at law school. Read a lot, including books that teach you about how to write a brief, and collect good examples, including those of the lawyers of your opponent. And learn how to speak before a group of strangers who will not simply believe what you are telling them. Don't be shy: the others are often not better than you are. If you are well prepared and if you have practiced your speech it might be you who leaves the impression that counts. Think first before you speak and structure your speech; it is better to be short and precise than long and confusing.

Seven: Learn languages

While English is the principal language you will need to know when practicing arbitration, it is helpful to have a good command of other languages as well, in particular those languages which the vast majority of other arbitration practitioners do not know. This may give you the kind of competitive edge you will need to make a difference.

Eight: Be organized

Arbitration has become a method of dispute resolution where the parties file extensive briefs, often consisting of several hundred pages, accompanied by hundreds of exhibits. Broad document production requests, by which a party is requested to produce often hundreds of documents in its possession, have become the standard. The now common use of e-mails has contributed to the fact that the pile of documents to be reviewed and considered has increased by the factor of 10. The party which is able to find, or to retrieve, the essential documents will often win the arbitration. This means that an arbitration lawyer not only has to be able to deal with a mass of documents; he or she must also be capable to quickly identify those documents which are really required and to distinguish them from the unnecessary ballast. If you are not organized, you will not master that task. And don't count on others: in the beginning of your career, you will be the one spending days and weeks in going through tons of documents.

Nine: Be different, do something else

Try to be different from others by having a skill that most others don't have. Learn a language that most other people don't speak. Get special knowledge and expertise in a field that makes you an expert compared to all those who have no or just general knowledge about that topic. And remember: life is (hopefully) long and so may be your professional career. At the end, it does not really matter whether you have been an arbitration lawyer for 35 or 30 or just 25 years. Use the time early in your career to do something else which does not have an immediate nexus to law. As a lawyer, you will be in close contact with all sorts of persons, and the more you have learned about people and the life in general, the better you will be able to see these persons' strengths and weaknesses and to appraise the way they act and behave.

Ten: Do what you really want to do and have fun

You may realize, at one point in your career, that being an arbitration lawyer is not what you actually wanted to be. If you don't have fun while being an arbitration lawyer, this will not add to your quality of life. Then, stop doing it! Life is never too short for not doing what you really want to do but never dared to try.

Annex

To download the current Vis Moot Rules, please visit: https://vismoot.pace.edu

Who We Are

The Editor

Prof. Dr. Jörg Risse, LL.M.
Jörg Risse is an eminent practitioner in the arbitration world. He represents clients in international arbitration proceedings before all major arbitral institutions. He is also frequently appointed as an arbitrator or mediator. Based on his extensive experience, Jörg Risse regularly lectures students and clients on advocacy skills such as legal writing and oral presentation.

The Authors

Dr. Markus Altenkirch, LL.M.
Markus Altenkirch has been part of the Vis Moot for many years. Starting his "Moot career" as participant in 2005/2006, Markus Altenkirch has been the coach for the team of the University of Mainz for seven years in a row. At Mainz University, Markus Altenkirch regularly teaches negotiating techniques.

Dr. Ragnar Harbst, LL.M.
Ragnar Harbst is dually qualified as Rechtsanwalt (Germany) and Solicitor (England & Wales). He devotes his practice to international arbitration and adjudication proceedings. He is also frequently sought as an arbitrator in ICC and DIS arbitrations in construction and commercial matters. Ragnar Harbst is also a lecturer on legal writing at the University of Frankfurt and regularly teaches legal writing to clients and students.

Dr. Annette Keilmann
Annette Keilmann is a counsel in the German Arbitration Group of Baker McKenzie. She focuses on international arbitration, in particular relating to plant construction. Prior to becoming a lawyer, Annette Keilmann worked as a research assistant at the University of Mannheim at a chair devoted, inter alia, to rhetoric.

Dr. Lisa Reiser
Lisa Reiser participated in the Vis Moot in 2004/2005 and has stayed in contact with the arbitration world ever since. She served as coach and advisor for the team of the University of Mainz and came back to Vienna as arbitrator. In 2010, she spent several months working with the American Arbitration Association in New York before she returned to Germany as an associate of Baker McKenzie's Frankfurt office.

About Baker McKenzie

Baker McKenzie's roots trace back to Chicago in 1949. Here, Russell Baker and John McKenzie – unknown to each other up to that point – had to share a cab on a rain-hit day. In a chat they found out that both of them were lawyers. They agreed that now, after World War II, it was essential to create a truly global law firm to assist American companies in expanding their business overseas. Since then, this idea of a truly international law firm runs like a golden thread through the work of Baker McKenzie, the law firm both men founded in the aftermath of their cab ride.

Now, in 2017, our law firm is home to more than 4,600 locally admitted lawyers. Our International Arbitration Group spans around the globe and is represented in every arbitration hub around the world. With our 77 offices in 47 countries, we share the international spirit of the Vis Moot and match the geographic outreach this phenomenon has today. Now that you gained the skills of an attorney working in international commercial arbitration, why not apply your skills during an internship in one of our 77 offices? Let us know via vis.moot@bakermckenzie.com.